For Real

For Real

THE UNCENSORED TRUTH ABOUT AMERICA'S TEENAGERS

by
JANE PRATT
and
KELLI PRYOR

NEW YORK

Designed by Helene Wald Berinsky

Library of Congress Cataloging-in-Publication Data
Pratt, Jane, 1962–
    For real : the uncensored truth about America's teenagers / by Jane
Pratt and Kelli Pryor.
        p.   cm.
    ISBN 0-7868-8064-3
    1. Teenagers—United States—Attitudes.   2. Adolescent psychology—
United States.   3. Youth—United States—Social conditions.
I. Pryor, Kelli.   II. Title.
HQ796.P725 1995
305.23´5´0973—dc20   94-46189
                                                                    CIP

10 9 8 7 6 5 4 3

Thanks

Tons of gratitude to Dan Strone for being the first person to believe that this was a book idea. Also to Robert Miller, Michael Lynton, Mary Ann Naples, Lauren Marino, Craig Nelson, Randi Rothstein, Karen Cohen, and a whole bunch of *Sassy* interns. And, thank you, James Seymore, Andrew Hurwitz, Richard Hofstetter, Frank Messa, Abby Adams, Jane Berliner, Jay Maloney for ongoing everything.

There are so many people who helped us out on the road, helped us find kids or told us what they thought of early drafts. Some of them we can't name to protect identities, but we thank them all anyway: Mary Huzinec, Tracey Conrad-Katz and Brad Katz, David Conrad and Ann Reynolds, Lonnie Delorme, Cindy Baggish, Brad Armstrong, Lou Tyson, Bob Foos, Marie Najikian, Ellen and Bill Pryor, Martha Ann Babcock, Tina Jordan, Jo Dawson, Nancy Dawson-Sauser, Nancy Goodman, Janet Brailsford, April Chapman, Danny Barrett, Ray Elliot and Vanessa Faurie, Robin Saex, Bill Gosch, Cheryl Schwartz, Tabitha Soren, Kate Meyers, Andy Postman, so much, Doug Coupland, Stephen Treffinger, Josh Patner, Suzanne Feigelson, Jennifer Drawbridge, Mae and Mory Moss, Florence Bernstein, Jill Bauer, Jeannine Landreth, Neal Carter, Stan and Barbara Rosenstein, Peter and Margaret Harriman, and Bob and Marilyn Conner.

Last and especially, thank you, thank you, thank you: Sheila Blake a.k.a. Mom, Vernon Pratt/Dad, Peter, Amy, Dan, Hill, Ben,

Debi, and Sarina. Also to Jerry Pryor, Dixie Carter, Robb Pryor, and Meredith Berkman. And to Andrew Rosenstein for, among other things, driving 21,925.4 miles.

And big thanks to all of the teenagers in this book and to teenagers in general for constantly challenging us and showing us it's possible to have hope in spite of it all.

Contents

Contents • *ix*

Not a Boring Introduction

A couple of marketing types who read this manuscript had a suggestion: Why not come up with a label for this generation of teenagers, you know, sort of like Generation X? My first reaction was, well, no thank you. I mean, the label *teenager* is damaging enough, especially when you've got people like Newt Gingrich blaming that group of people for a lot of what's wrong on the planet. Besides, this book is not about a category but about individual kids between the ages of thirteen and nineteen. Also, my friend Doug Coupland wrote *Generation X,* so why would I want to rip him off? The more I thought about it, though, the more I realized that if teenagers came up with the label themselves, maybe it wouldn't be so bad.

Eyes rolled. This eighteen-year-old named Zach, who lives in North Carolina, said, "We don't want to be labeled, because being gay or black or a rapper or redneck or alternative has only separated us, and those are labels previous generations have come up with, not us. We need to embrace our differences, not focus on them." That was pretty much the reaction, not always so eloquently put. Then a few teenagers indulged or humored me by coming up with suggestions: the Droopy Generation, the Contras, the Confused Ones, the Rap Generation, the Centurions, the Racers. And another guy commented, "I guess we'd be Generation Y 'cause that comes after X." Then his girlfriend said, "No, more like Generation Why, as in W-H-Y. For *Why* Label Us?" A few others I tried this Generation Why? idea out on thought it worked. "Yeah, like why are there no jobs left for us? Why can't I get into a good college even though my grades are good? Why is the environment so messed up? Why does sex kill? And why can't different races deal with each other a little better?" one girl wrote to me. Okay. So if they're anything, they're Generation Why?

I can relate to their whole problem with being labeled. Because even though Doug tells me I'm "dead center" Generation X, I've never really gone along with that (sorry, Doug). Partly because I've always related so much to this younger generation. I mean, it's been like a dumb joke: When people would ask me "what do you want to be when you grow up?" my instinct was to answer "a kid." But for the last ten years I somehow managed to make a career out of not growing up.

My mom's theory is that being a teenager is so troubling that most people just get through it and then block it out. They make a funny story out of the time they got drunk or dumped, and they romanticize the rest and go on perpetuating the myth that your teenage years are the best years of your life. And because they can't remember what it felt like to be a teenager, they treat the ones they encounter like some kind of aliens, doing things that are totally out of control and beyond any notion of reason. "He/she was the greatest/smartest/sweetest/wisest kid until he/she turned thirteen," I've heard from so many neighbors, bosses, counselors, fathers, mothers, and other assorted relatives.

My mom has no theory for why I can't forget that part of my life, why I'm "stunted," as a cool sixteen-year-old with dyed matte black hair and a few body piercings said. I've come up with a bunch of my own that I won't bore you with (fortunately, I have a therapist for that). All I know about it for sure is here I am, thirty-two, and I still feel closer to the insecurity and emotional volatility of being a teenager than whatever it is I'm supposed to feel at my age.

My teenage years were typically bad (with some typically bright spots), starting with my parents separating when I was thirteen, two years later going away to a prep school where I did not fit in big time, eventually doing what it took to fit in and having our dorm mother call me an alcoholic (as I lay at her feet with the room spinning so much I couldn't stagger up to contradict her), thinking I was the last living virgin at seventeen but finally thank god losing it before my eighteenth birthday. It was when I was fifteen, home for summer break from Andover, driving in the car with my mom, that I first said, "I know what I want to do for a job. I want to do a magazine for teenagers, like *Seventeen* but not." I'd read *Seventeen* since I was twelve. And I loved it in a way, couldn't wait to get it every month. But it also showed me again and again that yes, I *was* the mutant I always felt like I was. Real teenagers were those tall, skinny, blond girls with tennis rackets in their hands and boyfriends galore. Anyway, back in the car with mom, who blurted out, "Oh, no, you don't. Magazines are really superficial and trendy. If you're going to get into publishing, why not put your energy into writing the Great American Novel instead?" I knew she was just in a bad mood, so I ignored her and became even more determined to do it, to start a magazine that would make teenage girls feel their big noses, dark skin, wide hips, braces, and freckles are beautiful, and that what's going on inside their heads is a lot more important anyway.

One of the most satisfying things for me, and I think for the whole staff at *Sassy,* that made it feel worth it to be still in the office at 3:30 a.m., were letters like the one from a teenager in Virginia Beach who wrote, "I have to tell ya [*sic,* obviously], I love your magazine. I'm half black, part Indian, and a b-ball playing fool. And *Sassy* is the one mag that helped me realize that I can be me and fine the way I am instead of an anorexic-boychasing-bop." Or this one:

> Jane—I used to feel all out of it all the time—like no one really understood me. But somehow, even though I've never really met you, I feel like you do. See, people look at me and think that I have it easy. I'm popular, I have a 4.0 average (I'm not always so

into broadcasting my accomplishments, but since I know a lot about you, I figured I'd let you in on a few little details of my own life). But on the inside I feel like I'm somebody else. I know there's a lot more in there (good and bad) than I let on. Anyway, I feel like you understand why I have to spend three, count 'em! hours getting ready to go out, but you wouldn't judge me for it. *And* you'd also understand those parts of me that other people don't (that I don't even understand sometimes), like why I get depressed for no reason and how I worry I have no *true* friends. All this is to say: Thank you for being there!!!!!!

So when my critics (I've had plenty—more on them later) say that *Sassy* is only for "alienated teenagers," I feel like responding, "Well, isn't an unalienated teenager the biggest oxymoron?"

A few years after launching *Sassy*, when I started my talk shows (innovatively titled "Jane" on Fox and then "Jane Pratt" on Lifetime) and, more recently, started promoting a new series of TV specials and a new magazine, kids would recognize me and come up to me in stores or on the street. And within five minutes, they'd be telling me about how they'd gotten an abortion but could never tell their parents about it or how they're worried their girlfriend's getting high too much: "I mean we all do it at parties and stuff, but she smokes pot by herself in her room like all the time and should I say something to her about it?" Then, when adults find out I hear all this stuff from the same kids who won't say more than two words to them, I get the question, "What's your secret for communicating with teenagers?" Hmmmm.

Well, first of all, it's not about using "wicked," "straight up," "phat," and "dissed" in your conversation (and *definitely* not about using "def" and "rad"). The only key, I think, is really listening to them. Teenagers get talked at so often and told what to do and mostly what not to do. It's so rare for someone to actually take the time to listen to them with respect, taking what they're saying seriously, and not judging them first, that when an adult does that, they can't wait to be themselves. When Kelli and I were interviewing kids for this book, they'd say, "Nobody ever listens to me for this long" and "Hey, did you get that on your tape recorder, what I just said? 'Cause it was a pretty good point." Another thing teenagers seem to appreciate is when you open up about your own mistakes and short-comings, at their age and now—rather than trying to act like a per-fect role model, which only makes them feel more isolated with their problems. That's why my personal reminiscences are included here, not because I think it's so unique and fascinating what I was like at seventeen. And as I was rereading the journals I've kept since I was fourteen, to remember stories to put into this book, I decided it wasn't fair to the teenagers in here for me to only present my adult-slightly-wiser views of life. Plus I realized I could not recre-ate it all accurately now anyway. So as a sign of truth-or-dare style solidarity with the kids throughout this book who are revealing themselves exactly as they are, at this most unsettled time of their lives, I've reprinted some of my teenage diary entries too.

The truth is, these theories are pretty obvious. And I don't think that's just from my stunted perspective. They're about treating teenagers the way you like to be treated, not as you treat children or convicts. But I wish you could hear the tone in most adults' voices when they're asking me for advice about their kids. It sounds like fear. They seem intimidated by teenagers, and I can understand why. Teenagers, now especially, appear incredibly sophisticated. Their minds work like computers. They've tried designer drugs—like GBH—which we've never even heard of because they hadn't been chemically engineered when we were their age. They police their homes for environmental infractions or tell their teachers "it's *Asian,* not *Oriental* anymore." So they're scary. But at the same time adults feel more scared *for* them. After all, if they're fighting at school, the risk isn't getting punched, it's getting shot. Thirteen American teenagers die every day from gunshot wounds. And what we all worried about when we had unprotected sex (yes, "when" not "if," sorry to say) was getting pregnant. Now it's AIDS, and teenagers have become the highest risk group for getting the AIDS virus.

However, since nineties teenagers grew up learning about these dangers, I don't think they feel any more scared by them than if the risks were less severe, not life threatening. One fifteen-year-old from North Carolina told me, "We learned about AIDS when we learned the birds and the bees stuff. We've never known about sex without it. AIDS risk is just a given. It's not something we have to change our behavior for, just something we've always known we're supposed to protect ourselves against." So adults can't expect teenagers to sound so scared when they talk about heroin or guns or AIDS. But teenagers' seeming nonchalant about these issues makes adults even more worried for their safety, it seems. And less open to listening to them.

A lot of people disagree with me on this, but I don't think teenagers change their behavior because people tell them to. I think they change when they're given complete information and allowed to make their own decisions about what to do with it. So how does this whole communication problem get sorted out so kids can start asking for the information they need from the adults they count on even if they don't act like it? Well, don't look at me. But do as I say and do: Listen to kids. For this book, we went looking for a representative range of American teenagers. We called kids who'd written or phoned me. We called their friends and our friends. We called teachers and youth group leaders and social workers all over the place and told them we wanted to find teenagers with all different kinds of lives. We weren't looking for stereotypes, but a real multicultural, multisexual, geographical assortment. After we'd narrowed it down, we sent out a preliminary questionnaire asking the kids what ten issues were most on their minds. That's how we decided what issues to cover in the alternating sections. The topics that came up most often are the ones we addressed (not the onetime answers like the low water pressure in one girl's shower or "why my girlfriends are all so fucked up"). Afterward, we had teenagers name those chapters, from "Abs of Steel" to "Absolut Queer," which is why they're in quotes. Then Kelli and her husband Andrew spent four months driving around the country (plus a bush plane into Dan

Creek, Alaska), to stops where I'd fly and meet them, to see these kids where they live, work, go to school, hang out. For example, we spent one weekend shuttling between Quincy Jones's house, *Circus of the Stars* rehearsals, and an apartment shared by a couple of skinheads. We didn't go out with any preconceived notions about what we would find. And at the end of those 20,000 ground miles and more in frequent flier, we had met a group of kids whose lives, as you'll see, couldn't be more different from one another. But what's consistent is their brutal honesty—about everything from their morning hair gel routines to their favorite brands of condoms. (We did have to change some kids' names for legal reasons.)

What I hope to do in this book is to show teenagers as they really are. Not as a Madison Avenue market strategist excited about 27 million cyber-ready consumers sees them. Not as a politician discussing the link between gangsta rap and teenage violence rates sees them. Not as parents or teachers or aunts wish teenagers were—and therefore blur their vision to see them. But as if you could look through their bedroom keyholes or read their journals. I hope this book will provide some kind of bridge between kids and adults. Because, face it, we are a lot more alike than ever. Kids are adults, some before they ever were kids, partly because lots of adults have gone back to being kids, if you follow me. You hear a lot of media hype about teen pregnancy and teen suicide and teen violence, but you don't hear much about how these statistics are just mirror images of adults rates: From 1940 to 1990, unwed birthrates rose 4.7 times among teenagers and 4.6 times among adults. And 88 percent of all adult violent crime is committed by men and 88 percent of all juvenile violent crime is committed by boys. Twice as many white adults commit suicide as black adults, just as twice as many white teenagers commit suicide as black teenagers. So the more adults can learn to see themselves in kids, the better off we'll all be in trying to solve the bigger things we all face. Plus, I just think it's time to stop talking about teenagers as if they're not in the same room. Because as long as parents and stepgrandparents and mom's boyfriend turn away out of misunderstanding or frustration or intimidation, the kids are going to turn someplace else for the answers they want: They'll go into therapy or into gangs. Or they'll do what I did and wind up on a bathroom floor miles from home cutting my arms up with a knife.

I also want it to be a way for kids to take a close look at other kids and get, as one teenager put it, quoting from a T-shirt, "a knowledge that we are more similar than different." When I asked kids what they hoped would come of this book, their answers ranged from joking that they hoped it'd get them lots of dates to hoping "stereotypes about teenagers will be broken down a bit and won't be based on the way we dress and do our hair or our skin color, whatever." Nick Plummer said, "I hope that from this book, parents will understand the plight of the teenager and will give us a little slack."

I love Nick.

NICK PLUMMER, NAZI AVENGER

Nick Plummer is in a Nazi death camp trying to blast his way out with a machine gun. He blows away guards. He opens secret passageways in the shifting 3-D maze of bright blue and gold.

"I am a Death Incarnate," Nick explains, furiously tapping the keyboard of his color Core computer. "This is the hardest level."

Last summer Nick came home from summer camp in Maine, got off the bus and said, "Mom, you shrunk." Having grown nine inches in the last year, to 5´11˝, he's headed for 6´2˝ (he hopes). His Reeboks are size 11½. Nick has what he calls "box" muscles on his stomach and pecs that he calls his "pride and joy."

At age fourteen, he's the second best hockey player in his league. He can squat 185. He wears shorts further into the winter than any other kid he knows. He blasts Metallica. And he's had six—no, wait, only five—girlfriends in the past year.

Nick is also a straight-A student. He's been at this same computer most of the long Columbus weekend working on a biology paper about Lewis Thomas's *The Lives of a Cell*. Last year, he would have scoffed at spending all weekend sweating out a science paper. But that was eighth grade, when he could sleep through his Earth Science class and still have the highest grade point in the school—99.6. Other kids in the class told him he even raised his hand and called out answers in his sleep, but he only remembers doing it once. "I knew everything that was possible to be known," he says. That year, he was also getting up at six every morning to attend a ninth grade science class. He didn't get any credit for it, but he says it did him good anyway. It put him ahead for this year, plus when he watches *Jeopardy,* he knows a lot of the answers.

> *Nick's eyes are focused on a doorway at the end of a long corridor. He suspects there's a Nazi behind it. "He'll open the door," he predicts. "I'll just shoot him." Sure enough, a Nazi appears in the doorway, and Nick ventilates him with a cackle. "There's a cheating way, but I never do it," he explains as he pounds away at the keyboard, his Reeboks bouncing in time.*

This year, as a high school freshman at Montclair High School in New Jersey, Nick is having to work—hard. He has biology. The teacher gives one test per cycle, and as Nick explained earlier when he was sitting on his front porch, "If you screw up on that test, you're dead." He says his usual routine calls for taking breathers from homework by playing football in the street in front of his house or by punching a phone call into his Toshiba cellular phone, which he keeps in the back pocket of his jean shorts. But for this cycle's biology test, "I studied straight from six till like two in the morning," he says.

"The next day, I'm doin' my test, and I'm like, *I don't know this, I don't know this.* I did the whole thing. The teacher was like, 'Would you like me to grade it here?' And I was like, *'YES, please, please.'* He graded it; I got 8 wrong out of 82 questions, and I was just like . . . I went back to the desk and figured it out. [That time my score] was like 88. Then I did it again. It was like 90.2, plus there's extra credit, so in the end I might get 94, which is kinda, which I'm really happy about because this is my first year. I expected to get all *B*s and stuff. *I* expected to get *B*s. But my mom's like, 'You get two *B*s in a cycle, and you're grounded.' "

"Secret passageway," Nick shouts, surveying the brick walls on the game board. "Oh, I got it. Heehee." He's been playing this game so long that he knows where they all are on this board. He knows where the treasures are too. He's aiming to get 100 percent on secret passageways and 100 percent on treasures.

"I don't really like my parents that much," he continues. "They're cool until school comes up. They think I'm a genius or something. I don't listen to them. I study *for myself* because I know that I'll need it, *and* it feels good to be smart." Nick and his little sister, Samantha, live in Upper Montclair, New Jersey, with their mother, a writer, and her new husband, a lawyer who works in New York City. But they often spend the night with their father, a writer for *People* magazine, who lives in the next town over.

"I used to like my parents here, and my dad? *'I don't wanna go to his house,'* " Nick remembers. "Now I'm like, 'Oh, good, I get to go to Dad's house, get away from this place.' I can't stand it here."

Why can't he stand it here—where he has the master bedroom on the second floor with his own bathroom, a remote-control Kenwood stereo system, fifty-five CDs, a poster of "Penises of the Animal Kingdom," and a mini-refrigerator full of grape sodas?

"Third floor," he says, cryptically. "And the people who live there. Third floor. My parents' domain. It's just where they are all the time. It's like the only thing that's important to them is each other even though I know it's not true 'cause like . . ." He pauses. How to put it? "I'm not important until it has to do with school," he says.

His mom and stepdad don't like his habit of punctuating homework with loud Nirvana and video games. They don't like how he puts studying off until late in the night; they want his homework done right after school. They threaten to take away his phone if his grades slip. And if he argues with his mom about it, she says, "Speak to your stepdad."

"I don't wanna talk to him," Nick says, moaning. "I mean, he's okay. He's nice and everything, but I don't wanna have to talk to him about stuff because he always has some BIG thing to say. He's one of those lecturers . . . lawyers, *God!* He says I can be whatever I want, but I have to be a nuclear physicist."

Nick rolls his eyes. "I'm probably gonna be an architect, which is what I'm interested in. But still he thinks I have to get the straightest As, the biggest this and the biggest that, and I have to be perfect and join the Honor Society, which I'll probably do anyway because it's good. But, 'Join clubs; edit this.' My mom was like the chief editor of their newspaper in high school, and she's like, 'Why don't you do that?'

"I Don't Like Read-Ing," Nick says slowly, putting emphasis on every syllable, pretending he's speaking to his mom right now. "I *especially* don't like reading *bor*ing stuff."

Video fire rattatttats out and red blotches splash across the screen. "Oh, my GAAAwd," he cries. "Did you see that shot he did? Damn! He just totally destroyed me. The shot he took was from point blank range, so it took like sixty percent of my energy off. Might as well save it here cause I think there are some guys in there who could kill me."

Bleep, bleep, goes the computer. Nick sighs. Every time he gets hit, he does the computer equivalent of bleeding—he loses energy.

"I'll probably end up cheating this one," Nick explains, then, "Whoa!" as a Nazi surprises him, then, "HaHa!" He eludes the fire. But it's not easy because he's playing with low energy. "I'm an energy-expending kind of guy," he says.

He decides to cheat, bump the program up to more energy, get a bigger gun. "Like my machine gun?" he asks, his eyes glinting cockily.

Nick loves girls, skinny girls—5´3˝, 85 pounds, is perfection.

Of Nick's five girlfriends in the past year, he's still friends with four of them. Only the first is not a friend because she "pranked" him by phone for a long time after he broke up with her, which was partly because she cheated on him. He started paying people to prank her back and things tapered off. "I ended it because she was a zombie. It was good for like the first two weeks then I was just bored, very *bored*. She was just a blob, just there, literally too." But the rest of the girls, he's keeping around.

"I always got along with girls," Nick explains. "People are like, *'Nick, you're gay.'* I'm not gay. I just have a lot of friends who are girls. They all usually happen to be my ex's too."

Since that first girlfriend, he's given up exclusive relationships. "After a while I couldn't take that anymore because it was too much torment—you have to be faithful to this . . . It's not the faithfulness that's the problem. I mean I felt I couldn't even *look* at anybody else.

"I broke up with Claire. She's the one I went out with for the longest. I broke up with her, and I felt so *free* you know just like talking to all these girls and flirting my head off. I'm just like a tremendous flirt, just like my dad."

Nick stops to clarify something: "I never went out with anybody else while I saw her 'cause I don't feel that cheating is a thing but I just wanna have the option. It's nice to have the option. Always keep her in suspense. I don't want her to [have the same option] but still I'm not gonna say, 'No, you can't go out with somebody.'

"Claire wouldn't have done that anyway. She was like one of those people who liked to be faithful—as far as I know at least."

As far as he knows, 'cause lately girls are a tougher game than he's played in ten years of hockey, in a childhood of Mortal Kombat. He compares this time in his life to when he got hit by a speeding car stepping off the curb one morning on his way to second grade. ("I was okay," he says. "But my lunch box did take a beating though.") His mom took him to a therapist, who was supposed to help with any trauma. "I didn't need a shrink," he says. "The only time that I *know* that I need a shrink is nowadays when I do have a shrink. I just have all kinds of friend difficulties."

He illustrates with the story of his recent falling out with Kate, whom he once dated for a few weeks, and Jess, whom he wanted to date but didn't. He describes them as "two very close like best friends of mine."

Here's what happened: "I went out to dinner with Kate and Jess. And I was on time, and they were there early, and they just kinda ate without me. And they were like, 'We have to go soon so hurry up and eat.' I was just like, 'Okay,' and I just ate. That kinda annoyed me, but I got over that.

"I got over to their house, and they just kept patronizing me and everything. They normally do it. They just *over*did it, way overdid it. And I blew up pretty much. I was like, 'I gotta leave. Bye.' And I left, and I called 'em up and I screamed at them for about two hours. I shouldn't scream. I always scream too much. That's one of my big problems. I have big vocals, and I like to use them, and so I screamed at them a lot. They took very big offense at it. Neither of them apologized.

"I'm usually one of those people, I'll call them up. I won't give them the second chance. Five minutes later, I'll call 'em back and say I'm sorry, I didn't think about your side of the story."

He is being very earnest and deliberate, as though he's going over it for the zillionth time, as though he's telling it to his therapist: "Even after I called back . . . I was like, 'I'm sorry, I didn't think of your side of the story, you have your right to your opinion.' I apologized. I said that I had way overreacted I know, but they were really driving me crazy and I wished they would stop. And they said, 'We didn't do anything wrong.' " He repeats that, emphasizes it, to show he still can't believe they would say that to him: *"We didn't do anything wrong.*

"I don't know. Kate wasn't the friend I thought she was. But there's Jess who I miss very much. I miss her very much. She was very close even though she can be a very big pain in the ass."

Nick is anxious for his next appointment with his therapist, which was supposed to be last week, but his mom forgot to write it on the kitchen calendar. Nick says: "So I need to talk about it to the guy cause he said I should go call 'em up and state the issues like what should happen. And I did all that, and they still . . . Kate was like okay and then she just drifted away. She just like disappeared and then Jess was like, 'I didn't do anything wrong at all. It was all your fault blahblahblah.' "

Nick is proud of how this Wolfenstein game is going now that his energy level has been boosted, but he admits he's not as good as some people. "My friend Jon is a sicko at this game. He runs with the machine gun. He'll run up to somebody and right when he gets in somebody's face, he'll go ppppppppp. He does like a drive by. It's really funny."
Click, click, click, he goes on the keyboard.

Even though Nick is still dealing with this Kate and Jess stuff, he's also looking for a real girlfriend, because as he puts it, "Only a girlfriend and hockey can keep me pretty happy most of the time. Then I won't be very violent or anything." This week, he's checking out a quiet girl who sits at his lunch table at school. Plus, it's hockey season, and he's a high-scoring forward, which thrills him because although he's been playing for ten years, he only got good in the past two. No violence so far.

"But last year out of season, I had no girlfriend, and didn't have that many friends, a kid commented on my shorts," Nick says. "I had to kill him. I picked him up by his neck. I've never done this before. And I threw him into a locker. I did apologize to him as I walked him up to the infirmary.

"Now if somebody wants to pick on me, they don't. I'm not really picked on except last year . . ." He pauses and then says uncertainly: "Racial tensions."

Huh?

"Everybody thought I was a racist or something."

Why?

"It was just . . . I have a theory, kinda like . . . it's weird. It's like there are people. I don't despise black people. I have so many black friends, black girlfriends. My friends are black. I have a lot of friends who are black, have a lot of friends who are white. But there are a fraction of the black party which I cannot stand. The kids who steal bikes and beat each other up. And they go around calling each other nigger all the time and all that. And because of that, I hate them so much and the only word that I could use for them would be nigger. So there's this . . . So I did tend to express my feelings about that in school.

"In the middle of class, this kid stands up, he's like, 'I think that all white people are horrible and that blacks should rule' and all that and I'm just like, 'You know I don't understand you people.'

"And he was like, 'YOU PEOPLE?!'"

"And I was like, 'Yes, YOU PEOPLE, a certain party of the black people, which are just stupid. You're ignorant.' And I probably called him a nigger or something like that you know cause I got enraged . . . I don't know if I did or not. And everybody thought I was racist 'cause of that. Meanwhile, I'm in the hall hugging black people, hanging out with black friends of mine. And everybody still thinks I'm racist. It's just stupid."

"See that passageway," Nick says, indicating a brick wall on the computer board. There's a blood world in there. I'm not gonna go to it."

He cheats a little, though, so that he's got 100 percent energy.

"And," Nick says, "[the kids at school] all think I'm a Satan worshiper because I don't believe in God and I'm an anarchist." He holds up an anarchy emblem—a circle with an A inside it—on his necklace. "I just feel that there shouldn't be a central support of government. So anyway I had this on, and everybody said, 'Oh, it's a Satan sign.' *No,* it's not. They're so ignorant. Satan's stupid.

"There are a lot of Satan worshipers. I know many. They pray to Satan, weird stuff. One girl killed a dog. They're friends [of mine], except for the one who killed a dog. That was sick. They think of it one day. Oh, it'd be cool to worship Satan, and they read about it and read more. And they really start believing in it.

"I have some Satan-type music here. I only like it 'cause it's good music—Slayer, War Ensemble, Skeletons of Society."

When he goes to parties, he sings with his friend who plays guitar. "I'll sing Metallica," Nick says. "I can sing some Slayer." He went to a party Saturday night, took a break from his biology paper thinking he'd sing. But a hundred people showed up at his friend's house, and then the friend's mom showed up early. "It was supposed to be one of those beer-drinking, pot-smoking kinda things," Nick explains. Nick exited fast because his friend's mom "chews me out every time I go over there: *'Nick, I know you're a smart student. Why do you do this?'* I mean, I've gotten drunk," Nick admits. "I have tried pot, you know, whatever. What's wrong with that? There's nothing wrong with that, not particularly."

He says his mom and stepdad are cool about it. "One time," he says. "I drank beer and vodka together and I came home and I just like called my mom and said, 'I mixed. I'm stupid. I forgot about it, and I need you to come help me up the stairs.' And they helped me. Now they say—and this is one of their cool sides—we can't stop you from drinking. But don't mix, always have food in your stomach and don't overdo it. We don't like you drinking but if you're going to, just try and follow these rules so you don't really mess yourself up."

His dad was another story. "He was just like, I can't believe you're drinking at this young age. I was like, 'Dad, please, I've heard your stories. I know what you did when you were my age.' "

It's been twenty minutes since he started, and the game is over. "I got a 100 percent," Nick boasts. "Wait a minute. Eighty percent? I only got an 80 percent secret ratio?

"Anyway, that's the game. I was at the hardest level."

"Cartoons"

The first two adults who read early drafts of these chapters—
Kelli's dad and my mom—had the exact same question: *Are
you going to have any typical teenagers in here? We laughed.
'Cause we'd learned that these* are *typical teenagers, or rather that
there's no such thing as a typical teenager but this is a good mix of
who is really out there. We didn't go looking for extremes or anything.*

*What mom and dad meant, we guess, is what about kids like the
girls they saw getting their hair cut at the mall or those groups
playing pinball at 7-Eleven? Guess what? These are the ones. If we
told you that we were going to introduce you to a fourteen-year-old
who plays hockey and video games, you might conjure up a guy
who looks and acts a lot like Nick. But when he really opens up to
you, you see how complicated teenagers need to be to deal with a
pretty typical range of nineties concerns: Nick's got a therapist and
he's got two families and he's sorting through the race issue and
he's deciding what to do about sex. "I'm saving myself for when I'm
seventeen," he said when we asked him just what were his thoughts
on the whole sex thing. "Then it will be better, I think."*

*Now, meet Amber, whom you could describe as a fifteen-year-
old babysitter who worries about her grades. But we wouldn't.*

AMBER'S BOY BOX

Amber is leaning against her bamboo headboard in the cross-legged pose she uses when she lights candles, plays Tori Amos tapes, and meditates. She meditates to distract herself from issues like whether she should get an AIDS test or whether a seven-year-old kid she was babysitting at a birthday party sexually harassed her by calling her "hot stuff" while she was pouring his ginger ale. Today, she's not meditating. She's holding an old stuffed penguin toy, Opus from the *Bloom County* cartoons. Stuffed lambs and bears are arranged by her nightstand, and a Cabbage Patch doll is propped up on the pastel blue comforter. "I'm sentimental," she says, hugging Opus. "I can't throw *any*thing away."

To prove it, she gets out the shoebox she keeps hidden in her closet. Inside, there are a foam Hershey's Kiss from a guy who had a crush on her, a snapshot of her last kiss with her eighth-grade boyfriend, a business card advertising psychic services from a clairvoyant she smoked pot with (her first time) in South Street.

Amber is the first American born into her family, and the only person she knows who has never even tasted a peanut-butter-and-jelly sandwich—and now makes it a point of pride *not* to try one. Her father grew up in China and is now a computer engineer. Her Egyptian mother runs her own business out of their home in a "snobbish" suburb of Philadelphia. Her brother, Tom, is a decade older than Amber, who is about to be a high school sophomore and is as exotic looking in her neighborhood as the "politically incor-

rect" leopard rug on the family's front room floor. She's got on burgundy lipstick, a beaded choker, $5 China flats, and a black flowing
dress that is just a little darker than her long wispy-wavy hair.
Growing up, she's been called an "Oreo" and a "Spic." She also gets
called "cute." "I hate that adjective," she says. "I'm fifteen. I don't
wanna look *cute*. I wanna look sultry."

* * *

The first thing Amber pulls out of the box is a red ponytail. It
used to belong to a guy named Nick. "If fire could have a color," she
says, "[Nick's] hair would be it. Smell it. It smells so good, just like
him." She runs her fingers through it, brushes it under her nose
again. Even though Nick is now "slime," he did once quote a mono-
logue from *Romeo and Juliet* to her as she stood looking down at
him from her moonlit balcony.

As she strokes the ponytail, Amber tells how she met him at a
weekend conference for members of various Unitarian churches.
This cute guy, who reminded her a lot of the lead singer in *The
Commitments* and who turned out to be Nick, kept smelling her
hair. Finally, when everybody got into their sleeping bags on the
floor, he stretched Amber's hair across his pillow and slept all night
on it. "It was kind of endearing," she admits. After that, she went to
his house and saw his red ponytail hanging up in his room. She
admired it; he gave it to her. That was before he dated her for three
months, then dumped her one night, after which she ran upstairs
and threw up five times. "It was like he was my drug or something,"
she recalls, then adds wistfully: "His hair was *the* most *glor*ious
thing in the face of the world. So he gave me the ponytail, and I'm
glad 'cause I got the funnest part." She shrugs as a grin spreads all
over her face. "Apparently," she says, "there wasn't really much
else."

Meaning?

"I met one of Nick's old girlfriends, and we had this huge bash-
Nick fest," Amber says, giggling, "and she told me the *best* thing
about him. She said, 'You know how he walks around like he's like

completely the male gift to women.' And I said, 'Yeah.' She said, *'Amber, his penis is so tiny.' "*

Amber squeals and squeezes Opus till one of his little button eyes almost pops off.

*   *   *

Amber pulls a condom out of the box. It's in a cellophane package that says Bare Back. "Isn't that *hilarious?*" she says. "Bare Back."

Amber explains she's a virgin even though "some people think that if sex were fast food, I would have golden arches over my bed." But, really, before she went on vacation this summer she had only been to "sloppy second" base. (Her sexual base system goes like this: "First base is French kissing. Second base is over/under blouse. Third base is digital and genital contact. And in between second and third is sloppy second, which is I guess contact with mouth and breast. And then sloppy third is oral sex, which is of course a very sophisticated way of putting it. It's all incredibly sophomoric but *what*ever.")

Then, in July, she went to Hawaii with her parents and big brother. Amber was bummed when they got to the island because it rained the first night and she had to stay in and read. But the next day, she put on her cut-offs and a tee-shirt. "I went to the beach, which is a pretty good place to meet people when you're looking for people to know," she says, talking even faster than usual. "So I see this big group of kids who are like seventeen and over, and I was like, *oh god,* because at this point I was only fourteen. So I'm sitting around, and this kid comes up to me." The kid looked like Keanu Reeves, but his name was Jed and he was from San Diego.

He asked her name; she answered. He asked where she was from; she told him. He asked her age.

Here she shudders and looks around her room dramatically. "I was like, *Oh, Godddd.* I'm thinking to myself, What am I gonna do? If I say fourteen, I may as well just lock myself in my closet and just not come out. So I go, 'Well, how old do I look?'

He goes, "I don't know, eighteen, nineteen."

She goes, "I'm gonna be seventeen at the end of the month."

"Oh," he says, "I thought you were older."

"Well, how old are you?" she asks.

"Oh, I'm sixteen. I'm sixteen too," he says. "When are you gonna be seventeen?"

She goes, "July."

He goes, "I'm gonna be seventeen in October."

She arches her eyebrows, loving to tell this story. "I just go, 'Ooh, *younger man.'*

"So we like spent all of this time together," she says, her voice rising and falling with all the drama of it. "That night actually, everyone was gonna get drunk on the beach which is a stupid thing to do. I always find it's much better to be sober and watch people that are drunk than to actually *be* drunk yourself 'cause everyone's doing these stupid things. So we're just there, and we're just talking and watching everyone totally looking *ab*solutely ridiculous.

"And I asked him about his life and he was like, '*Well . . .'* He was a Dead Head, and he had a little drug problem, and like he told me all about this stuff about his life. He was in rehab for a while, and he told me about his mother and like his mother's second husband beat her and all this stuff. He kept telling me and I thought, *I* have nothing interesting to say.

"He said, '*Tell me about your brother.'* "

She smiles here because she knows Jed must have been worried about how protective her brother, Tom, was of her. Tom looks like a bouncer. "He's a big burly guy. He's really short but big. And so I told him that we Sumo wrestle each other all the time. I said, '*Oh, he tickles me all the time.'*

"[Jed] goes, '*You're ticklish?'*

"I go, '*No.'*

"So he like *jumps* on me, he starts tickling me, and I tickle him back, and we're like *roll*ing around and stuff. We stopped. And we were in that classic black-and-white movie pose: I'm looking up at him, he's looking down at me." She sweeps her arms up into the air, trying to conjure up just what an epic moment of romance this was.

Next, he asked if Amber wanted to go skinnydipping. "So I take off my bathing suit, and I put like the arm straps around my neck and he takes off his boxers and throws them up onto the shore. So we're swimming for a while, keeping distance. And he looks up and he goes, *OOOmigod.* There was this *huge* figure just like on the beach. This guy was just like looking at us. My *brother!* Jed's boxers were NnnEXXT to his feet. Tom picks up his boxers and just *looks* at them.

"And Jed's face was like something out of *Hellraiser.* He was *so* scared. And I'm like putting on my suit, going: *'Hi, Tom, how are you doing?'* I come out of the water. I was scared to death I'd have my bathing suit on like inside out or something and he was like, *'Oh, good, you're wearing clothes.'*

"I say, *'Tom, come on, I just met this guy today. What do you think I'm doing?'* " She grins sheepishly.

"Then [Jed and I] just spent days and days and days together and like we had a really *really* good relationship, and we also had a physical relationship. We didn't have sex. We're still *pure.*" The way she says it, she doesn't want you to think she means pure-pure.

"So after a while we're sitting on this dock. It was very nice. It was very very romantic. And he goes, *'What would you do if you knew someone who lived with someone that had a really contagious disease?'*

"I'm just like, *'Well, I'd ask them if they had it. If they didn't, then nothing would change and if they did then you know we might try just doing something different . . . Why do you ask?'*

"He goes, *'My mom has AIDS.'*

"I'm just like, *omigod"* Her voice is barely a whisper here. She clutches her face with both hands: "I mean, I had put myself at risk at this point. We had oral sex. But we were protected, but I guess I put myself at risk. At the time, I was so like *stunned.*

"And he goes, *'But I don't have it.'* And it didn't even occur to me to ask. What I'm saying is that I wasn't thinking about myself about whether I'd be at risk. But I was thinking, *Omigod,* his *mother* has AIDS. She got it from her second husband who abused her and also had a lot of affairs, so that's how she got it. He's like, *'But I don't have it.'*

"Then I started thinking to myself you know, here's this kid who's told me about the most intimate details of his life and even the most basic thing about me—my age—isn't honest, and I just started really getting upset about that. I said, *'Jed, can I say something?'*

"He's like, *'Sure.'*

"I'm like, *'All right well um you know, I'm not seventeen.'*

"He's like, *'Okay.'*

" *'I'm fourteen.'*

"He just got up. You could see him like pacing, *Omigod, omigod, omigod.* And I just sat there, and I just started crying. He didn't swear *at* me. He was just like, *'Oh shit, oh god.'* I just sat there, and I just cried and cried and cried. I was like, Oh *no.*

"He said, *'I turned fifteen in May.'* "

*   *   *

Then vacation was over. Amber was back in Pennsylvania. "I told all my friends you know, I met this guy and they would all say, 'Well, what did you do with him?' And when I told them, my friends said, 'You did what?' 'Cause at this point, I hadn't done *anything* like *any*where *near* this. I had boyfriends before and we had done stuff but nothing *any*where near this. So I told my friends what we had done. They were just like, *Are you high?* They're like, *Amber, you met this guy on vacation. What are you stupid?*"

She shrugs. "Actually," she says, "we had talked about having sex. He was the second guy that I had ever actually contemplated it. In the end, we decided not to because you know if it was meant to happen, it will. Later. The condoms in Hawaii weren't very good. They were like, they were more like novelties than anything else. They had names like Bare Back and Wet & Wild and Rough Rider. There's like a deli, a little convenience store, and they had these really cheap condoms. They didn't have Trojan or anything that I had known. So all these names were just like Bare Back and Kiss of Mint and Wet & Wild. And I was like, *'I don't want to do this.'*

"This time last year I wouldn't have ever thought that I would even contemplate it. I mean, I've known most of the people [in my class] since kindergarten and when I hear rumors about them having sex with people, it's just *omigod."*

She is thinking. She is quieter. Her hands, for the first time, are lying still in her lap: "And like I want to get tested for HIV, you know even though I know, I mean, Jed told me that he wasn't infected, and I know that he would not have done things to me if he thought I might be infected. So but I mean . . . He had a condom on. Because we didn't have any dental dams, and we did *that* once. And we didn't have one. And then the more I reflected on it when I got back and figured *omigod.* So I want to get tested. Actually the next time I go up to the city, I probably will.

"But you know it wasn't really until now that I really realized that teenagers really are capable of getting AIDS, and I mean when you're young you kind of think that you're totally invincible and nothing bad can ever happen to you. And *sex* seems like such a natural thing that you don't even think about it. But now I'm like telling all my friends, *If you're gonna go out with your boyfriend and do this, make sure that you've got at least one condom with you."*

* * *

Next, she pulls out an envelope. In the upper left corner is the logo from the resort where she met Jed. She starts trying to explain why she kept so many little things from that vacation, even a stupid envelope. It was like that time dancing with Jed in Burger King to Annie Lennox, "feeling so in sync." Knowing he thought it was adorable when she did some simple silly thing like lean against a wall in a certain way. And because before that vacation, "actually, I didn't really before have much luck with boys because . . . I guess when you've lived in a town for so long that people sort of get used to the way you were, like in sixth grade. I was a different person in sixth grade than I am now. But apparently people remember the past, and in sixth grade I was kind of a slut."

Her mother was away in Europe on business for six months that year. "She abandoned me," Amber says. "That was the year I started my period. I was incredibly big in a classroom of flat-chested people. I started developing a lot earlier than everyone else did so I guess my hormones were just sort of like flying out the door a lot of times before anyone else was. I was different from normal regular people. The way I dressed was different. I wore makeup before everyone else did. I was a big flirt." That year a girl in her class walked up to her and said, "Amber, you are so terribly ugly."

Guys were the only ones offering comfort. "Guys would be like, *'You are SOMEtimes attractive, SOMEWHAT on alternative bank holidays and in certain shades of light,'* and I'd just be like, *'Wow. Do you want me to remove my shirt or my shorts first?'* So I basically, what I used to do is repay compliments with physical . . . a lot of guys used to say, *'Oh, Amber, you're a beauty'*—with like an ulterior motive.

"I'll basically do just about anything you know, which is actually kind of a bad thing. Nick, who cheated on me, I guess he knew that I was kind of insecure and that I needed someone to *have* for like security. He just said, *'Oh Amber, I'll help you'* and so then that's basically all it really took at first for me to really open up to him. I think a lot of guys, when they find that out, that they'll sort of take advantage of it.

"But with [Jed] . . . Jed's the first guy, excluding my doctor, who's seen me naked," she says. "I mean, until then, no guy has ever really seen me . . . anything. I mean, I just knew so much about him, and like he knew as much interesting stuff as there is about me. So it was totally nonthreatening. I mean he got naked before I did. And then back in his room one day . . . but I mean he like didn't pressure me into doing anything. In fact, at first, he's like, *'Now, you sure, you don't mind this?'* I'm just like, *'Yeah.'* *'Like if I do anything at all that makes you feel uncomfortable, I just want you to tell me. Please.'* So I trusted him, and I'm really glad I did."

But after she got home from vacation and wrote Jed and didn't hear anything, she wasn't so sure. "I felt really lonely," she says. "I was like really scared. I was scared that I had like let myself get used again." Jed finally called, said he had needed time to "reassess" his feelings. Now, even though the boy next door still calls her weekly asking for sex, Amber thinks dating Jed has been a turning point. "I think that this summer actually is when I really started to grow up because now everyone knows that I'm dating Jed and everyone knows that I would never cheat on Jed and, I don't know, I think I'm starting to shed this image that I used to have. I'm kinda happy. It's a new year."

*   *   *

Yep, next week, in fact, the school year begins. Her braces come off soon. Her skin just cleared up miraculously, and she's praying her dad's going to let her trade glasses for contacts. Who knows, maybe some magazine—she writes lots of hint letters to *Sassy*— will do a makeover on her. "I'm hoping for this cataclysmic thing. The planets will realign," she giggles.

School isn't easy for Amber: "I'm the one that basically sits alone when I go to the library or to the cafe. I associate the cafeteria with *hell*. All the football players and their cheerleader girlfriends are there, and they all sit and talk about the mad drug party they went to a couple of days ago and like how smashed they got and how they're so glad that they managed to sober up just before their parents woke up or something like that."

She describes the other kids from the feet up: "Their shoes are always by either Converse, Bass, or Teva. Their socks are always made by Champion. Their jeans are always Gap, never Levi's for some reason I still don't know. If the person wears stuff by like The Limited or something, they most likely listen to pop or rap. If they wear stuff by The Gap, then chances are they're either alternative or classic rock, depending upon the shirt or jeans or whatever. If they dress in black, most likely heavy metal or alternative depending upon the eye makeup or the rippedness of the clothes. If they happen to wear long flowered dresses, they'd probably be just a lot like me.

"Sometimes I might get a little bit lonely. At first it used to really get to me, like I would make extra effort to befriend a member of the popular group and like suck up to them like a vacuum cleaner," she says. "I think I'm actually pretty alienated even from most of my friends. I've met friends who also feel alienated. So we've sort of unalienated each other."

Amber is trying more and more not to cower just because she feels excluded from most of the cliques at school. Instead, she's joined the Martin Luther King Jr. Action League, the Gay-Straight Alliance. She goes three times a month to Philadelphia to work in a soup kitchen. She has solicited signatures for Gays in the Military. "I think that one of the things that we [as teenagers] have to do is to make ourselves visible in helping the planet, not just ecologically but socially and racially and stuff like that," she says.

Sometimes the other kids tease her about her Birkenstocks and all her beliefs. "The next time somebody calls me hippie chick," she says, "I'm gonna look them right in the face and say, *I hope you get drafted.*

"What I'm gonna do is starting this year, if there happens to be a Friday night or Saturday night that I'm not going out, I'm gonna study and the way I figure it is that then the kids that go out every Friday and Saturday night, they're gonna wind up at like the state college of like Northern Bumblefuck and I'm gonna wind up at Harvard or something."

She only has to get her *B*s up to *A*s this school year and start touring "pretty high up" colleges next summer—the University of California at Los Angeles or San Diego or Berkeley, Rice in Texas, and Penn State. Her father already brought home "this huge packet" put out by *U.S. News & World Report* on the best colleges. "So I looked them over, and I figured out what kind of standards I want to achieve," she says. "My father really pushes me a lot. It's not like negatively. He doesn't say like, 'Oh you're so stupid. Why'd you do this?' But he wants to make sure that I succeed." He tells her stories about kids at the college where he works who don't speak English, whose parents work in rice fields. He tells her they work harder. " *'And they wind up getting into Harvard,'* " she quotes him. " *'They wind up building these big corporations that whip everyone else.'* He tells me about girls that have been beaten by their boyfriends and stuff like that. I don't think he's trying to intimidate me into success, but I think he's just trying to keep me aware of all the things that are going around and things that I have to make sure that I avoid.

"I sort of think I put more pressure on myself to be a good student because I know that nothing is going to be handed to me. I have to work for it."

She calls herself a daddy's girl, and one of the things she hates most in the world is disappointing him. And she's pretty sure she did in Hawaii because her mother mentioned to her—*casually*—that she and Amber's father had seen Amber by a fountain. And Amber already knew right then what her mother wasn't saying. "I don't *make out*," Amber says. "I *kiss*. Like I don't do a Sharon Stone–esque thing. So Jed and I were just there. We were at this fountain. It was really nice and quiet and romantic. So we just started kissing. We weren't just like all over each other you know. It was really sweet."

When her mother told her, Amber says, "I wasn't really ashamed of it, but there was nothing I could do about it now and I mean I had gotten to the point that if people wanted to . . . if people were like really anxious that I was going out with Jed they should just *deal* with it because I didn't really plan on dumping him. So, but, she said that my dad had seen us, and he just said, *Omigod* and they left. So after a while, I was kind of in a guilt trip. I was like, *Omigod,* I disappointed my father. What am I gonna do?"

There's still a ton more stuff in the shoebox. Old flower petals. Snapshots of a crush who looked like Waldo from *Where's Waldo?* A Signet paperback of *Romeo and Juliet,* which reminds Amber of Jed again. "We wanted to have some sort of a song. He's really sentimental, and I'm like, Ah, it's like "Romeo and Juliet," by the Indigo Girls. Because he used to say that I look like Juliet. He talked about how we were similar to Romeo and Juliet, although it might be sort of hard to see. We met, but it's just gonna seem really hard to be together because you know, it's as though the distance between us is like our parents. Our distance is like feuding with us."

They talk on the phone now. Amber sends him condoms. "I sent him like a green one, a purple one, a blue one," she says. Amber plans to marry him someday. It annoys her that her mother "trivializes" her relationship with him, but she's got someone now she hopes will take her more seriously. "I'm going to see a therapist actually next week," she says. "I'm not incredibly troubled. I'm not suicidal. I was just talking to my physician." She pauses. "Just that I thought that I was bisexual. Actually it was really funny. I said well you know, *'I think I'm bisexual.'* And she said, *'Oh, well, there's nothing I can do about it. Sorry.'* She was just joking."

Amber is knitting her fingers together. "I just have this feeling that I am. I've never pursued a relationship with a woman, and I've never been pursued. I think probably once I get into college, I'll probably do some experimentation. The advice that has been given to me by a lot of adults that I know—not my parents, my parents have no idea—most of the advice that I have received is that I shouldn't do it with someone who's older than me. Someone that's maybe three years older than me probably has a completely different agenda than I do. I just have this feeling that I am. I mean I don't know anyone in my family that is. I figure you know . . . there must be one somewhere. But I'm probably the only one that I'm familiar with. I just have this feeling that I am. I just . . . I think I'm gonna get sick of having a boyfriend. I sometimes get sick of guys in general.

"I've felt this way since I was eleven. I remember when I was like little, when I was like seven, I used to go up and down the dressing rooms in like department stores and peek in them."

Has she tried telling anyone else?

"I told my brother. The first thing my brother said was, *'I can't* wait *till you tell mom and dad.'* My parents, they're not homophobic but they don't get as intimately involved in like the gay rights argument as I am. Because they just think that you should just live and let people live.

"I guess I just first became involved in gay rights through the news. I don't really think that anyone should be tormented. I don't think anyone should be discriminated against. I just think that everyone is entitled to live their own life. And I think that gays are being really violently opposed. No one has to really like what they do, but I think they're entitled to their respect. I think that they shouldn't be denied jobs or housing or anything just because. Their sexual preference really isn't anyone else's business anyway."

At her high school, two lesbians kissed in the hall. "They were confronted with this huge angry mob," Amber says heatedly. "I mean, people if they'd had rocks, they would have stoned them to death undeniably.

"I would never come out to people in my school. A few of my friends know. But I just . . . I don't even know if it's fair to call myself bisexual. But if word got out that I even *thought* that I was, I would have death threats, people taping things to my locker, and I think that there are a lot of straight people who deserve to die sooner than I do."

∗ ∗ ∗

She puts the lid back on the shoe box and shakes her hair, runs her fingers through it. She feels like grabbing some fried mozzarella sticks and then a sundae at Friendly's. After that, she says, "Let's go play" in the dark on the wooden playground equipment at the elementary school.

On the way through town, she points out her long brick high school and the white-steepled church she attends. When she gets to Friendly's, she says that this is it—the only form of recreation available on a summer night in her suburb. She slides into a booth, and as she's spooning up some of her cookies-and-cream double scoop with jimmies, she spies a boy from her school walking in.

He's wearing a tie-dyed shirt, little John Lennon wirerims, and jean shorts. And Teva strap sandals. "Oh," she whispers appreciatively, then admits she has a bit of a crush on him. His name's Micah.

On her way out the door, she makes a point of saying hi. She asks if he has a quarter so she can call and tell her parents she'll be a little late. He does. She says maybe the two of them should take a walk some night this summer. He says yeah.

On the drive to the playground, Amber says, "Micah would be a Grateful Dead type." She's got this big grin.

So what about Jed?

"Actually," she says, "Jed and I got disconnected a couple of weeks ago, just when we were talking about how committed we were to each other."

Pause. "I personally don't like Tevas, do you?"

Nine Months Later

Nine months later, in a taped-shut envelope with the return address: "From A Chick That Owes You A Serious Apology," we got a letter from Amber asking if we could get together again because, she wrote, "So much has happened since we talked that, in reflection, I have figured out that the person you interviewed was not really me." She wanted people to read about how she was now, rather than how she was then. She asked us to call her.

When we called, Amber was in the middle of studying for her biology final exam, "stuff like pig dissection and genetics and the endocrine system." Even though she was getting a D ("I've got As in everything else. Could this be that Amber is stupid third period every day?"), she said of course she'd rather talk on the phone. After saying, "I'm sorry, I'm sorry, I'm sorry, I'm sorry," she asked if we could please not use her name because of the stuff she told us about maybe being bisexual: "I don't know if I want to come out in the book. I've sort've figured out that labels restrict you, but in my heart I think that I am. But since I saw you, my mother indicated to me that she thinks homosexuality is WRONG. She's really intense about it. I don't think she has a clue about me. See, 'Amber brings home a boyfriend every week.'" She added she was also worried about hostility at school because a gay friend got his car smashed with a brick when he left it in the school parking lot to go volunteer at a homeless shelter.

Then she forgot to breathe for about ten minutes while she listed the ways she's changed besides that:

My confidence has gone way up since the last time I spoke with you. I wanted everybody to like me. I got my braces off. That's pretty cool. And that guy Jed turned out to be a total prick. I got really upset about it. Then I noticed weird things happening to me, like my waist swelling and my breasts feeling tender, so I consulted a medical book. A lot of what I was feeling were common things for the first trimester of pregnancy. I hadn't had my period in three months. I'm really irregular. But when you spend a week with a guy, more time naked than dressed, you get worried that maybe you got too close. I called Planned Parenthood to see if you could get pregnant without actually having sex, and they said, Have you taken a pregnancy test? So I took $5 or $10 to CVS and went to the handy family planning center, conveniently located across from the candy, and the pregnancy kits were $25. I had to leave. I couldn't go ask my mother for that much money. So one day that week I was coming home from a shelter with a neighbor who was chaperoning us and it was this outpouring of emotion, and I just asked her. She stopped at her house and gave me the money. I bought the test, and then my best friend and I went into the locker room of school really early. You're supposed to pee on the little strip for ten seconds but of course Amber didn't read the instructions. So we had to go back later and try it again. If it turns purple then pink, you're pregnant. Mine turned turquoise then pink. Oh, shit. Then it turned white and I got my period two weeks later.

And you remember that guy we ran into that night at Friendly's. We both thought he was cute?

(You mean Micah?)

Yeah, in the end, we kinda hooked up. We would stare at each other on the bus, this incredible glorious tension. Then on Christmas Day I went to his house and thank god. But then he wrote me this long letter and poem, saying, "Amber, you're so beautiful and I totally value you as a person" and whatever else crap they always say. He doesn't want me. He says he knows I'm the one. Just not now. Anyway, he smokes so much pot it's ridiculous. He's incredibly deep, considering his brain doesn't work anymore.

So another thing you should know is that not only are the kids profiled here just basically randomly selected and not definitive or meant to represent more than themselves, sometimes, often, teenagers don't even represent themselves for more than a minute. And then they change. That's one thing that makes them so challenging for people trying to sell them eye shadow. And one thing that makes them so much fun to hang around.

January 7, 1981

Death is black and birth is green. While the thought of a birth that is unwanted can be a blacker black than I've known until now. The ugly side, the realization that I am not invincible, the pain, the cost (in many many more ways than one), etcetera. But now only the question: Am I?

*   *   *

January 8, 1981

NO! (now maybe I am invincible after all . . .)

FOLLOWING NICOLE WOOLF
UP THE MOUNTAIN

Nicole Woolf is hiking up Timpanogos Mountain. She's wearing a sweatshirt and cutoffs, and even though it is July, she's also wrapped in a piecework quilt. The night air in Utah is cold enough to make her breath hover like a guardian angel. The mountain stands out black against the dark blue of the near-midnight sky. The moon is low behind it, but the starlight is bright. It makes the flowers along the trail glow white. It makes the snowfields loom out of all the darkness.

The incline is steep, but seventeen-year-old Nicole's burgundy Converse All-Stars zig upward, then zag around an outcropping of rock, then climb again. Her tanned legs are taut and strong because she runs seven miles a day, seven miles straight up, to the huge white Y (signifying Brigham Young University) that is mounted onto the brushy hill above her Provo neighborhood. She hikes or runs to keep in shape; for real fun she goes rock climbing, water skiing, skydiving.

Suddenly, Nicole notices that one of her shoelaces has come undone. She stops and turns to the tall blond guy following her. "Jake," she says. "Tie my shoe." Her tone is playful, but she means it. She points her toe in his direction.

Jake grins and bends over to tie her shoe—even though his best friend, Cody, protests with a loud groan; even though Cody's girlfriend, Kerri, snickers.

Jake fixes the lace, gets up, and they all trudge on past another rock outcropping and then another—until Nicole's other shoe comes undone. "Jake," she says, crossing her arms. "Tie my shoe." This time, he complains with a dramatic sigh, and Cody prods him: "Don't do it. Be a man, Jake."

But Jake gets down on his knees and ties Nicole's shoe.

They hike on, Jake and Nicole seeming to float ahead on the trail as Cody and Kerri climb slowly, murmuring to each other. This is a double date. Cody and Kerri are a new couple, still amazed they are together. Nicole and Jake are something else. This is maybe Jake's last ever date with Nicole—*if* he can even call it a date.

Next week, Jake is going on a mission. As a member of the Church of Jesus Christ of Latter-Day Saints, he is being sent abroad for two years of spreading the word about what it means to be Mormon. Guys usually become missionaries when they are nineteen, but Jake wanted to be different. Just like when he stopped rollerblading and snowboarding because everybody else started. To him, a mission seemed like what *everybody* did. And it's not like it's a required thing. It's a freewill choice. So at nineteen he had exercised his free will and chosen not to go. Soon after that, he was eating an ice cream cone in the mall one night, and this little blonde with snapping blue eyes and a broken arm came over and asked where he got that "superman" cone anyway. That was Nicole.

Just the day before, Nicole had both broken her arm and broken up with her longtime boyfriend, Rob. She was healing. A "superman" ice cream might help. And that good-looking guy with the corkscrew hair and the loopy grin sure wouldn't hurt either.

But that all happened a whole year ago. And Nicole's best friend Lynn, who makes sandwiches with her at Subway, says that Nicole isn't over Rob. "She's in the best mood if she talks about him," Lynn says as proof. "*Everything* reminds her of him."

Nicole protests: "Well, I was goin' out with the guy for a year and a half. We went out too long. He was the first guy I've ever really liked a lot, that I liked equal," she says. "Usually, I let the guy like me more than I like them. That's how I always keep unattached."

* * *

So, Jake is following Nicole up the mountain for the last time. They've done a lot of hiking in the last year. They've also gone to concerts and to the mall a lot. They bought funny hats at the Dollar Store, Jake got her a chia pet for Christmas, and on New Year's they got his car stuck in a humongous snowbank. Nicole graduated from public high school. And sometime in there, Jake decided he would go on a mission after all. Nicole takes a little credit for that. "I told him he wouldn't get a good wife if he didn't go," she says. Anyway, Jake sent in his paperwork to the church bureaucracy, and the church sent back word that he'd be sent to of all places—Russia. As he spends his last free days in Provo, and as he hikes up the mountain at midnight, he cracks jokes about nuclear waste and Cyrillic.

He'll be learning Russian for two months in the locked-down school in Provo before he'll be flown away to some remote town in Russia, where he'll be teamed with only one other missionary. He'll be able to send and receive letters. On Mother's Day, he will be able to call his mom. If he's lucky, the church will let him call home on Christmas. And who knows where Nicole will be when Jake gets out—studying the Scriptures in Jerusalem "where Jesus walked on the water." Or dating some guy who walked up to the Subway counter and offered to take her skydiving. Or *marrying* some guy who walked into the Subway shop and offered to take her skydiving.

* * *

A sign on the mountain warns hikers to stay off the snowfields, which are riddled with killer crevasses. But instead of turning back, Nicole and her three buddies go out onto the snowfield, which has lasted this long into the summer because the past winter's snows were so deep. They skate around on the snow for a while and then climb farther up the mountain to another snowfield, where a waterfall thunders. They shout above the sound. They giggle. Nicole goes right to the lip of the ice near the rushing water, and Jake pulls her back. Then they slide down the icy snowfields and race each other back down the paths until they find a clearing where they can have a fire.

Jake piles up some wood he brought from home and gets out a lighter. It's low on fuel because earlier at Nicole's house he was using it to toast ants on the sidewalk. ("I killed an ant. Will I go to hell?" he asked Nicole provocatively. "Animals can talk in the after life," she told him. "Ants can testify against you.")

Nicole sits on a log near the woodpile, wrapped in her quilt. Cody and Kerri huddle against one another. Jake gathers kindling and finds some bug spray in the trunk of his car to douse the wood, hoping for a lighter-fluid effect. A flame ignites. Smoke billows out.

"Smoke follows beauty," Cody chokes out as the smoke moves over to him. "I hate rabbits!" he screams, a childhood saying that's supposed to make smoke veer away.

"Don't be a jerk," Jake scolds the fire.

"You know what you're supposed to say if somebody calls you a jerk," Nicole announces. She sing-songs: *"A jerk is a tug. A tug is a boat. A boat floats on water. Water is nature. Nature is beautiful. So thanks for the compliment."*

Everyone laughs, and Jake says, "My favorite is, *'I'm rubber, you're glue, whatever you say bounces off me and sticks on you.'* "

"What's that one about *in your underwear?*" Nicole asks.

A huge laugh bursts out of Cody. Jake says wryly, "I think that's a Woolf family one."

"No," Nicole insists, giggling. "The one where you're like naked."

Kerri offers: "You say, *'What are you eating under there?'* "

"No," Nicole says. "It was like something you said as a come-back."

Cody interjects. *"There's a place in France where the naked ladies dance. There's a hole in the wall where the men can see them all."*

Nicole interrupts him. She has just remembered: *"So, so suck your toe, all the way to Mexico. While you're there, kiss a bear, and don't forget your underwear.*" She finishes with a stagey hand flourish. She grins around the fire at her friends.

"What?" Jake says with fake disbelief.

"You've never heard that?" Nicole asks.

"Like *look at my thumb.*" She does. He makes his voice a cartoon pitch, *"Gee, you're dumb."*

"Look at my pinky," Cody and Jake recite together. *"Gee you're stinky."*

"Stare hard, retard. Stare on, moron." Everyone is giggling.

"I hate rabbits!" Cody screams at the smoke again.

"Does anyone want marshmallows?" Jake asks, tossing a bag of them from hand to hand.

"Does *anyone* have any sticks?" Nicole asks him, meaning him, meaning does he have any sticks.

"No," he replies. "But the trees do." She looks at him, meaning *what are you waiting for?*

"Sure," Jake shrugs. "I'll be back." He heads into the woods.

Nicole squeezes a marshmallow. "These are great if you put 'em in the microwave and let 'em blow up real big and then take a knife, you have to have a knife because with a fork it's too hard to get 'em out and you go like this"—she stabs at the marshmallow with an invisible knife—"and you try to peel it off the knife for like an hour 'cause it gets hard."

"Another Woolf tradition," Cody deadpans.

"Ouch, stinging nettle," Jake yelps, limping back into the firelight, rubbing his leg. Cody starts whittling the branches into skewers.

They stab marshmallows and hold them near the embers until the sugary skin bubbles black. Nicole knows a game where you make letters with your backside. She gets up and demonstrates: "Guess what letter I'm doing?"

Jake snorts: "She really is gonna spell a letter with her butt?"

Nicole twists around in the firelight.

Everyone cracks up.

She sits down, grinning hugely. "That was an *A,*" she says.

"That was an *A?*" Jake asks, mystified.

"Yeah."

"Oh," he says. "A *little a.*"

Cody protests, "You have to tell us if you're doing a big letter or a small letter."

"Okay, here's a big letter," Nicole swivels around.

"Oh, sit down," Cody groans.

"That was a *B,*" she says triumphantly.

"Mormons play Butt Game," Jake blurts out an imaginary headline making them all gasp with laughter.

Nicole shrugs. "I only played it once."

"That's what they all say," Jake teases. *"I only did it once."*

"It was fun," Nicole tells him. "We played it at my house. My family."

"You are kidding?" Cody erupts again.

"Your family," Jake shakes his head. He has seen the Woolfs in action.

"I think we had like a party," she explains. "I can't remember."

"Oh my gosh," Cody says, laughing hard. "Some kids standin' up by the fireplace, makin' letters with their butt. *'Hey, mom, spell a whole word.'* Oh, my gosh." He is gasping for air, barely keeping himself on the log in his hysteria.

"I don't think it's *that* weird," Nicole says. She leans her head onto Jake's shoulder. It is the first time she has touched him all night.

* * *

Nicole's family has tons of their own funny traditions—like all eleven kids wearing matching pajamas on Christmas Eve and acting out the Nativity. "It's just so weird how much *love* we have in our family," she says. Her family has always been the most solid thing—a big, energetic Mormon family integrally involved with the church.

That's why her parents' divorce almost three years ago affected her so harshly. Her mother was crying in the master bedroom. Her father was meeting with the older kids. And finally he called the younger kids in, including Nicole ("I was daddy's little girl," she says more than once). He told them that he was leaving, moving to California alone. She remembers thinking, "Wait, our perfect family?"

Having her father go from the man who held her and called her his princess to someone who left has also changed the way Nicole looks at the boys she dates. After she goes on her own mission at twenty-one, she wants to marry a man strong in the faith, someone who will "honor his priesthood" and be able to bless his children (five of them, she hopes). She is aware that she herself can only reach the highest realm of the Celestial kingdom if she is married in the temple. It is the highest good. "Later," she explains, "you become a god, and you get to have your own earth—only if you're married in the temple."

She feels confident she will find the right husband. Eternity hinges on it. When she marries, she is binding herself to that man for all eternity. They will be together forever. And only after marriage will she know the fullness of the Mormon faith. As a child, there are still many covenants of the temple she has not been told. But once she marries, she will go to the temple and there learn the sacraments in which only married people or those who have been on missions can participate. She is looking forward to growing in God's will, to being an example, even "just by being happy."

This past year, she entered into a ceremony that gave her confidence that it will all happen. She had her patriarchal blessing, which means that she went to a patriarch in the church whose calling is seeing into people's futures. She fasted and then her mom took her into the patriarch, who laid his hands on her head. "It was so neat," she recalls, "just 'cause I was like hearing things about my husband and how he was gonna be a great guy and all this stuff. The spirit was *so strong.* I was bawling."

So far she hasn't found the guy for her, though she has found at least one who wasn't. "With Rob, I probably wasn't doing the things I was supposed to, and I just wasn't happy," she says. "He didn't really care about the church and just being around that. And his friends . . . and kissing him too much, I don't know. We [Mormons] don't have sex outside of marriage, which I'm glad. I never had sex with Rob or anything, but you know how you have those feelings and stuff."

That's why she shook with tears as the patriarch told her that her husband would be "a man of sterling character." She was just *so* relieved: "I don't wanna jerk husband, like Rob," she says quietly but with conviction. Then she adds haltingly: "That's kinda my fear, that they're gonna leave me—someone that I love a lot, that they'll leave me. That's my biggest fear. It's not like I'm afraid to love people, but like I'm afraid to get attached and stuff cause I was close to my dad, and I'm afraid they're gonna leave. And I was afraid the whole time: *I'm pressing Rob too much. He's just gonna leave.* I was always afraid of that. And I didn't want to go out with Jake just because, then you're just gonna leave."

* * *

Their last night together is getting close to curfew, and they get quieter around the fire. Soon, Jake will leave for Russia. Nicole will go to California to work in her brother-in-law's dental practice for a few months. Then she'll start college, then go to Jerusalem to study religion. She and Jake will write. But they won't find each other again some day and marry. Nicole can't see it happening.

The fire dies away to embers, and Jake finally douses it by peeing on it. And then everyone crawls into the Jeep for the ride back to Provo. Jake puts on Bob Dylan singing: "Everybody must get stoned" and weaves in and out of the broken yellow line on the deserted highway; the kids sway against each other as the car rocks from side to side.

"I want to watch *Mary Poppins,*" Cody says wistfully.

"I have the videotape at my house," Nicole says.

"No!" Cody shouts, shocked at this beautiful luck. "Can we watch it?"

"Sure," Nicole says. And they do.

Step–Grand–Surrogate–Adoptive–Dysfunctional–Test-Tube–Parents

These days you don't see many moms in aprons happily frying chicken for dinner at six o'clock sharp so dad can get out in the backyard to play catch with the kids before dark. Maybe you never did; maybe everybody only sort of agreed to pretend this scenario really existed somewhere. You sure don't see a lot of nuclear families anymore—with such an ominous label, I guess they couldn't have lasted long. Anyway, because of all the changes that have taken place in the last few decades, I think a lot of people assume the family has less influence than ever today, and especially on teenagers. You hear about gangs described as surrogate families, and you hear about seven-year-old Tommy letting himself into the house after school every day (by the way, what's a "latchkey" exactly?), then going back out to the A&P for some milk to have with dinner with the sitter. And it's true you could hang out with a teenager, have in-depth talks with them about curfew laws or their fights with their girlfriend, and realize at the end of it you don't even know if they *have* parents, since the mention of them has never come up.

But even though most teenagers' families don't follow that traditional old model, they still have a huge, if more distant, influence. When you ask about their parents, you see how much *teenagers define themselves by where mom expects them to go to college or even by not ending up in jail like the dad they've never met. Sure, you hear some of the old complaints about not getting enough money for the weekend or dad not liking their new boyfriend, but a lot of what they say has to do with comparing and contrasting their goals, opinions, tastes, actions with their dads, moms, stepdads, foster moms, legal guardians of whatever type.*

From what I've seen, it's clear that a single mom or two gay dads or a stepdad, three half siblings and four steps can all be great, supportive, healthy environments or abusive, nightmarish ones. Most are somewhere in between. Same as it ever was. Same as it was for me. And actually, one reason I relate to teenagers so much might be that unlike most people my age, my parents were not fifties-mentality but more hippies. Mom says that's not the best description, preferring we be called a family of "artists." You can see what you think.

I was born in San Francisco after my mom moved out there with just her baby son, Hill, and the stroller she bought from Goodwill. She was twenty-one and had been living in an East Village walk-up while going to Cooper Union for painting, taking breaks and playing guitar in Washington Square Park. She got pregnant at twenty, married the father and named Hill after a drop out neighbor who used to say to Baby Hill, "Hey Hill, say motherfucker." Hill slept in a basket on the floor of the sandal shop on MacDougal Street mom owned with her husband. One day mom stretched the phone into the back room of the shop so she could call her friend and whisper, "Bob Dylan is playing my guitar!" But after less than a year, mom ended up leaving her husband who was cheating on her, and she chose San Francisco because she had a friend who'd let her stay. It was a duplex on Chestnut Street and there was an art student from North Carolina living on the other side. That was dad.

After mom got pregnant with me, she and dad got married. And when dad graduated from the San Francisco Art Institute, we moved to North Carolina where he had a teaching job at Duke Uni-

versity. In Durham, we were the weird artist family. We had a two-story house with every wall in every room painted a different bright color with contrasting trim. I think I learned to read off Fillmore posters about The Grateful Dead and Janis Joplin concerts. And at the top of the red-white-and-blue stairway, there was another one saying "War Is Not Healthy for Children and Other Living Things." There was a beanbag chair in the living room and beaded curtains and tapestries. My brother Ben was born in '65 and then two years later my sister, Amy.

We kids were kind of wild: We melted crayons on the radiator in the playroom and laughed that the other neighborhood kids needed permission to go to the park when we roamed anywhere and stayed out as late as we wanted. I thought a curfew was some quaint outdated Wally and Beav notion. When six-year-old Amy scrawled, "Shit man, I love you" on the dashboard of our VW van, dad thought it was a cool statement so he traced over it in indelible Magic Marker and left it there till we sold the van years later. And once, when we were in Washington and went to see the White House, the guard wouldn't let me in because I had no shoes on. I told mom I hadn't brought them, and she tried to send me back to the car to get them, but I said, "No, I didn't bring any shoes to Washington." Meanwhile, we'd already been there two days.

We were a family that did everything together, from lots of camping at the lake to elaborate scavenger hunts on our birthdays. Nobody ever expected my parents to split up. I remember talking about it with my two best friends on the jungle gym at school one day. Kate's parents were already divorced, but Debbie and Kate and I all agreed my parents had the best marriage and were the least likely to break up. I also don't recall a long time of them fighting, but I do know it got really tense on a cross-country camping trip we took, the summer before they separated. Like the Great Salt Flats in Utah, when mom made dad stop the van, she got out, and dad just kept driving. I can still picture mom as this little stick fig-ure receding into a blinding white desert. So it wasn't any big sur-prise when about six months later they called us four into their bedroom for a family conference and said they were going to marriage counseling. Actually, right afterward, Hill and I walked outside and said to each other, "Marriage counseling? Why don't they just get divorced?" Then we headed down to the park to play on the merry-go-round.

We were kind of psyched about the possibility. We thought it meant we'd have two of everything: two TVs, two houses, two people who wouldn't consult each other if one said no to something we wanted. And didn't divorced dads take their kids out for dinner all the time and stuff like that? But when they did separate, it was less than half of everything. Dad was sleeping in his painting studio, and mom went on food stamps because she only had a part-time teaching salary from Duke. For a while, mom took a paper route, and we kids rode along in the back of our bashed-in Rambler. I'd roll, and Amy, who was nine and had the best arm, flipped the papers over the roof of the car onto people's porches. We didn't really have regular meals anymore. Mostly the four of us would just skip breakfast and lunch. Then after Hill drove us home from school at about 4:30 in the afternoon, we'd all head straight for the kitchen and cook up one of our specialties: spaghetti or hot dogs, fighting over whether they were best broiled, boiled, or fried.

I think parents and kids tend to have really different takes on divorce. After Kurt Cobain died, one newscaster I really like and agree with on most issues said something that to me exemplifies a common parental perspective: "Well, Kurt had been very depressed from a young age, which any child of divorce can understand." Maybe in Kurt Cobain's case that was true, and maybe it's true in a lot of cases. I can't really speak for anyone else's psyche for sure. I know a 1995 study showed that children of divorce were more likely to skip school, drop out, and were more likely to get divorced themselves. Even my brother Ben feels the divorce was more devastating for him than I think it was for me. But many kids have told me that divorce has been much better for them than the alternatives. I think it has much more to do with how the divorce is handled, how much fighting goes on, and whether there's contin-

ued contact with both parents and any siblings. Plus, it's so common now that they know it's a really good possibility all along, so it's not some huge shock. Half their friends' parents and even grandparents have been divorced at least once, if they even had two parents to start with.

I tell parents who ask that they might as well be honest with their teenage kids all along about the problems they're having, since the kids will know it anyway. I don't mean dumping specifics on them about who did what to whom, how he threw the saucer at you and how you threatened to kill the woman he's sleeping with, or even that you always disagree over where to spend the inheritance. Do give teenagers a general sense that there are problems between you but you are working on them or whatever the truth is, so kids'll know what they are dealing with.

Divorce or separation or finding out about a parent's affair or watching mom go through a breakup with her boyfriend lets teenage kids see their parents as fallible, perhaps for the first time. And seeing your parents more objectively usually makes you grow up faster. But a lot of parents who are divorcing, or who have always been single parents, take that too far and treat their kids more like friends, people they can rely on as they would adults. I've seen some try to turn their kids into their primary companions. One mom I know who was divorced for the second time and had only her fourteen-year-old daughter living at home with her not only asked her daughter to go shopping with her for new clothes and makeup so she'd look cool going out to clubs or, hopefully, on dates, but she constantly asked her daughter to double-date with her. I understand why this may be tempting, especially since I saw in both my parents the loneliness that comes with the breakup of a marriage. But relying on your kids to be your support or your regular companion or your friend or shoulder to cry on, while understandable, is totally unfair and won't serve you well in the long-term. Teenagers still need their parents to be parents, probably more now than ever because things are confusing at home. Try not to ask them for reassurance, acceptance, companionship, advice, or love. *Instead, show them you love them, like them, and are interested in how all this is affecting them, and make clear you're there to talk to them about it whenever they'd like.*

Obviously, it's also unfair for parents to ask their kids to take sides. Or even to hope they will. This same principle applies to not only divorcing parents but to foster parents, stepparents, surrogate parents, legal guardians—any situation where a teenager is potentially in the middle of two or more feuding adults. My own mom admitted this to me recently:

> *No matter how much you hear that it's bad to put your kids in the middle, it's really hard not to think, 'Well, my case is different.' I wanted you kids to know that it wasn't my fault, that your dad made it impossible for me to live with him. You want your kids to love you, not the guy who made your life miserable. I think you feel that if your kids are on your side, that makes you feel better about this terrible thing you're doing by breaking up the family.*

In her case, it may have worked somewhat because as you can see throughout this book, my dad was much less present in my life following my parents' divorce than my mom.

For me, and for teenagers even more now, I think, the initial ways divorce affects you are mostly practical. Divorce means you take on responsibilities faster: You probably already knew how to shop for food but now maybe you have to do it more often. You learn how to fill out a check that your mom's made out to K-Mart. You learn to be a parent to yourself maybe more of the time, since your parents are probably around less. You have to start running the carpool for your little brother's soccer team. And you may struggle with these really confusing family trees (my brother Hill has five sets of grandparents, four of which showed up at his college graduation).

I don't mean to say it's all about the grocery shopping either. Of course there are emotional reactions to the whole situation, probably a lot of things you've never felt before. First of all, to teenagers whose parents are splitting up, or whose stepmom is making her mom miserable, or whose dad and his boyfriend fight constantly: You're not responsible. You are entitled to your own life with one or more parents or responsible adults who are focused on your well-being (and not adults who need you as a friend). If the atmosphere at your house is really tense, get away from it if you can by hanging out at a friend's family's house, having meals there, staying over. You don't have to be around all that tension you didn't create. Also, forget family loyalty. What I mean is, it's okay to talk about problems inside your home with someone out-side if you think they will be able to listen and help: a friend's dad, a teacher, a counselor, your adult ear of choice. Likewise, if you have two lesbian moms (which will be increasingly common) or never had a dad at home (already very common), it's okay to find yourself a reasonable facsimile of one. Know that if your mom or dad is a single parent, no matter how great they are, they're just one person and they can't offer you everything or necessarily be right about all their decisions. So don't feel guilty about talking to other adults about problems or questions you have, and don't take responsibility for your mom or dad feeling threatened that you seem so much closer to Laura's mom or you'd rather talk about your problems with your track coach these days.

Something else that happens a lot in broken up families, which I didn't have the luxury of experiencing firsthand, is parents' brib-ing kids for their affection. "My stepdad gave me a car so I wouldn't go away to Yale, even though that's a much better school for me. He did it so I wouldn't be near my dad, who teaches there," one girl told me. Lots of teenagers say they know there were ulterior motives behind their new leather jackets or vacations, and even that they've allowed themselves to be manipulated by more lenient rules, like being able to get high in your room at dad's. I'd say that in those cases, you really have to be your own parent, and decide for yourself, thinking long term now, what you really want. Is it really worth a leather jacket to not be able to see your mom for months? Or is staying out till all hours or being able to get away with trashing the house or getting smashed the night before your Achievements really a good move, even if your parents are saying it's all cool by them?

The truth is, everyone involved will be figuring out as they go along how to deal with this situation. And probably feeling like they're failing everyone else. One eighteen-year-old told me that her mom recently apologized, teary-eyed, about getting divorced when the girl was seven. The mom said she felt really bad she hadn't been able to give the kids more financially, and that they'd moved a lot and things hadn't been more stable. And the girl told her, "Mom, don't worry about it, you guys splitting up just made me more resourceful. Please, I don't resent you for it." This girl is definitely resourceful. She's in tons of groups at school, created her own school paper because there was none, plays soccer, and has worked since she was sixteen to make money for college. She also said she couldn't tell her mom this but her mom really wasn't around much, and so from a young age she learned she could rely on herself: "The fact that I didn't have one place I could always go for emotional stability made me create my own home inside."

Not that emotional instability is something to wish on anybody. Not that you'd wish for anyone to have to go through some of the really tense and painful experiences that come with divorce. Even as Kelli and I were talking about this chapter, I started crying thinking of my dad coming back over a little while after he'd moved out. He'd asked if he could have dinner with all of us like old times, and he sat at his old place at the table, but his beer and his food sat there completely untouched while he just cried.

But I guess, really, divorce is just another one of those realities that kids today aren't shielded from. You know sex can kill. You know the earth's resources can get used up. You know everybody has to work and things are tight a lot of the time and jobs can disappear just like that. You know some dads are in prison, some moms have babies out of test tubes or petri dishes, sometimes two dads adopt kids, plenty of kids inherit a different race from each of *their parents, some fathers can't see their kids anymore because they hit their moms or sexually abused their daughters, and even when it is a married mom and a dad having a biological child or two together, the chances are only about 50-50 they'll stay that way.*

WHEN KYLE TWOHORSES SPEAKS

*K*yle TwoHorses is watching *The Young and the Restless* with his
mom in the living room of their trailer. There is a doily on the
19-inch television set and on the wall above it there is a circle of
pictures, all of Kyle at ages four, ten, fourteen, and, one taken just a
few months ago, at sixteen. The house smells clean as bleach. The
green curtains blow in a breeze.

This morning Kyle told his social worker he didn't want to be in
a book, but then he changed his mind and said he would. His social
worker promised he would get to eat lunch out during the interview. But so far Kyle has just kept his eyes on the television. His
long ponytail is still wet from the shower and as it dries, the shorter
pieces of hair fall over his eyes. He twists them around a finger.

His mother watches him more than she watches the TV. She
named him after a town on the Pine Ridge, South Dakota, Sioux
reservation where she has a friend. He is her only child, conceived
with a Comanche man from Oklahoma who hit her one night when
they were at a bar and then disappeared before Kyle was even born.
Since his birth, she has only left him once—for a ten-day trip to a
Washington State reservation. While she was gone, four-year-old
Kyle sat every day on the steps of her apartment, waiting.

As the closing music comes on the soap opera, Kyle stands up.
"I'm ready," he says. "I want McDonald's."

In a park near the Bismarck, North Dakota, zoo, Kyle unwraps a
Number One Super Value meal. When he has the Big Mac ready,

when he has the French fries laid out, he looks up and asks, "Where do you want me to begin, when I was born?"

He begins to talk solemnly. His voice has a Sioux cadence even though Kyle says he never learned to speak the "Indian" that his grandmother was speaking on her deathbed, when none of her children knew exactly what she was saying. Still, he is a storyteller, same as she was.

"Okay," he says, "I was born in Fort Yates on March 28, '77. And then we lived in Cannonball [on the Standing Rock reservation], and my mom told me she did a lot of hitchhiking like all over, like Denver and Cheyenne and stuff when I was small with me in a backpack. And then we came and moved to Bismarck and I started kindergarten, first grade, then second grade, moved back to the reservation and then we lived down there until I was about sixth grade. In sixth grade, I went to the Indian school in Wahpeton for one year, and I liked it, but I don't know why I went back [to Cannonball]. I shouldn't have but I did. And that summer I came back from Indian school, that same summer, that's when I start getting into trouble.

"Like my older friends, they were all drinking, and I never drank anything, and they gave me a can of beer, and I opened it, and I started drinking it, and at first I didn't know if I didn't want to but I did. Pretty soon, I musta got drunk, 'cause that was my first time I got drunk. And I don't even remember what even happened that night. I woke up. I was sick. I was throwing up. All day, I was just sick and then I don't know after that I must've, I guess I just started getting used to it and I started drinking and I got in trouble with the tribal court down there and they put me on probation you know and so I had to be in at ten and stuff. I was about twelve."

He is almost chanting, his voice is so steady as his fingers twist at the hair fringed along his forehead. "And then seventh grade, I was drinking the whole year, and then like in May, the last month of school, I almost got sent to South Dakota for treatment 'cause I started huffin' gas and rubber cement. Everybody was doing it, so I was doing it. They said, 'Here, you can huff this. Inhale it.' And so I did, and then that got me high and seeing things that weren't there. I seen snakes one time when I was high, and I dreamt I got—this scared the crap out of me—I got put in this box and there was this hole in the ground and I just went down it, and I was going down there, and I was seeing, oh, no, all kinds of ghosts or dead people. Soon as I got hit on the bottom, I seen the devil and stuff and holy cow. I must've been so high I was crying. 'Cause I came out of my highness and I was still crying. That's how scared I was.

"We used a bread bag or any kind of bag and you poured rubber cement you know, and that's what we used to inhale or White-Out or gasoline. Gas in jugs or in bags. We'd put like rubber cement or White-Out in a bag and huffed it. We tried spray paint once, but it didn't get us high. You inhale and you get high. But I haven't did that since that time I seen the devil. I was high on rubber cement. I always like see this green mammoth, like he's like right in front of me and stuff. But the time I didn't see him, that's when I seen the devil.

"And then there was this one time, when we first started, we were outside and it was like evening out and there was like these clouds going by, and then I don't know what made me see this but I seen this cloud going by and I looked at it again and it was Snoopy the dog, and then it was going by and there was like this thing on his neck you know. It was like a collar, it had a paper and it was hanging out like this and it had somethin' on it like, *I'm Gonna Tell Your Mom on You.* And oh I just let go of that bag and I was just sittin' there watching it and then the highness must have weared off and I just looked and that cloud was just a regular cloud. I told everyone else and they just start laughin' at me. The stuff I seen, boy.

"There was one time it was dark out and we were sittin' outside and I was gettin' higher and all of a sudden, that high musta hit me and I just see these big snakes, they're just all over in the sky and they all come right towards me and I just get up screaming hollering, crying. I run inside the house and you know when I was running inside the house, it seemed like one snake went in my mouth and I just grabbed it and I was just screamin' and crying and I ran inside and I call my mom and they got mad at me and I had to go to bed. I was in this trouble. And they told me I wasn't sposed to huff anymore, so I didn't do that. I haven't did that since what, since I was what? Thirteen now. I haven't touched that.

"And then that seventh grade, school's out, and then my uncle died in May. You know, I never really thought that was gonna happen to our family but surprised me. He was drinking. I think his heart or something, how do you say? It was enlargement, enlarged, and I guess it just stopped so . . . He was like forty-one, I think."

Here he pauses to outline his family tree, tracing it out on the wood of the picnic table with a fingernail. "My mom, 'kay. There's my grandma, but she died. My uncle, but he's dead. My mom and my auntie are the only ones left with their dad—my grandpa. And my auntie has five kids and my uncle had what six or seven kids. All my cousins."

"Anyway," he says, "[my uncle] died. And that was kinda hard on my grandma, her only son.

"And then that fall of '91. I was gonna be an eighth grader that fall, and we moved up here because my mom wanted to get away from the reservation cause she said there was too much drinkin' and stuff. So we moved up here, got that trailer, and then started to school.

"I didn't know nobody. That's when I started gettin' into trouble in school you know. This wasn't the reservation, but I was like walkin' out of school, you know swearin' at my teachers and stuff and gettin' in trouble, detention, truancy and stuff. I start drinking, running away from school and I don't know, running from my mom and school.

"And then once, I threw up but I was layin' on my back and it wasn't coming out, so I almost choked. This was at some party, some apartment building, where they were all drinking and I guess I almost choked on my own vomit but somebody turned me over on my stomach. So I was okay on that.

"Me and my mom weren't gettin' along, so I just drink and go

out and drink and get in trouble. I didn't know then what I was gettin' myself into you know under Burleigh County." He pauses here.
He doesn't even like to think about Burleigh County.

"And then that Christmas I drank. New Year's I drank. Then February I got put under Police Youth Bureau, some people that talked
to me and stuff and tried to help me stay out of the Burleigh County
custody and stuff. But I didn't listen you know, and I just kept gettin' into trouble, doing stuff wrong and doing stupid stuff to get
more in trouble. And finally I got put to a probation officer, and she
told me to take an evaluation and then they sent me to treatment.

"There's a treatment center in Mandan called Heartview. And I
was there for what, thirty days. Gosh, I was just scared you know. I
was crying and everything, but I guess it was for the best. My first
night I was really scared, and I felt embarrassed you know 'cause I
was only like fifteen and I'm going to treatment.

"I just wanted to leave but I couldn't 'cause the cops took me
there. I got used to it. I just wanted to do what I had to do just to get
out of there. I just went there just to make my probation officer
happy. I didn't try to help myself.

"I got out March 13, right on a Friday, Friday the 13th. I didn't
drink till like the first part of April. I was going to aftercare and they
all said I was changed and stuff, and that got me mad. They all tried
to say that I was drinking, and I wasn't. And so I just got mad and
told them that I was not gonna go back to group and so then I just
started drinking again in April '92.

"And then May of '92, still drinking. You know, I didn't think
anything. My mom told me that we were gonna have to go see my
probation officer. She started talking about group homes and then
pretty soon she said, 'You're going to another home.' And I started
crying, and two police officers walked in there and handcuffed me,
put me in a car, and they took me up to the group home and oh I
just, I was just mad at my probation officer for puttin' me there.

"I don't know how many citations I had from the Police Youth
Bureau—from school and running away at home and like minor
possession and stuff, curfew and stuff. I got that all built up and

against me. I was mad and scared, and [my social worker] said I was only gonna be there for a month. So, like I got there June 26. I didn't know nobody and then that July 29, I went to court, me and my mom. Burleigh County was petitioning for custody of me, and that's when my probation officer handed me over to the County social services. Then I was *under* them, and they said I had to stay at the group home, and gosh I was just mad."

He straightens his back, as if bracing himself for the rest of the story: "Home wasn't an option, they said, right at that time. The group home's just like a regular house, you know, regular house with bedrooms and then there's a house parent. They watch us, cook for us. It isn't like prison or anything. It's just like a house.

"I'd do good for a while. I had a job out at this plant material center where I had to plant like you know big fields and hoe and stuff. It was my first time on a job and I didn't really, I didn't like the people 'cause they were all older than me, and I was the only youngest one.

"Each time I took off, I would run to Cannonball, the reservation, but that didn't do me no good. I'd catch rides with my cousins or either there's a bingo hall, and a lot of Indians gamble, and that's where I'd catch a ride. And then I got caught and brought back.

"And then I took off in August and I went back to the reservation. And the tribal court, the tribal police caught me down there and they put me in jail for one day and then somebody from the tribe drove me back up to the group home.

"And then I straightened out. I didn't want to take off, but I was just mad 'cause I had to be in there. And then I kinda thought that that was my fault. I'm the one that put myself in there. And then September, I was doing good in school and I didn't take off or anything and then I guess I kinda got tired of being in a group home. And so I was takin' my clothes, all my stuff to school slowly. All my stuff was in my locker at once.

"October 1st I remember, I said, 'Well I'll see you after school.' I just said that 'cause I was gonna take off that day. Last period, I put all my stuff together and I left from school and walked through the mall, thinkin' about *what* am I doing? Then again, I'm thinkin, *I'm just fine.*

"I was comin' out of the mall," he says, "and there was a cop car standin' right there. And I was thinking, *oh shit, what if they're already lookin' for me?* It left and so I was walkin' over to my friends' and there was this cop car. It just turned my way and oh I was thinkin', *oh oh, I'm busted.* It went by me and so I just got to my friends' and we drank and they said I could stay there until whenever I could get back.

"I caught a ride with people who were goin' back to the reservation from the Bingo. I didn't even eat. I just drank every day. I'd drink one night and get up the next morning and drink again. My cousin's car, I was driving it and I was drunk and I don't even remember. I guess I was racing some other people that were in another car. And that kind of scared me.

"And when I was on a run, what a stupidest thing to do, I enrolled myself in the school down there. I went only two days. Solo High School. I got caught and so they kept me in jail and my aunt down there wanted to take custody of me and the tribal court was gonna take over jurisdiction to keep me down there but then again my aunt didn't want to 'cause I stayed with her like before and that's when I started to get in trouble.

"[My caseworker] came after me. It was on a Friday, I got out of jail. They don't feed good in the jail, and I felt dirty and there's a Taco John's in Fort Yates and she took me there and, oh, I just ate, ate. I was so happy. She didn't want to take me back to the group home she said 'cause I was gonna take off anyway again. So she just said, Well, she was gonna place me with my mom. But my mom was drunk. She was too drunk to watch me. So she brought me back to my aunt. I was supposed to stay there till Monday when they were gonna take me to treatment in Minot. I drank Friday night and Saturday, and Saturday night I was supposed to have watched my little cousin, he's like only what, two or three. I was supposed to watch him, cause my aunt was gonna go someplace and she'd be right back, she said. And my little cousin was sleeping—well first I gave him a bunch of Tylenol. I don't know if I knocked him out, but he was out like that. He was just sleeping and so then I just left him all by himself in the house. And then I went to the Bingo hall and I caught a ride back to the reservation."

His mouth is set in a grim line when he stops before saying: "That's when my caseworker said I had to go with them. I told my mom, I said, 'Okay, mom, just please tell 'em I'm not here.' And my mom, she said, 'Well I don't want to get in more trouble, Kyle,' so she just told 'em that I was there.

"They told me to get all my clothes. I got all my clothes. I got in the back. They took me to Hardee's and then we got on the interstate, Highway 83, I think that is, and then we went to Minot, and gosh I was just, I was cryin' all the way up there to the chemical dependency unit. My caseworker says, 'I'll call you as soon as I get back to Bismarck and if you need me or if you need to talk to me, just you know where and how to get ahold of me.' So there I was. She dumped me off with my clothes, and she just left me there. Oh, I just didn't know what to do. It was twenty-eight days.

"I'd call my mom, and I'd tell her I miss her and she said, 'Well you should never took off.' Then I kinda felt, I should never took off and then I made everything worse and I missed out on like a month and a half of school.

"Then like the 2nd of November, I remember them calling to tell me what the news was where I was going, 'cause I didn't know where I was going. The group home didn't no longer want me back. So we go to my addiction counselor's office and we sit down and he told me, 'You're going to be going to Home on the Range for Boys.' And I just start crying. I just felt like killin' myself, I don't know. I just felt lost and just mad at myself, at my social worker, at the county juvenile guy.

"Then 11th of November, the county guy came after me and I didn't wanna go, but I had no choice. I got in the car, put all my stuff in the trunk and then we started out. We got out there in the evening time and I seen this big ol' sign, HOME ON THE RANGE. I was just crying, I said, 'Don't leave me here.' I'll never forget that day 'cause I thought that was the worst day of my life. It was my fault 'cause I'm the one that took off and got in trouble.

"He said, 'Kyle, you'll only be here for a couple of months.' He said, 'Then we'll try to get you closer to Bismarck, a foster home.' He left. And you know I had longer hair, and then I had to get it cut like up to here." He holds his hand high on his neck.

"They let me come home for Christmas. I left the 23rd and I was supposed to be back the 29th of December but I kinda took off again. I drank at New Year's and then that 4th, I finally caught the bus back.

"And then my mom, they told her that if she wanted me back she had to go into treatment. So she said she was goin' to treatment for me and her. Just to get me back. And it was like her last week of treatment and I was supposed to go back for her family week. And some old man, I think he's a priest of something, he's this real old guy, he drove me back to Bismarck. I guess they weren't expecting me so everything was unorganized. I felt like taking off from this old man because he was so old. But I didn't. I just, I kinda felt bad. We drove all the way back to Home on the Range. I guess I kinda, how do you say that monipu-, manipulated? They said I was good at manipulating people then, and I guess I did that. They said that, and then so I just got mad and I just said, 'I don't care. You guys can just send me someplace else.'

"I just slammed that door, and I just start running toward the Interstate. And guess who was running behind me? There was this ranch dog. His name was Bear. The staff out there were chasing me, and I got on the Interstate and then it was like gettin' dark and I couldn't see no more and this dog was still with me.

"I was tryin' to catch a ride. Some car stopped. I think they were white people, but I'm not sure. The sheriff came and so they stopped that car and they said I was a runaway and so they put me in that cop car and they took me into town to the police station, whatever. My social worker came up to the jail and said that there was a mental health center in Dickinson. I was there for like a week and one day. Then I said I'd start all over.

"I was doing okay and stuff then one night I got a phone call from my mom's friend and she told me that my grandma was in the hospital. And they didn't think she was gonna make it through the night, and so I was really worried cause that's my only grandma.

"That next morning, they let me call to Fort Yates to the hospital again and my mom told me that my grandma passed away at like five o'clock that morning, and I just started crying.

"I went back to Cannonball. We had her funeral. That was kinda bad cause everybody was crying and I was crying. My grandpa, I just felt sorry for my grandpa cause that's his wife you know, and she died. She was like sixty. But another thing too is that she kinda drank herself to death. 'Cause she was an alcoholic, just like my uncle, and they told her not to drink. I think she had like cirrhosis of the liver. And then she had cancer that spread all the way up to her brain or something.

"That Monday, they had her funeral, closed her casket, and they took her out to bury her. My grandma's friend, my grandma's drinking partner, she was just drunk and then the holes you know, how deep are they, six or seven feet, aren't they? And my grandma's friend was just crying, screaming, and she's standing by where they're gonna bury her you know and she was standin' there and they told her to leave 'cause she was drunk and she almost fell in that hole but luckily somebody grabbed her otherwise she woulda fell way in there. I kinda got mad at her. There was a lot of people that were drunk. I kinda got mad cause there was like a lot of drinking people."

Kyle leans more and more forward as he speaks. "I was supposed to go back to Home on the Range. That same February 25th, I had a permanency planning with Burleigh County again, to see, talk about how I'm doing. And that day, that Thursday morning, I wrote stuff what I wanted to tell 'em about you know, what I wanted and stuff and what I was gonna do and change and stuff about myself. So I went.

"I told 'em I didn't wanna go back to Home on the Range. I said,

I'm willing to start school and just start over and change everything. Oh, then I read this thing I wrote about what I was gonna do
to change everything if I got to stay home and then finally it was
over. You know I was just sittin' there waitin' for the county guy to
say, 'So Kyle, when are you gonna catch the bus?' And I kinda
wanted them to just hurry up and say that and then finally they
said, 'Well, so Kyle how are we gonna get all your stuff back from
Home on the Range?' And you know I'm sittin' there almost in tears
now and you know it didn't hit me till after. I kinda got excited.
They said, you get to stay home and they were gonna give me
another chance at home. So February 25th was the happiest day of
my life. I got to come home.

"And then April, I started getting in trouble in school again and
then they said I might have to go to group home again. And you
know I just kinda came in one ear and out the other ear. And I just
started drinkin' and stuff and I was lying and I got in trouble and I
was at the police station that one time for, 'cause, oh, I swore at
the teacher at the school and I walked out of the school and I was
there at the police station and my new social worker came over and
and he was nice and stuff and I thanked him for everything he did
for me. I kinda used him I guess. You might as well say that and
um that was the first time since I met him he was mad at me. And
he was swearin' at me. That kinda surprised me but I guess I
deserved it. And then I got put in a group home the 8th of April.
That April 15th I took off, and I was gone like the 26th of April and
then I got caught in Fort Yates. They faxed something to [my social
worker] and so he told 'em just keep me until the Burleigh County
sheriff's department was gonna come after me. So they came after
me and another boy that took off too. Me and this boy, they put
these chains around us, handcuffed us like this [around our wrists]
and handcuffed us on our ankles and gosh that was so . . . I sat like
this all the way up to Bismarck. They brought me back to the
group home.

"And then I thought, If I wanna get home, I've gotta straighten
up. So I wrote all these letters to my social worker, saying *yeah*, I'm

gonna behave now. May was my last month, and they told me I had
to really work to pass, get out of ninth grade and so I did. The last
day of school, got my report card, and it said I was promoted to
tenth grade, and I was happy. I told my mom that I passed and she
just told me to behave so that I can go home now.

"In June, I kinda messed up cause there was this carnival and I
seen all the old friends and stuff from Cannonball and I didn't go
back to the group home. I was supposed to go back at twelve, but I
didn't, I stayed on and got drunk and stuff.

"That's when I had to fill out all the applications for the Dakota
Boys Ranch [DBR] placement for boys. It's in Minot, and that's
where they were gonna send me. I had that hangin' over my head,
and they said, 'If you mess up once you're goin' to Minot.' I didn't
wanna go you know cause I was tired of going here and there. I was
kind of tired of getting sent here and there, like a box.

"I was in a room by myself at the group home, and I had this
paper—and another consequence was I was gonna be under
Burleigh County till I was eighteen years old. And I'm only sixteen
and I thought about that: They're like takin' away a whole two years
of my teenage life.

"So I got a paper and a marker, and I put "DBR" in big letters
and I put "One year stay" and I put "Under Burleigh County until 18
years old." And then every morning I thought about that. I looked at
that. On the wall, on my calendar. I was thinkin'.

"I was gettin' off probation July 29. The 29th was gonna be one
year, I was under Burleigh County and I was gonna finally be off.
And I was really excited 'cause I could go home and there was
nothin' else they could do and stuff. Then that June went by and
July was finally here. That morning, my social worker came after
me. And I was going home and I was just excited. I couldn't sleep
that night. I got up real early, and I took a shower, got dressed and
was waitin' for him: *I'm going home, back to my home home.* Okay,
at nine o'clock he came, and he was real happy. I left the group
home, said goodbye to everybody and I said *HaHa.* I was happy. He
said, 'You can rip these papers up or burn 'em up'—those applica-

tions to DBR and there were some papers that said that I'm no longer under Burleigh County. I was finally off and I was happy. And then ever since then, it's real nice. I've been stayin' out of trouble. I haven't been drinking.

"When I go back [to the reservation], like this last weekend, I went back, I wanted to [drink] again but again I was thinking. I was thinkin' about Burleigh County and stuff and tribal court. 'Cause tribal court said if I got in trouble down there, they're gonna put me at the Industrial School until I'm eighteen. So, either way, I'm . . . Sometimes you know I feel like takin' off again, just takin' off just . . . but again I don't want to because . . ."

* * *

Kyle is finished with his story. His Big Mac is still sitting whole in front of him. His fries are cold. He eats a few of them and small talks about the crude tattoos on his hand that he did with a safety pin and India ink. One of them says, *I love mom.* Another says, *word.* Some are just dots on his knuckles. "I wish they all weren't there now," he says.

He says he can't wait for school to start. He describes himself as "one of the kids who sits in a corner and smokes," but adds: "I gotta try to graduate. My last name is TwoHorses and my family all call on me, cause all the other TwoHorses didn't graduate you know. I guess it's up to me. I guess I'll be the first TwoHorses to graduate. I kinda have plans for like when I get older: Try to finish school, and if my grades are good in high school, I'll ask the tribe to lend me money so I could go to college, and I want to be a social worker. I want to maybe work with the tribe cause I don't think the tribe's— how you say it?—running their court good. Like last month, okay, there was all these people that were Native Americans that were coming back from Southridge. They were all drunk and she was drunk, the driver, and she rolled the car and her boyfriend or her husband that was on the passenger side, they all got thrown out of the car and he got killed. Isn't that like manslaughter or something or whatever? And then she's . . . I seen her that other weekend I was down there. She was just walkin' around on the reservation, and see that ain't right I don't think."

Kyle has saved money for new clothes and fresh Nikes. He says there's nothing to do but watch soap operas and drink all summer. But he hasn't had a drink in months. Neither has his mother. And they're trying to keep each other strong. That means staying away from the reservation as much as possible. But Kyle says he left his good jacket down there, and wouldn't mind riding down to pick it up. He'll give the directions.

*　*　*

Outside of Bismarck, heading south, Kyle says, "Guess whose house is here?" Cocking his head ironically, he answers: "Custer's."

It is on the right side of the road—big with lots of windows looking out over the grounds where the soldiers slept in tents. Kyle has passed it most weeks of his life, going back and forth from the Standing Rock reservation to Bismarck, but he has never been inside. "I wouldn't mind going through it," he says. "But that costs three or four dollars."

He says he's not much up on the history of his people. He knows the name Sitting Bull. He's seen someone demonstrate how to skin a dead buffalo. "It was pretty gross," he says. The only "Indian" word he knows off the top of his head is the pet name his grandma called him, Chepaw, which he thinks means chubby. His grandma used to tell him stories about how you had to keep the curtains closed at night or "the dead people, the ghosts" would watch you. And how if you ate at night, you should always toss a little meat out the door to the ghosts. His grandma always used to spill a little of her wine on the ground when she drank. Another thing, when you dream about the dead and they talk to you, just don't accept anything from them to eat because then you'll wake up dead yourself.

Sunflowers are blooming along the road, turning west toward the sun. The Missouri River parallels the road. Kyle narrates all the points along here where people from the reservation have died in car accidents—or killed someone—because they were driving drunk. Here, a baby girl thrown through a windshield. Here, three bodies hidden in the grass while his cousins searched with only two weak flashlights.

* * *

His grandma's grave is still covered with crosses and plastic flowers that have faded. The cemetery stands on a knoll overlooking the river. The grasses bend in the wind. A crow croaks overhead. Kyle points out his uncle's grave and the grave of a baby who died when its parents left it in a hot car with the windows rolled up. His grandma is probably the oldest person in the cemetery. And she was only sixty.

Kyle keeps a photograph album. It is his most prized possession. He kept it with him in the group homes, in the treatment centers. But he rarely showed anyone. On the cover, he has written: *If you look at my photo album, please don't steal any of my pictures. Bad enough you should be glad I'm letting you look at it. Thank you for your cooperation.* On the inside cover is a picture of his grandmother in her coffin. She looks eighty years old. Stuck in next to the picture is a poem that ends with the lines: "Leave me in peace, and I shall leave you too in peace. While you live, let your thoughts be with the living."

As he heads over to the little community of Cannonball, he passes the tiny brown shack where his grandfather lives. "My grandpa since she died, my grandpa has been drinking, trying to drink mostly every day, even drank Lysol I guess, from what my cousin said. I guess he wants to die."

* * *

Cannonball's houses are painted turquoise and fuchsia and cobalt, all strung around some looping, intersecting roads. It looks hunkered down and small under the stretching North Dakota sky. The ground between the houses is dirt, some places worn more into paths, and in the late sun, people move along them, slow as cats.

Kyle points out where he lived as a child. Then he stops at a gray house. The screens are torn at most of the windows, and someone has written letters on its siding. Kyle goes to the ripped screendoor and knocks. A five-year-old girl comes to the door and stands precariously with one foot on top of another. Kyle is trying to open the door, but it's all twisted up with the frame.

"Where's your mom?" he asks the child.

"She's in jail," she answers and goes to get her nineteen-year-old brother who says that their mother, father, and two older sisters are in jail. Kyle can't find out why.

He gets his jacket and leaves.

*   *   *

As the car heads north toward home and his mom, Kyle looks out the window at the neat rows of corn ticking by in the fields. "Sometimes," he says, "I would just like to run away down the cornfields."

JAMES COLZIE III
ON ATHLETE-OF-THE-YEAR
AWARDS NIGHT

*E*verybody in the family is trying to get James Calhoun Colzie III
dressed up. His mom keeps reminding him what time it is. His
dad keeps checking to see whether or not he's got his suit ready.
Tonight is a big awards ceremony in downtown Miami, where the
Miami Herald will announce who it has picked as Dade County
Athlete of the Year. It may be James. He has already won what his
father calls the Emmy of Dade County, the Silver Knight award,
given to fourteen students who excel in business or languages or
athletics. James won for athletics. The ninth grade was when he
decided he wanted to get both these awards. But no one student
has ever taken both awards. So James is coursing around the
low-slung blue stucco house the way he moves on a basketball
court, on a football field, around bases on a diamond. Tirelessly.
Not stopping long enough to change out of the MIAMI T-shirt and
blue parachute-fabric sweat pants he has worn all day at South
Miami High.

His mother, Earnestine, is on the couch, tired out from her day
teaching thirty-one second-graders. His little sisters, eleven-year-
old twins named Shandra and Shaundra who look exactly alike
except one of them has a scar over her eyebrow, are putting on purple pleated skirts and gray stockings. His father, James II, a big guy
with a serious face but a smile that he metes out liberally to his children, is wearing shorts and leaning against the kitchen counter
thumbing through a sheaf of papers that documents James's career:

All-American in football, 2,000 career points in basketball, McDonald's All-American High School Basketball team. James II is athletic director at South Miami, and he watches closely over James III, academically and athletically.

James comes in and drapes a tie over his father's shoulder. "Here, Daddy," he says, surging on out the door. His best friend, Steve, is following him around. Steve has been one year away at college, but he is here for James's big night, hanging close just as he has for most of the past five years, since they met at Gulliver Academy. They have a friendship based on cruising surreptitiously past the houses of girls they like, of washing their cars together for twenty weekends straight, of being the only black guys to eat in (and leave fast) a fancy pizza joint.

Big James puts his son's tie around his own neck and knots it as he talks about the eighteen-year-old's career, which began when he was six years old. James II is the one who keeps track of his son's accomplishments by stapling together the papers that document his career. And they aren't just clippings about sports. There are letters of recommendation from teachers at South Miami High praising his *A*-average in advanced placement chemistry and from Sunday school teachers at the Greater Saint Paul African Methodist Episcopal Church commending him for his work with the homeless. "That's James in a nutshell," his father says, fanning out the papers in his big hands. James II is a modest man, who tends not to brag, so he adds: "But he can't tie a tie." He pulls the knotted tie over his head and tosses it to James III, who is swinging back through the room, Steve right behind him.

James disappears into his small bedroom. It's crowded with his trophies. A mural of a baseball stadium and diamond wraps around the wall over the neatly made water-bed. James has carefully decorated the other walls with pictures from preschool and grade-school classes and teams. Little James is usually easy to pick out in the pictures: often, he is the only black child among all the white ones.

When he next appears, he is wearing a dark pinstriped suit, the tie, and tasseled loafers. James has a steel wire build, curly eyelashes, and a flat-top haircut that sits on his head kind of like a pillbox hat. "Are you nervous?" his mother asks. He shakes his head showily, as if to say: How ridiculous.

The family streams out the door, and a neighbor waves to them from over the side fence, out by the basketball hoop that James II put two inches higher than regulation—so the arc on James III's shot would improve. "Is tonight the night?" the neighbor calls.

"Yes it is," Earnestine answers.

"Well, good luck," the man says.

"Thank you," the family answers in chorus as they climb into their white Chevy van and settle into the plush burgundy interior, which has curtains and a television set. James closes the gate in the chain link fence after his father backs out and then gets back in the van. His twin sisters are in the farthest back seat, sitting on either side of his friend Steve. They all three giggle and sing along with Whitney Houston on the radio: *"I will always love you."*

As James II drives toward downtown Miami, Earnestine calls over her shoulder to her son, "Do you wanna rehearse your speech?"

"I'm not gonna win, Mommy," he says softly.

"What?" she says.

"I'm not gonna win."

"Don't you wanna have something prepared?"

He just wags his head no. In the back seats, the sisters are singing. *"Always loove yoooooooooooooooooou."*

On Biscayne Boulevard, the family goes into an International House of Pancakes to eat a quick supper before the awards ceremony. James orders a hamburger and chocolate milk.

"Don't you want steak and eggs?" his mother asks him, looking at him with one of those looks that says, *I know you so well, and I'm sure you would rather have steak and eggs.* She is clearly proud of this son, proud not so much because he is an All-American athlete but because of things like the time when one of the recruiters gave him free tickets to the big University of Miami vs. Florida State game, James didn't go with a buddy. He took his little sisters, who don't much care for big-time football but who adore their brother. His mother is proud that her boy is kind.

James says no he just wants a hamburger, and his parents grin at one another. Ah, their look says, he's nervous.

James and Steve go off to the restroom, and when they come back, James notices that his father is writing something on an envelope that he has unfolded to get more room. James III figures out that he is writing an acceptance speech.

Just as James is finishing his burger, his father tries to hand him the speech. James shakes his head no. He is polite but adamant. One of the girls takes the paper and reads it. "It's good," she says to her brother. He shakes his head again.

When the family finally pulls up to the Gusman Cultural Arts Center, James is sitting up straighter. As everyone piles out, his father says: "Good luck, babe." His mother tells him good luck too, and he says, just a touch irritated, "I'm sitting with you."

Inside the gold and velvet ornate theater, the Colzies are greeted by relatives and other well-wishers. James's grandparents are there. His granddaddy played ball in the "Negro" leagues and is featured in the book *Only the Ball Was White*. If it hadn't been for racism, he could have done so much more with his athletic career. But he did raise two boys who played professional ball: Neal Colzie played football for the Raiders, Buccaneers, and Dolphins; Rick Colzie played baseball for the Cleveland Indians. So James Colzie Sr. is proud tonight, wearing a tie and saying little. James III kisses his grandmother. He says hi to his aunts. The principal at South Miami comes up and asks him if he is nervous. He says no.

He sits way over against the wall, with his family lined up between him and the aisle. Steve is next to him. The hours begin creeping by with awards going to all-stars in water polo, badminton, bowling, etc. James and Steve amuse themselves by wiggling their eyebrows over the volleyball players with dressy side-slit skirts, the swimmers with tight dresses. They make noises and follow the girls with their eyes. They crack each other up. But James's eyes sweep over the audience more than once. He is looking for his girlfriend. He doubts she'll come. He had to miss her private school graduation last night because he had an awards banquet at South Miami. He was named the school's athlete of the year and its scholar athlete. But his girlfriend cried because he wasn't coming to see her graduate, and she hasn't called since, even though they usually speak every day.

When James was still in private school at Gulliver Preparatory, before he transferred because the draft agents wanted to see him play at a big school, he and his girlfriend used to walk to class every day holding hands. She came from Spain, and when James, as an eighth grader, first saw her and asked for her phone number, she couldn't understand. So he learned how to ask in Spanish and called her all the time. Her sister translated at first. They've been going together since then, off and on. Sometimes one of them cheats or something, and they break up. The only time Steve has ever seen James cry is over her. Until last night, things had been going pretty great.

Earlier in the day, Steve teased him: "Even though he doesn't want to admit it . . ."

"Shut up, man," James said, putting up his hand to stop what was coming.

"You know you're in love with her, man."

James shook his head. "I don't know about that love part. I love my parents. You can't really get in love with . . ." Then he gave up and said what he meant. "Okay. I'm in love with the girl, yes. Yes. We talk about marriage all the time. That's all we talk about. That's all *she* talks about really." He gets out his favorite picture of her: The sun in her blond hair, wearing only a bathing suit, the Atlantic Ocean gleaming behind her.

* * *

He looks around the theater again. She still isn't here. But his family is, and as James gets up to take his place in the line of nominees, his father squeezes his hand. The principal at South Miami has called this night "a family affair" and said of the Colzies, "His father is a dynamite teacher, a man of high expectations. And he's got a whole family that participates in one another's lives." Indeed, James says that his mother is his role model, for suffering the loss of both of her parents and carrying on. But he's closest to his dad because of the sports. "The first time I was in the paper, I was like four. My dad was coaching basketball, and there was me chillin' on the sideline," James says, laughing.

He grew up knowing what they expected of him. "If there was pressure, I only felt it when I was in ninth or tenth grade. I've grown into it now." His parents have strong Christian beliefs as well as a strong work ethic, and they instilled them early in James. They sent him to an academically challenging private school because they wanted him to know that books came before sports. They take him to the Methodist church every Sunday, and afterward they go to his grandparents' house. "We're trying' to keep him smooth, and let him know that it's rocky out there," James II says.

James III says he stays clear of the rocky part, like drugs and even alcohol. "I've never touched it, and I never will," James says. "I made a promise to my parents; I made a promise to myself that I'd never be that way. I've never even taken a sip of beer. I know you ain't gonna believe me, but I never have. If you don't want to do it, you just don't." His blunt sincerity is not actually hard to believe. "I've been tempted. But if it's there in front of me, I just can't do it. I don't."

* * *

One by one the emcee calls the names of the athletes who might be Dade County's Athlete of the Year. Out of 337 eligible Dade athletes, there are eight finalists. They walk to the stage. James stands with his head down, his hands deep in his pockets.

Shandra and Shaundra hunch in their seats. James II straightens his tie. Earnestine is motionless. The whole standing-room-only crowd is hushed.

This is an extravaganza: A trophy on a pillar rises with smoke from the stage. Colored lights play. Music swells. The tuxedo-clad emcee is making an introduction, saying something about a family tradition, about the will to work finally paying off. And then he says: James Colzie III.

The aunts scream. His mother shakes her arms in the air. The twins bounce to their feet and leap around. His father sits absolutely still, grinning.

Finally the whole family gets up onto the stage. James is thanking his parents, his school. His mother is holding dozens of peach roses. His father is shouldering the three-foot trophy. In his excitement, James shakes hands with his mother, hugs his dad, then corrects himself. The cameras are flashing and a reporter who covers high school sports for the *Herald* is telling James II confidentially that "It was not even close. This one, we knew." James II is laughing heartily and saying, "All in a day's work." Coaches and well-wishers congratulate him and tell him things about James III like, "on the field, he was like a man against those guys."

Next year, James will be out there on the field, this time at Florida State University, where he decided to go instead of Stanford or Cal Berkeley or Georgia or all the other places that tried to recruit him. He chose FSU because he could play football there on scholarship, but the school would also let him play his grandfather's sport, baseball. Also, he thinks it will be a good place to study acting, which has been his ambition ever since he played the scarecrow in his high school's production of *The Wizard of Oz*.

On the stage now, James III is shaking. "He's overcome," his grandmother whispers to his mother. "I'm nervous," he admits.

Somebody asks him what he was doing up there, looking at his shoes, not looking up. He seems surprised. "I was praying," he says. "I was praying."

June 6, 1979

*HOME is certainly the
nicest place this side of
Heaven.*

*   *   *

October 4, 1979

*A girl in my English class gossiped about her parents.
Another girl in my dorm screamed and cried with her mom
on the phone, "I am not a spoiled brat!" At times I wish that
I could cut my wrists and spill your blood from me without
also spilling my own.*

*   *   *

January 2, 1980

*Home on break. Although I love and miss my friends, this is
where my other me lives.*

HOW GABI PHILLIPS SPENDS
SEVEN HOURS A DAY

Gabriella Phillips has a callus at the square edge of her jaw. Pretty much every day since she was three years old, she has tucked a violin under that left side of her chin, as she does now. It is a June night not long after her graduation from the North Carolina School of the Arts and not long before her first trip to Europe as part of an orchestra. Tonight her audience is different from the ones in Frankfurt and Florence where she will wear a delicate black dress that her grandmother made especially for the trip. Tonight Gabi is wearing cutoff Levi's and a plain barrette to hold back her black hair. She's playing for her family: mother, father, and both grandmothers who all call her The Gabriella, as in The Storm. "Here comes The Gabriella," one of them will say as she runs through the house. "I'm very fast," Gabi says. "I always have a purpose. I hate this period in my life—two weeks with nothing to do. It makes me nervous. I just hate wasting time. Life is short."

As she pulls her bow across the strings, she hears more than the Mendelssohn concerto that her family hears. She has learned to listen to music in a different way during days that start with violin practice at 6:30 a.m. and end as late as eleven with orchestra rehearsal. She doesn't so much listen to the music as to the hiss of the horsehair along the strings, the plunk of each finger as it hits the neckpiece. Her fingers move as if reading Braille as she concentrates on the width of her vibrato, the angle of the bow. Her lips purse and quiver in silent conversation with the instrument. The family sit in a semicircle around her—except for her father. He is in front of her, holding her sheet music, as if he were her music stand. He is in a wheelchair, has been since childhood, because of a bone disease. He's the only one besides Gabi who is not still: Mike Phillips conducts his daughter's music with subtle motions of his head, and with expressions that pass like weather patterns across his face. His daughter may hear things in her playing that he doesn't, but he feels it most intensely.

"Play the Fauré," he tells her, after she finishes the Mendelssohn piece.

"It's part of a quartet," she tells him. "It will sound dumb."

"Play it," he says.

The Gabriella looks to her mother, Judy, who is also in a wheelchair (because of childhood polio), and they smirk together over something so much a part of their lives it needs no words: *Oh, Dad.*

Right then, Gabi's grandmother tells her: "I can remember [your father] sitting in front of the music system, just a little tiny thing. He didn't walk then either, and he would just sit for *hours.*"

Gabi has heard this before. She also remembers being three and having her father carry the ⅟₁₆-size violin to her Suzuki lessons. She remembers being eight or nine and refusing to let him go to lessons because he was so intense. She remembers when he learned to play the cello so he could perform with her orchestra, the Santa Fe children's orchestra. And she can't count how many times he's called her into his study to hear the "perfect melody" of something like "A String of Pearls." Gabi knows her father loves music, loves her music, and tonight as she plays the Fauré, she stays turned toward him, even though she knows the piece by heart.

"There is nothing better that the human mind, that the human body is capable of," Mike says of Gabi's music, of anybody's music. He is proud that his daughter's success is somehow his accomplishment too. He moved his wife and two older sons here to Winston-Salem from Santa Fe, New Mexico, so Gabi could get the finest musical education. He drove her to class and picked her up until she learned to drive. He finds the $7,000 for a new violin, the $2,000 each for two new horsehair bows, the $40 every month or so for new strings. This year he even got her a car phone for her 1982 Ford Fairmont so that if she got a flat in the dangerous Happy Hills section on her way home from late orchestra practice, she could call her parents for help (which she did not long after they installed the phone). His daughter teases him: "I know when I come back to him after a performance his face will be red and his hair will be messed up. He played every note with me."

Mike grins. He admits it. "I used to be tense waiting for every note," he says. "But these last few months, I've just relaxed and listened." He means these last few months since The Gabriella got accepted into the highly respected Cleveland Institute of Music.

*   *   *

Earlier in the day, Gabriella and her two best friends from school, Amelia and Ramona, took over a high Naugahyde booth at a vintage coffee shop eating pizza and mozzarella salad, and reminisced about the teachers at the school of the arts. They had only graduated the week before, but they were already nostalgic. They remembered how their white-bearded old English teacher wore these flamboyant blouses and huge rings and told stories about Vivien Leigh and Sarah Churchill and nervous breakdowns in taxicabs; how the biology teacher "used to be an activist—equality for everyone—and she throws that into cell division"; how the math teacher let them come to class barefoot, called them all chickees and used to dismiss them after five minutes on a whim.

Ramona said that the school's arts emphasis gave them a way of seeing people "for different things than what clothes they're wearing."

"Boyfriends," Amelia added. "There's not a peer pressure thing for that or for going out on Friday or for cruising. It's nice to go home . . ."

"And sleep," Gabi joked.

"And we don't hate our parents or anything," Amelia went on, "I don't hate them or *say* that I hate them."

Still, for everything they loved about the school, it wasn't easy. Three times a year they had juries, which meant playing for all the string teachers or all the piano teachers. They had academic tests in English, math and science, as well as weeks of intensive arts practice. They had to juggle orchestra and theory classes and private lessons. "The suicide rate is pretty high apparently," Gabriella said.

Her friends gave an example about a visual arts student who tried to hang himself from a dorm window with piano wire. The wire broke; he fell but lived. And then the year before there was a guy who slit his wrists and somebody else recently who took too many pills.

So when they got a break, they took it. In the spring, Gabi and her friends rented a condominium on the North Carolina shore. And, they admitted sheepishly, they drank. To relax.

They planned spring break the way Gabi plays the violin, the way Amelia plays the piano, the way Ramona plays oboe: Details were important. First, they got an older friend to buy them alcohol. They stashed it in a locker at school. Then came The Blizzard of '93.

Amelia was supposed to drive her new Saturn. "I was sure my dad was not gonna let me drive," she said as Gabi peeked over the side of the booth to make sure nobody they knew was around. "But my brother drove my car and my dad drove his, and we went and picked up these guys." She indicated Gabi and Ramona, who were both grinning sort of guiltily. "Then my dad followed us to the highway. He was sure the highways would be clear." After her dad left them safe on the highway, they looped around and headed back through the icy streets of town.

"We had worked so hard to get the stuff," Amelia said. "It was like a big deal . . . when you can't drink. We were all cool, and then it snowed, and then we didn't think we'd get to school. Then we thought they'd lock the school and we wouldn't be able to get to it. And then we got there and the security guards were there. We were like, 'We just need to get some groceries out of our locker.'" They got the suspiciously shaped brown bags.

"And we skidded on ice with our precious cargo," Ramona laughed.

"I was like really scared the whole time," Amelia said. "I just knew we were gonna have a wreck and my dad was gonna get so mad. He was gonna find out *why* I had not stayed on the highway."

But they made it to the condo and went out to rent videos to watch on the VCR Gabi had brought. They got *Mystic Pizza, Aliens, The Hitcher, Arachnophobia,* and Gabi's favorite movie, *The Competition,* about a piano contest. They got carded trying to see *Peter's Friends* because Gabi "looks twelve" even though she's eighteen. Another night, they saw *A Few Good Men.*

They drank beer, although Ramona had to mix it with Sprite to get it down. They drank wine, although Ramona had to heat it in the microwave to make it taste better. They saved the Jack Daniel's for St. Patrick's Day, then drank it all—and even turned on a tape recorder so nobody would be able to deny anything embarrassing that happened.

But really, it was all a big strain. None of them was used to drinking alcohol. None of them was used to doing anything but what she was supposed to. "I was so paranoid," Amelia admitted again. "My mom had rented this condominium for us, and I could just see these people calling my mom, saying that we were in there and we were *drunk.*"

"And I was being so loud," Gabi said.

They all started to laugh at the memory of that. "She was on the floor, and she could not get up," Amelia explained.

"See, I'm little so if I'm drinkin' the same amount . . . I was gone," Gabi added. "That was the *worst,* man. But you were the one that got sick." She pointed to Amelia.

Amelia nodded, still giggling breathlessly. "I know I got really sick . . . *Four* times." That set them all off again.

Plus, Ramona has a phobia about vomit. "If she thinks somebody's gonna throw up she like starts humming and puts her fingers in her ears. She like cannot deal with it at all," Amelia elaborated. "And there I was on the bed with a trashcan. It was really gross."

"On *my* bed with a trashcan," Gabi groaned. "We have a tape of it, of her like puking in my bed."

The next day, the phone rang early. Gabi answered it and started jumping around yelling, "Holy Shit! Holy Shit!" It was her parents. She had been accepted by Cleveland.

*   *   *

After Gabi plays the Fauré for her father, her mother brings out napoleons and everyone starts going back over the story of her getting into Cleveland. Mike says, "It was scary to have her work this hard."

Her mother adds: "But when she's not working, she's not as happy as she is when she's doing it."

"She's not being asked to be more than other kids," Mike says. "She may be tired. But she's not stressed out. The whole Gabriella isn't unhappy about what she's doing." He talks about how in tune he and his daughter are. "Gabi and I share the same brain," he says. "I'm real proud that she's able to do this. I don't pin my hopes on a particular goal. She's already surpassed any goal." He looks at her often as he speaks. "We don't have a plan. If there's a plan here, it's Gabi's."

Gabi herself is quiet. Earlier, in her room, which has a poster of James Dean and some reproduction Renoirs, she confessed that she is scared. She is worried about her parents spending so much money and about the competition there. "It's too much," she said. "I feel like I don't deserve it. I could get to Cleveland and totally freak out and become a belly dancer."

But as apprehensive as she is, Gabi knows she has gone as far as she can in North Carolina, where she could have stayed on for a college degree. Here, she plays first violin. "At Cleveland, I'll be the bottom. But any day I would pick to be the worst than the best," she says. It challenges her to get better. "I don't want to be less than spectacular. Sometimes you just think it's not worth it. There are so many good violinists who could just kick my ass. I can't beat them. I just can't. But it's a personal challenge that I set for myself seven years ago. I can handle it. You have to be like steel.

"Right now, I pretty much have everything I want. I never

thought that I would get [into Cleveland]. Nobody at my school thought I would. They take ten violinists out of sixty or one hundred. And I'm the one."

So as her family goes on about how Gabriella's plan is paying off, her father brings up an old memory. He says that when she was a little girl, he used to talk her to sleep. "I'd tell her the story of the Cleveland Gabi who went to Cleveland and had this brilliant career. Isn't that eerie?" he says.

But it's not so eerie to Gabi. She remembers how many times she has pulled her bow across the strings. She knows how many times she has held her violin against the callus on her jaw. She knows just how many times it takes to get to Cleveland.

"Advanced Placement"

I never knew exactly how I wound up at Andover, and why I stayed there when I was so completely miserable. But it has something to do with when you're a kid and people ask you what you want to be when you grow up, what you want to major in when you get to what college was it you wanted to go to? Long before you actually have a fully formed clue of what you really want, you do know what other people want you to say. Plus, you have a strong sense of wanting to please the people you care about and respect.

Most of the time what your parents expect from you is not a real spelled-out kind of thing, but kids are especially good at reading what might seem like subtle messages, even facial expressions. You somehow know that your parents would love for you to follow them into their field, or you sense their remorse over things they didn't or couldn't do with their own lives and feel like it's up to you to make it happen for them through you. Whether you do it consciously or not, you'll usually try to meet high expectations or even sabotage yourself to fulfill a poor opinion. Sometimes it's the world's poor opinion based on where you live. You see that happening all the time in places with a reputation for poverty and violence. Occasionally, you'll think you've found an exception, like this amazing guy I met from the outskirts of L.A. whose parents had deserted him when he was just a kid. But then as we were talking, he kept mentioning a man from his neighborhood who really believed in him. ("He's the one I take after," he said.) The guy had pushed him to get an education. *"You've got to think about the future," he said, probably echoing his friend.*

But expectation can mean pressure. Gabi knows how much her violin playing means to her father even though he would never force her to keep working as hard as she does. She seems genuinely to love playing the violin and to love what she's achieved. But it reminds me of the dynamic that made me think I wanted to go to Andover. By the end of the ninth grade, I had gotten through most of the upper-level classes at learn-at-your-own-pace Carolina Friends School. So on a trip around Europe with dad that summer after my parents split up, I was probably bragging a little about that to dad, and then we got talking about how I might want to change schools, for a new challenge academically. I didn't know anything about Phillips Academy, Andover, where dad and his brother Joe had gone, but dad and I made a plan to visit some prep schools to see if I might want to go away. Out of the four that we visited, I applied to Phillips Academy, Concord Academy, and Phillips Exeter Academy, and got accepted to all three. Even though I remember feeling more comfortable at Concord during our visits, somehow dad and I decided that Andover would be the best for me—if I chose to go through with this plan at all.

But it's still impossible for me to determine how much going eight hundred miles away from my family when I'd only ever been away from them for a week tops, was my idea and how much was my wanting to be in sync with dad and his ideas. Especially because I'd been told, and felt, since I can remember, that I was a lot like dad—both really organized, the only two out of the six of us with blue eyes and lighter skin, both got headaches—I don't know, it felt significant to me at the time. And I liked that connection.

From the time we got the acceptance letters, it was like perpetual motion took over, and there were deadlines for loan applications, dorm assignments, dad saying he'd just go ahead and send in the $100 deposit to hold my place while I made up my mind, etc., etc., until I felt too deep into it, and like I had put way too many people out to back out now. I spent the week and a half before I left *crying and not being able to sleep or eat—I ate like a peanut and a half the whole time.*

At first, Andover was academically overwhelming for me. The policy was an hour and a half of homework for every hour you were in class. Every other week was a six-day week, meaning classes on Saturdays. We'd sit around and figure out that with all the sports teams and extracurricular activities you were encouraged to participate in, that officially left us about three hours a night for sleeping. But worse, I didn't know who I was there. Friends School was all about non-competition, "Free to Be You and Me" kind of love yourself and your neighbor, be true to yourself. At Andover, I felt like you needed a lot of things I didn't have and would never have, like a dad who owned a corporation.

That first year, I had maybe two or three friends, and I think even they didn't know how to deal with how depressed and withdrawn I seemed. I'd wake up and be flooded with such doom that even if it was four in the morning and I'd been working until one, I couldn't go back to sleep. I was so terrified of the dining halls, even the one known for feeding the nerds and the teachers, of standing there in front of the room with my tray while looking around for anyone who would want me to sit with them. So I skipped most meals, and lived off pizza deliveries and chocolate chip cookies from the grocery store in town.

Before my second year, I was determined to turn things around, so that was my makeover summer. I came back in the fall with bright pink sweaters, five-inch-heels, and this hair and makeup routine that meant I had to get up at 6:30 if I had a 9 a.m. class, earlier if I went to breakfast. I used under-eye coverup, powdered bronzer, and a few different shades of blush for contouring. I had bright turquoisey-blue eye liner for the inside of my bottom lid, then lighter sky blue under the bottom lashes, and dark blue over the top lashes and tons and tons of mascara. Plus a lip pencil, then lipstick, then Strawberry Kissing Slicks, which I carried in my pocket for constant touch-ups. I had to curling-iron my hair to make it flip away from my face, and depending on the weather, I'd first stick my head over a sink of steaming hot water to give it more volume. By the time I went to my first morning class, I had spent two hours looking in a mirror. And I knew every good reflective surface between my dorm room and German, German and English, English and the library. But it worked. Or maybe the veneer of confidence it gave me worked. Other students thought I was a new kid, and I finally got some friends, got invited to parties, made out with guys, took illegal trips into Boston to pursue these guys at Harvard we had crushes on. I still got depressed really easily though. Like that year at Dartmouth Winter Carnival when my friend Kathy and I got into a fight—I think it was about whether or not I would sneak into the infirmary with her to visit the guy she liked—and I wandered into some dorm bathroom and broke a beer bottle that was sitting in the sink and cut my arm a bunch of times with the glass.

I didn't actively want to kill myself and every time I did that (starting at age fourteen with an S that I still have on my arm, the first initial of a boyfriend I'd broken up with), the cuts were pretty superficial. But in a passive way, I wouldn't have minded dying at all, like the day I ended a journal entry with "As a filmmaker, as a person, I would like to be invisible. Maybe I will be." Similar to the suicide-attempt stories Gabi and her friends knew, I remember hearing that one kid had hung himself from a light fixture in our dorm a year or two before I got there and that at another prep school, they closed off the belltower during finals weeks so kids wouldn't jump. But obviously, teenage suicide is not a prep school phenomenon. In fact, the third leading cause of death among people age 15 to 24 is suicide. More than 5,000 die this way each year, up 20 percent from ten years ago. Most anxiety disorders start by the age of 15. And even if they don't suffer from a clinical mental disorder, almost all have mood swings they can't explain and many go through periods of intense depression that feel more scary than when you have them as an adult because you don't have the perspective to know they'll end.

And all the pressure teenagers are under now doesn't help.

Where kids used to pretty much follow their parents in a path that started with high school graduation, then college and/or marriage and a job that lasted decades, things don't work that way now. High school educations don't qualify you for a lot of jobs, while college costs have risen to an average of more than $12,000 a year. And because there's less government loan money available to students, most schools have had to drop their blind admissions policies, making it harder for a kid without money to get in. Plus there are all the "boomlet" teenagers, those kids of the baby boomers, applying to them. I've seen a bunch of Sassy *interns a lot more qualified than I was not get into my alma mater, Oberlin. Afterward, there's only an iffy chance of a high-paying job as a reward anyway. So any teenager's life can take any course and the pressure of not knowing which way is best is compounded because most parents need to spend more time working and have less time to muddle through these decisions with their kids. More significant, less contact between parents and teenagers means it's harder for parents to instill in their kids the sense that they're valuable no matter which turns their lives take.*

The bottom line is that we need to expect things of teenagers while keeping in mind that what they want is most important. I remember my mom telling me over and over again I could do anything I wanted to do. I didn't realize until five years ago or something, that like 90 percent of parents use that line. I actually believed her. Now I'd be lying by omission not to say that her statement also made me feel that I had all the equipment to be really successful and that I'd better use it. But for good or bad, through panic attacks and anxiety and total joy at accomplishing things that I went after, definitely her complete and continual faith in me was a huge force behind everything I did.

One day in the last weeks of writing this thing, I was so burned out and decided to seek inspiration and a break by going to see Fred Wiseman's documentary, High School II, *filmed at Central Park East Secondary School in Spanish Harlem. From the moment the movie started, I was in love with these kids, every one of them.*

As the first kid on the screen used the trial of the police officers who beat Rodney King to explain to a few teachers his thoughts about how socialism could increase democracy, I realized I was laughing too loud. Then one after the other, kids who had babies at home and guns pulled on them on their way to the store were shown attacking learning with such energy and genuine enthusiasm, usually not to please their parents or teachers, but for themselves and their futures. The teachers and whole school staff worked to earn respect rather than demanding it, running the school on philosophies that reminded me of a lot of what Carolina Friends was based on: tolerance, learning for learning's sake over competitions or grades, taking a critical stance toward studies rather than memorization, and always incorporating the larger context of the complicated world outside the classrooms. Now, I don't mean to say that Andover was just about how miserable I was socially that first year. I crammed more information and studying methods into my brain, probably more than in all the years since, which have helped me in every class and job since. And though I'm a big wimp saying this next to kids who deal with friends getting shot, having gotten through Andover made me know I could live through anything.

Anyway, this was a while ago. Andover has also changed a lot— they have their first female president and a group for gay students now and I'm sure they're having to include all of the same sorts of issues in their curriculum that Central Park East was handling so beautifully. Becoming the kind of school we need so much more now than ever, one where that excuse doesn't apply, the one about, "Well, they should learn about that at home." So, whether that's about sex. Or about morals. Or about taking care of themselves. Especially not while, at the same time, most of the people who say that are decrying the lack of stable homes for kids these days. Whether it's a boarding school like Andover, where it's literally the kids' home, or any public or private school anywhere, we need schools that help kids integrate what they're learning in class into their increasingly complicated lives.

February 12, 1980
(First written in GB's memory book)

a PA depression—

schizo,
crazy,
I don't care,

destructive
moods and
rip out hair,

those tears
from sneers
of smilers rare,

hard work
on papers
that need repair,

PA—
you make us
as we are,

with talent
and brains
but o so far

from those
things real
and how you mar

distinctions
that make us
more than smart,

our few
yes, true
desires and goals,

replaced
by space
by emptied holes.

JEP

WHAT ERIN CONRAD DID
ON HER SUMMER VACATION

*O*ne day earlier this summer when Erin Conrad was sitting here by the lake outside the University of Wisconsin student union, she was reading *Henry IV* ("boring") in preparation for her AP English class and this guy with dreadlocks and a guitar walked up and wanted to test some lyrics on her. He played, sang, asked about her. She lied: *"Yeah, yeah, I'm going to graduate school next year."*

She grins now, pulls her brown hair back from her forehead, and says: "I make up all these little . . . 'cause I can relate to them. And they'll ask me, and I'm like, *Yeah, I'm in political science.* And they'll ask me about it and I'll be like, *Yeah, blaaablaa.* I can relate. I'm a little liar but *ehhh* . . . It's fun. I get the biggest kick out of it."

Sitting here in her old Birkenstock sandals and a Save the Wetlands T-shirt, she has a lot on her mind, such as whether she would most like her college application to be accepted by Colorado College or by Kalamazoo. Also, she can't stop remembering a question that a friend's mom asked her yesterday: "Erin, are you having fun? Are you making sure you're having fun?"

She sits motionless, then says. "And I *don't* know. I think so. I *guess* so.

"I have a lot of trouble relating to kids my age—although I have tons of acquaintances and many friends. Friends aren't a problem and I can get on their level.

"But I'm a very motivated and I would almost say driven person.

I mean, everything I do has a purpose and it really does. It really does if I think about it." She looks at the water.

* * *

Erin, seventeen, lives in a cul-de-sac neighborhood where all the houses have trimmed lawns and big shade trees and two-car garages. Her dad, whom she mostly calls Clif, is a college professor who travels across the country doing ethnographies on people involved in racially motivated incidents. Her mom, Pam, is a school psychologist. She has a little sister named Abbi and a dog who freaks out every time strange men come around because when he was a puppy the famous-in-Madison "patio burglar" robbed the house while he watched.

After eighth grade, Erin switched from public school, where "kids were mean to me 'cause I didn't have the clothes," meaning Esprit and Guess. So now, she gets to drive the family station wagon that has 140,000 miles on the odometer and a bumper sticker she put on that says, "Friends Don't Let Friends Vote Republican." It takes her twenty minutes in morning traffic to get to the small private Catholic school where "all the kids are from well-off families, very preppy, polo shirts. They're just like clones," she explains. "I mean, sure they're my friends, and I love them to death. But they all look the same, and they act the same and their views are the same." In a mock election at the school during the 1992 presidential campaign, Bush won. But, despite that, enough of the kids voted for Erin last year to make her president of her class and chairman of the Prom committee.

It's an *"ab*solutely wonderful" life, Erin says. She spent last summer being a Senate page in Washington D.C., and then rode on the Senators' train to the Democratic National Convention in New York, where she went to tons of parties and speeches with her dad's cousin, Senator Kent Conrad of North Dakota. She sat two seats away from Jesse Jackson in the "very very very important persons" section. *"Three V's,"* she reiterates. She watched Clinton give his acceptance speech. "It was so moving. We're all clasping hands. I'm clasping hands with Jesse Jackson's sister. We're all singing a song. I mean, that stuff just doesn't happen. I felt so united. It was a neat experience." She met Al Gore and LBJ's grandchildren. She ate more dessert than she'd ever seen in her life and stayed in a suite where they put chocolate on your pillow.

And this summer, she spent a month in Costa Rica studying Spanish while living with a family who never had a television until two weeks into her stay (and then only because they got paid for having her). She loved the family. The mother, who only had sons, braided Erin's hair at the dinner table. Her first night with them, the "crazy off-the-wall construction-worker" dad turned a cart-wheel in the kitchen. Erin had to take cold showers, but, she says, "I was so independent"—traveling with her sixteen-year-old cousin (who was living with another family) and staying in a $3-a-night cockroach-infested shack on the beach and then missing the bus the next day and having to hitch a ride in a cow truck back to San José. Almost every night she went out to the disco with a twenty-one-year-old American guy who was also staying with the family. "I got down. I really know the disco and the taxi cab language," she says with a little smirk. She also got drunk for the first time in her life and kissed ten different guys, who told her how beautiful she was with her blonde hair (even though by American standards she is a brunette). "There was Frederico and Mario and Roberto and I liked them all. They all told me they loved me. I kissed 'em all. I mean, what the heck. I'm in a foreign country," she says giggling and shrugging.

But the whole time she was away, something was bothering her: "I had a very very extremely big big confrontation with my dad before I left, a day before I left for Costa Rica," she says. "And he was really really hurt by it . . . he never admits he's wrong; he thinks he's always right. And it sounds like, *You can live with that, Erin.* But you can't."

Her tone is solemn. "Once, we were going to Minneapolis, and he was driving, and he had the map, and he took a wrong turn, and we ended up going to Iowa. But somehow it's *my* fault. And I told him all this and I said, It hurts me.

"It was the day before Father's Day. Things had piled up and piled up, and I'd been wanting to say this like forever. And I said it, and he called from work and he left a message on the answering machine and he goes, he said, 'Well, let's just not celebrate this goddamn Father's Day thing.'

"So you know I went off to Costa Rica with a father who hated me."

The whole time she was there, Erin cried when her family would call. She missed her mom and dad and even promised her sister that she would spend all her time with her when she got home. After getting back through customs with her stuffed suitcase, she watched TV constantly, which she had never done in her life. She had gained eight pounds on fried foods and was happy to get back to her routine: "Fifty-calorie no-fat Yoplait yogurt for breakfast and then for lunch I have my two pieces of forty-calorie bread and my two pieces of cheese and two pieces of turkey and an apple and that's it. And then I have a big dinner. After dinner, I have fifty-calorie no-fat frozen yogurt. It's perfect." She was even happy to be back to the family ritual of watching *MacNeil/Lehrer Newshour* every night.

Right after she got home, the Conrads took a family vacation to Colorado. Erin even got to take her best friend. But little things drove her crazy. "Like on the trip, my friend and Abbi and I were playing the game *Who Am I?* and *Twenty Questions* to guess a person, and we were doing people like Bill Clinton. My dad says, 'Let's play the game *Name the Revolutionaries.*'" She sighs. "I mean . . . my mom, she's like 'Oh, shut up, Clif.'"

Erin still hasn't talked things through with her dad. And she knows he's still hurt about their pre–Costa Rica encounter because just last night, he left an article on her nightstand. It said, "To: Erin Conrad. From: Mr. Know-it-All." "I'll read it. And I'm sure it will be interesting." She grins. "But I won't tell *him* that.

"I think I've always, up till now, I think every single, *every* thing

I've done has been to please my father. And that's the wrong way to go in life because you have to be out there to please yourself and I'm glad I realized it."

She realized it partially because of her best friend, Traci. They got to be close last year after each broke up with a year-long boyfriend. "She helped me," Erin says. "She has no work ethic. She has no motivation. She's absolutely the most rebellious person. Yet she thinks about things and different ways of looking at things and she's helped me so much."

When Eric contrasts her life with Traci's, she feels cheated. "We watch *MacNeil/Lehrer* and although I appreciate it, it's always been forced upon me. In sixth grade, I was handed like *Moby-Dick* and these big books. Reading. When you read, you read to learn. Reading has never been considered enjoyment. So I have always resented reading. And I've hated it because it's always been so forced. And like my friend Traci, she's never had that. She's enjoyed reading. And writing has always been forced upon me and 'You have to write to be successful, Erin.' And so I didn't like to write and my friend Traci, just writes journals every day. And she's the most talented writer. She makes me absolutely . . . she makes me sick. I sit down with a paper and can work three days on it to just get it in writing, and she'll do it in an hour. That kind of learning, reading, and analyzing and critical thinking is . . . since I was born. It's important around my family. I've been able to be a kid but not completely. I mean, what other family sits down and talks about— *with my eleven-year-old sister*—homosexuals in the Army? During dinner, we'll talk about these kind of things. It's not very normal."

Normal would be if you made a list of colleges and your dad didn't mark some of them off, saying, "Only stupid people go there, Erin." Normal would be if you wrote a paper and your dad didn't edit it. She says: "He'll just go, 'Ooohh, this is trash, trash, trash.' And that's been really hard on me. The other day my mom said, 'Erin, do you realize he's comparing your work to graduate student level writing?' I was like, 'Well, I guess I never knew it.'"

Erin shrugs now. "My teachers have said my writing is good compared to my peers. But it's not good enough for my dad."

* * *

At home that evening, Erin and her dad are playing some sort of running game in the front yard with Abbi and her friends. There are hamburgers on the backyard grill, and her mom, who is in the kitchen, has made a cake and some fruit salad. There is fresh corn. It looks like a Norman Rockwell painting.

"No family's as good as this one, Dad," Erin teases him.

"Why don't you move away from that notion of the ideal family which you can become a prisoner of—I think we all do," he responds. He adds that Erin's been going through "a phase of using, not a 1950's standard, but sort of an absolute ideal of *nobody ever raising his voice, nobody having a difference.* And you *try* to live up to *that.*" He tells her: "It's taken *me* a long time to grapple with that—not to be a prisoner. We sure become prisoners of these kind of romantic ideals—fairy tales we read."

At supper, he talks about an essay Erin is doing about how teenagers need something fun to do if anyone ever expects them to stay out of trouble. She woke her dad up to show it to him after she wrote it in a late-night inspiration. Clif says: "She has a kind of lyricism that I long ago rooted out of [my writing]. So when you see it, you still kind of like it, and you don't want to crush that because there's something in that liveliness. What she has is sort of three parts of an essay where she doesn't quite have the segues or logical connections between them, but she's got the pieces. It's much better for her to get it down in the first place. Me, having written for many years, I do it this way: I think about it a lot and then I do a general scaffolding. For me, within that order is freedom."

Erin has been watching him intently as he speaks and says: "But I can't do that. I get myself so worked up about *how* I have to write."

Her father nods, conceding: "Other people get so worked up that it's almost better to just get it out. That's how most fiction writers do it."

Someone else at the table says, "I've never met two writers who work the same way."

Pam looks at her daughter and smiles. "Keep that thought. Your father is not the only one."

Clif scoffs. "She's already dismissed me." Then going back to her essay: "The thing I liked about it was the ending—a feminist kind of rage about how basically, who decided what social activities were available for kids was a bunch of white males. And then the closing line is something like—she didn't quite use that word—but a lot of feminists and others these days feel that instead of silencing the voices of kids they ought to be invited into the conversation. She had the idea."

Erin beams.

* * *

Dessert is over, and Erin announces that she and her friend are going to see the movie *Much Ado About Nothing*. It's the Sunday before her senior year starts. Tuesday, she'll have to start getting up at six so she can go to the gym and work out before school. This year, she'll also have a job at a deli, which her father doesn't approve of because she won't be "learning anything." And she's already sort of in trouble at school because when the new dress code was announced at a preliminary assembly, Erin was wearing five violations—Birkenstocks, a T-shirt untucked, frayed jean shorts, two inches above the knee, a shirt tied around her waist and a hat. She got up and said to the principal, "Well, I'm just wondering, what is your vision of diversity?"

She jingles her keys and heads toward the front door. Clif says: "There are some nuts down on State Street, I noticed. And I hope you're careful." He fixes a serious look on Erin. She nods. "Yesterday there was this one guy who had brass knuckles and he had a shirt that said *Fuckin' Angry* on the back," he continues.

"His name's Jedediah," Erin says cheerily.

"You know him?" Clif doesn't quite hide his surprise.

"Yeah."

"You're not good *buddies* with him?"

"No," Erin shakes her head. "But I know who he is."

Clif says: "He has a little chip on his shoulder. Those *are* brass knuckles, aren't they?"

"Yeah," she answers.

"Aren't those against the law?" he asks.

She shrugs. "Probably, yes. He dropped out of school last year. He's one of the biggest drug dealers in the city, in the county."

Erin turns and rushes out the door. "What time will you be home?" her dad calls after her.

"I won't be home late," she yells back as she opens the car door.

"Abs of Steel"

Depending on which studies you listen to, the number of teenagers with eating disorders is anywhere from 1 in 100 to 1 in 3. I think one of the reasons for this discrepancy is there's now less of a distinction than ever between kids with eating disorders and kids without. Although kids with anorexia, compulsive overeating, or bulimia (which can mean vomiting or taking laxatives, or even exercising a lot to burn off food they ate) are still in the minority, I'll add my own statistic here, based on lots of anecdotal evidence: I'd say closer to 95 percent of teenage girls have an eating disorder if you take that to mean that they are intensely preoccupied with the way their bodies look and they don't just think of food as healthy and fun, but rather something to be avoided or manipulated or burned off climbing fake stairs. And there are fewer, but still a majority of, guys with distorted ideas of what their bodies should look like who no matter what they do, feel their bodies are never good enough.

So they may not be kids you'd pick out on the street because they weigh 15 percent below normal body weight (the official definition of anorexia nervosa) or obviously overweight kids stuffing themselves with Big Macs. They may not look totally pumped up with steroids. But I'm talking about things teenagers consider normal: wishing to get sick so they can lose 5 pounds, intentionally not eating all day, drinking protein drinks or taking amino acids to try to bulk up, eating only fat-free foods, doing five hundred sit-ups *every night before bed, smoking to keep from eating, thinking they're worthless unless they look like Mr. Olympia or Stephanie Seymour. And Erin being glad to get home from Costa Rica because at home she can get calorie counts on her yogurt containers and work out every morning.*

Almost every teenage girl I know is unhappy with her body in one way or another and can tell you down to the minutest detail just what's wrong with it. "That little wiggly part under my arms, like when you wave, should be tight," one tells me. "I try to work my triceps to help it, but it's still too wobbly." Another girl likes her "abs" but hates her "gluts" (translation: abdomen and butt). A seventeen-year-old girl I know says that when she goes to the mall, "I can't help it, I compare myself. 'Did you see her waist? It was so tiny. I wish I had that. Did you see her legs? They were perfect. I can't wear skirts that short 'cause of my thighs,' etcetera, etcetera." And the guys are that way too, although they express it differently, more in fake bragging tones. "These six-pack muscles are my trophy," one sixteen-year-old football player said, making his stomach ripple. "But I've gotta do more bleachers training before my butt is fully buff."

This obsession with making your body look a certain way through diet, drugs, and exercise starts much younger now too. We've all heard about those studies showing girls who are seven years old and dieting. One report found that 55 percent of girls ages ten to thirteen think they're fat, even though only 13 percent are technically overweight. So by the time they're teenagers, it's ingrained. They know every inch of their body that they hate, just in time for it to whack out on them because they're hitting puberty anyway. Also, while models have always provided unrealistic images for girls to try to emulate, now models have become supermodels and everyone knows who Christy, Cindy, Kate, and Naomi are, eclipsing some of the other maybe-less-body-beautiful role models we used to have.

Another reason more and more teenagers seem to be obsessed with their bodies came to me from one girl from California who visited me up at Sassy *one day: "It's about control. When you're five pounds over where you want to be, you feel totally out of control. And there's not that much we can control these days," said this sixteen-year-old whose mom is a therapist. It's true—on top of all the out-of-control body changes that have always come along with adolescence, there's the combination of teenagers' increasing awareness of global problems and their less predictable families to exacerbate everything. Abigail, who's fifteen and looks like she falls right into that insurance company chart of acceptable weight ranges, told me she cries intermittently about the way she thinks her body looks. "It's better when I have a boyfriend," she says. But even then, she'll feel bad if she eats anything she doesn't consider "diet food." Another fifteen-year-old who's 4 feet, 10 inches tall and whose weight fluctuates between 70 and 74 pounds always knows exactly where she is in that range. "I weigh myself every day. I'm constantly thinking about it—exercising, scrutinizing what I eat. I don't see myself as thin, and I'm only happy when I weigh 72 pounds. That's not technically an eating disorder, but it is an obsession. It's a mental thing."*

Same thing for guys. "I love it when girls squeeze my biceps and say, 'Wow, you're so big and strong!'" says one fifteen-year-old, "But they don't that often because I'm not that good, like I'm not some huge-o beefcake. I'm not ideal." Then after making sure I won't use his name here, he admits, "It bothers me a lot more than I let on." He's thought about using steroids and knows guys at his school who do. He knows they can cause problems like acne on your back, but that doesn't really worry him. Steroid use, like anorexia and bulimia, is increasing. And like eating disorders, it doesn't just cause superficial nuisances but also serious and lasting physical problems, like heart disease and kidney damage. Though guys have traditionally done it to try to excel in sports like wrestling and boxing, more seem to be doing it strictly for looks. One guy I know said his sixteen-year-old brother got steroids from their older brother, who deals them, a couple of years ago and has been taking them ever since. All his friends do. "It's what you do," he tells me. "It's like, if you've got a headache, you take aspirin. If you want to get buffed, you take steroids. It's no big deal."

Plus guys aren't the only ones taking them anymore. I recently heard of a high school sophomore in Texas who, along with her volleyball teammates, takes steroids. Some other kids said all the girls on their high school's basketball team take them. Meanwhile, another way more and more girls are disregarding their health to get that "healthy" look is with cigarettes. Smoking has declined in every single demographic group—except among teenage girls, many of whom are using it as an appetite suppressant. Teenage girls' smoking rates are actually increasing; every day, two thousand of them smoke for the first time. (Interestingly, smoking is much less common with black teenage girls, maybe partly because their body ideal is generally not as skinny-skinny.) More teenagers are also undergoing another potentially dangerous procedure: plastic surgery, most commonly nose jobs, liposuction, and breast augmentation. The latest thing is getting your face sculpted into what some doctors are calling "the waif face." For $3,000, surgeons remove the fat pads from your cheeks, which hollows out your face to make it look more gaunt.

The temptation for a lot of adults is to dismiss the seriousness of fat-gram-and-StairMaster obsessions or even their kid wanting a cheek job as just a shallow vanity that's kind of cute. But it goes much, much deeper than that. While going back through my old journals, I was surprised to find an entry from when I was seventeen comparing my makeup and hair obsession with anorexia. Even though I'd been thin, if not skinny, my whole life and never worried about what I ate, I saw the connection between the all-consuming obsession I had with my makeup and hair and an eating disorder. After I got to college, I slowly intentionally weaned myself off all that makeup I used to wear daily. It was just ruling my life too much. And now that we were in coed dorms, it became harder and harder to control the image of myself I wanted to present. Like the time freshman year that a guy walked into our room when I wasn't fully made up and I jumped into the closet and didn't *come out till he'd left a half hour later. But even after I got rid of most of my eyeliners, it was a while before I started admitting to people what I realized at seventeen—this was my version of a body image disorder. It had practically all the components: The way my head looked was more important to me than anything else. I fixated on it constantly, but got good at pretending I was actually engaged in other activities, like reading a book or having a conversation. It seriously curtailed my life. For example, rainy days were a nightmare because of the potential for my face to run. And I had a totally distorted idea of how I appeared, how ridiculous I looked with all that makeup piled on; even when people like my dorm mother at Andover said to me I'd be so pretty without all that junk on, I couldn't believe her. I would be obsessed with minor flaws that changed from day to day. The big difference, obviously, is that I wasn't doing my health any severe damage with all those face and hair products; I just looked ridiculous.*

So it's important for adults to deal with this issue as though it weren't about Snackwell's Fat-Free Devil's Food Cookies or how much someone can bench-press. Because it's not about that. It's about self-image and self-worth and self-esteem and all those other overused terms for the toughest teenage issues. If you think your daughter, nephew, friend, anyone, including yourself, has an eating disorder, there are places you can go, like the American Anorexia/Bulimia Association (listed in the back of this book). I said nephew *specifically because in general I think there need to be more places that boys with body image problems can go—for both steroid abuse and eating disorders. They're less common, but that much harder to admit to.*

On the flip side, if you know a teenager who wants to lose weight (and some should for health reasons), they should learn how to do it right. They need to learn about nutrition and about exercise from a health perspective. Often, they don't have good role models at home—mothers and fathers getting liposuction, tummy tucks, and face-lifts, and the message to their children is, "You're not pretty

enough or thin enough or good enough without all these proce-
dures."

If you're a teenager who does some of the exercise/weight control things I mentioned, here's my advice: First, there's not one
good thing I can say about smoking. Realize that tobacco companies are exploiting this dangerous cultural ideal that says you
should weigh less than you naturally, healthfully would and con-
vincing you to do something incredibly unhealthy. As far as plastic
surgery goes, I have to say that the cheeks you hate now may be
way in tomorrow. But I also feel most strongly that if you go on
steroids or get plastic surgery, you're not only risking your health,
you're contributing to the Barbie-ization of this country. By mold-
ing yourself into this physical ideal, you're intensifying this epidemic and making other teenagers, and your younger brothers and
sisters, feel their quirks are even more outstanding and unaccept-
able. I'd love to say that instead you should flaunt what you think
of as flaws, make individual statements about what's beautiful, but
I don't know how I would have reacted to that advice in the midst
of my own obsession. I will say this: If you don't fall into some tech-
nical definition of an eating disorder but you are preoccupied with
your weight, face, muscle definition when there are a lot more
interesting things going on, talk to a therapist or someone else you
trust who'll help you figure out what's underneath it. It can turn
out to be a short-term problem that doesn't end up following you
through your adult life. Exercise and good food shouldn't be rigid
disciplines but pleasures.

But don't stop with yourself and your own health. Try to change
things in whatever way you can. Right from the start at Sassy, I
implemented a policy of using more human-looking models
because I didn't want teenagers measuring themselves against
these largely unattainable standards. I also decided never to print
diets, calorie counts, fat grams, or spot-reducing exercises, anything that would perpetuate the idea you need to do unnatural
things or put in inordinate time to feel okay about your body. We

always wrote about food in terms of health and exercise and having fun. I remember at one point getting a letter from a girl who said, "I weigh 95 pounds and just want to lose 5. Why won't you print diets in your magazine?", and thinking, "You're why." But there's still a lot more to be done, and I'm sure you can teach me new ways of doing it. So start your own magazines and TV shows and model agencies and production companies and other outlets I haven't thought of and show all types of bodies. Get yourself into positions of influence where you can expand all of our definitions of what's beautiful. We need it badly.

May 5, 1980

I know what it feels like to have anorexia. Vanity. It's an obsession and a sickness just like anorexia. It's just as serious, just as time-consuming, just as lonely, every bit as consuming. That terrible feeling of knowing you could never leave your room (or any room for that matter) without checking the mirror first. Knowing where the bathrooms are in all of your class-buildings so you can go make sure everything's ok before going to your next class, and then again after that one, etc. Starting to get ready a half-hour before your friend comes to get you for dinner or lunch, so that you can be all ready by the time she gets there. It means lying to your friends. It means never thinking you look good enough, and yet thinking your looks are your best asset (that's not conceit, that's self-degradation).

* * *

November 1, 1979

Why am I so screwy? Maybe I should move to China where they don't canonize models.

CASSIDY HILL, "PLAZA RAT"

*C*assidy Hill is looking for his bong. It's not on the loft above his bed that opens onto a porch with a view of the Sangre de Cristo mountains that ring Santa Fe. It's not in his top drawer or the second or even the bottom. He thinks his dad may have hidden it, like that time when he buried it in Cassidy's shirt drawer and got "bong oil" all over the clothes. The only reason his dad would stash it is if the real estate agent was coming over with someone interested in spending $225,000 to buy this house. Cassidy, fourteen, has lived here for a year with his father and ten-year-old sister, Amanda. They rent, and the landlady informed his dad that Cassidy's room had to look like a "Southwestern studio," not a teenager's bedroom. Down came the posters of Jimi Hendrix. Down came the centerfolds from *High Times* magazine. And now his dad must have done something with the bong again because it's not under the blue geometrically patterned sheets that cover the twin mattress on the floor where Cassidy sleeps. It's not behind his rolled-up sleeping bag.

"Ewwww!" Cassidy shrieks. "A dead lizard!" He gags and runs to the kitchen for a paper towel. "That cat," he cries as his best friend Max Schön shields his nose from the stench.

"How long has that thing been there?" Max asks, as Cassidy lunges out the sliding screen door to toss the stiff carcass.

"It wasn't there this morning," Cassidy says.

"It had to be, dude. It couldn't get *that* ripe *that* fast."

Cassidy shrugs and sprawls on the carpet next to Max. They forget the search for the bong. They've already smoked a joint earlier tonight anyway, before Cassidy's dad got home from working as a projectionist on a film about Wyatt Earp. He brought the boys each a hamburger and some nachos and salsa in a cardboard box. They're out of school for the summer, released from what they call "the most radical highly alternative school in Santa Fe." They switched there this past year because they say they were "slippin' through the cracks" in the vast public school they went to.

Tonight they're "hangin' at home" in their baggy plaid shorts and loose T-shirts. They call themselves "Plaza rats," but if you're flat broke, there's no sense in going downtown just to deride the tourists. If you can't go under the bridge and pay $35 for Mexi or $110 for "the kind," if you can't smoke dope, why go? Yeah, they need money, so they're waiting for a phone call about whether they're getting up first thing in the morning to help some bricklayers who are building a house out by the Santa Fe opera. They were supposed to work today, but at the last minute, their boss called and said he didn't need 'em. So they played some Streetfighter II on Nintendo in Amanda's room and kicked around aimlessly until they spotted a pool hall where they could play a round for a buck-forty, which was just about all they had between them. They make $5 an hour with the bricklayers, which isn't bad for a couple of guys who don't qualify for minimum wage 'cause they're under sixteen. But Cassidy spends 90 percent of that on drugs, he says. The "primo bud" they just finished off cost them $20 for a quarter-ounce.

Cassidy and Max, who's fifteen, are together more than they're not. Cassidy says the top three things they talk about are sex, drugs, and rock and roll, but admits he's off girls now. He had a girlfriend until last week, then she changed her mind about him. He's a virgin who keeps getting hurt. Max too. Sex is nothing but "wishes" right now, they say. Max says the top three things should really be drugs, videogames, and rock and roll. Cassidy chuckles, psyched. These guys are in sync. They hang out everyday, philosophizing about the meaning of the world according to Herman Hesse or Kafka or Jim Morrison or Clive Barker. They read the sci-fi books that go with

Amber, the role-playing game they're into with kids at school. They've been total best buddies since eighth-grade typing class back in public school. "We were both troublemakers," Cassidy says.

"Yeah," Max agrees.

"Fuckin' around in class," Cassidy adds. "We're both skaters and we'd go out skating after school. We've progressed."

To what?

"Tenth grade," Cassidy says, snickering, then adds, "To working for our money and riding mountain bikes or wilderness backpacking."

"Backpacking," Max says. "That's what we do."

"As often as we can, basically," Cassidy adds.

They get one of their parents to drop them off at a wilderness area, and they hike up and build a tent and boil water to activate the six-dollar, feeds-two Alpine Air freeze-dried Summer Chicken or Beef Stroganoff.

"Boy it was cold last time, though," Cassidy says. "But that's cause we went in winter. We climbed Santa Fe Baldy in the middle of winter."

"Twelve thousand, six hundred feet," Max adds.

"We had to climb in our snowshoes. There was not even a trail. You follow cross-country ski tracks. After four days, we were sick of snow."

"We do psychedelic drugs when we go backpacking up in the mountains," Max goes on.

"Mushrooms."

"Well, we've only tripped once in the mountains. It was just sssshhhhhmmmm. It was great."

"LSD," Cassidy says. "We took LSD in the mountains and found that there was nothing like it."

"LSD," Max says with this sort of serene smile. "It was a very good trip. Before, like in seventh grade, we'd take acid in school, munch it up in school. It was no big deal, sitting there in school."

Cassidy laughs. "I told you, man, we've progressed."

Max cackles. "Yeah, into eating *lots* of LSD."

"We used to fuckin' be into it, man."

"Eighth grade, not seventh grade," Max says, correcting himself. "But then this one trip came along." He slaps the floor Judge Wapner-style.

"Changed my mind about everything," Cassidy says seriously. "I saw the light."

Max giggles. "Yeah, that's how you could say, saw the light."

"Whoa!"

"Everything," Max says, blown away by the memory. "I could say before, I guess, I never really hallucinated. It was never really tripping very hard. But this time, it was . . . Colors were moving and sounds were ddrrrrraaaaaAAAAgggggggiiiing. I guess it was. . . . No one was up there in the mountains. No one was up there but us."

"We didn't know you could trip that hard," Cassidy says. "We didn't know that could happen."

"I now feel that I could eat a little bit of mushrooms and trip as hard as I would've if I'd eaten big quantities."

Cassidy agrees. "Like before, I took the drug with a different attitude."

"Yeah, different attitude."

"Took larger quantities of drugs and didn't get off nearly as hard as we did when we took just a little bit of acid . . . flipped out. So I guess it changed our mind about everything."

"Like about drugs in general," Max says.

. "These things are hard to explain." Cassidy holds his long bangs out of his eyes, thinking.

Max tries. "I used to think I could trip every week, you know?"

"Every weekend," Cassidy says.

"No, not every weekend."

"I used to trip every weekend," Cassidy says.

"Yeah," Max says. "You used to do it much more than I did. You did it a lot. We did it often. Now, I do it once every month or two."

"It's a special occasion," Cassidy explains before launching into a description of that trip that "blowed our mind again and again and again":

"It was our first day hiking up Hamilton Mesa in the Pecos Wilderness area. We'd left so late in the day that it wasn't worth hiking anymore so we stopped about four o'clock, set up tent. There was nobody around which was a biggie—just like no one to bother you. You could run around and act like complete fools on the mountain. No one cares."

"There were big fluffy clouds that day," Max says. "It was during the light still. And it just started out weirder than any other trip. All of a sudden . . ."

"When it first hit us," Cassidy talks over him, "we couldn't speak."

"I couldn't believe it," Max rushes on, "I'd be thinkin' about something, but then I'd start to say something else . . . We climbed up to the top of a big hill and sat there."

"We were having minor telepathic experiences," Cassidy continues quickly." Even though we couldn't talk to each other, we could know what we meant. *Oh, yeah, jtttjtttjttt."*

"Oh, yeah, jtttjtttjtttt," Max answers.

"And we understood exactly what was going on even though we were laughing hysterically because we couldn't talk." Cassidy starts laughing now.

"I saw my first like real hallucination," Max says, on top of him. They are rushing over each other, as though hurtling down a hill, one faster than the other. Then in unison, they go, "OOOOOHHHHHH!"

Max continues: "I saw this motorcycle woman, I guess it was like on a Harley-Davidson. It was definitely on a Harley-Davidson. It said Harley-Davidson on it, and it was crystal clear. I could see everything. There was this like Grateful Dead woman riding on a Harley-Davidson down the clouds. This little bear was dancing beside her. I've never seen anything like that before and then from thereon. We developed something called the elevator."

Cassidy gets this high-pitched giggle. "Boy, we went up and down the elevator, even though we weren't going anywhere. We were just kinda standin' there, but we had our own elevator that could take us to different floors of . . ."

"Mental thought," Max finishes.

"So much was going on in our mind that it was all jumbled up. So we developed an elevator to go from one conversation to another, from one plane of thought to another, skipping around in our different worlds."

"It worked good."

"It was flat, grassy," Max says.

"Trees and flowers," Cassidy remembers.

"Lots of flowers."

"It was the perfect setting," Cassidy assesses.

Max nods. "Lots of purple and blue and pink and flowers and trees and everything. It was great."

"We've had plenty of other trips that were pretty miiiiind blooowin'," Cassidy says wistfully. "But that one just seems to be the best one sticking out above all of them."

"I smoked pot for the first time in summer of seventh grade," Max explains.

"Yeah, summer of seventh grade, I smoked pot my first time too," Cassidy recalls.

"I didn't start doing acid until eighth grade," Max says. Around the same time, he went through a phase of smashing mailboxes, shooting BB guns at cars, stealing, and setting fires. He spent two weeks in a juvenile detention center. "It was supposed to shock me. And it sure did. I don't do pointless destruction." Now he and Cassidy might indulge in a little nail-the-tourist-with-a-snowball, but, as Cassidy says, "We're much more innocent now."

They both get kind of mad when they talk about friends who aren't allowed to hang out with them anymore. Cassidy had a close friend whose parents "took her up to Utah and left her there in some rehab center for two months. She came back and they had her by a leash. They sent her to a Christian school. Her parents just fucked her over. She goes to get drug tests every two weeks."

Another kid they know has a "born again" Christian mom who

wouldn't let her kid watch the Smurfs because they contained sorcery and who "whacked him bare butt with a stick." Now, she gives her son a urine test every week.

"How else are you gonna tell?" Cassidy says. "If the kid's denying it, and you think so. You'll find out for sure. My dad knows just what he'd see on the urine test."

"My parents know," Max says.

"They don't hassle us unless we were gettin' out of control doin' nothing but drugs, waking up in the morning and doing more." Cassidy's mom lives about an hour away. His parents, who named their son after Neal Cassady from the Merry Pranksters, got divorced about four years ago. "It was kinda troubling, and I guess I kinda had a pretty emotional state," Cassidy says. "In sixth grade, I was pretty touchy, and I think that mighta come from the divorce. Now, I'm glad they're divorced. My mom and dad, they don't work together." His mom has what he calls an "alternative lifestyle." She's intense, Cassidy says. "I get worn out just visitin' her for five days."

His dad is "caring" and "lenient as long as it's reasonable." For Christmas, he gave his son "a 1930s anti-drug prop film" called *Reefer Madness* that Cassidy and Max love: "First you laugh and you can't stop. Then you're paranoid and scared of everything. Then you just wanna kill people," Cassidy says, recounting the movie's theories. "It's a hilarious movie, man, especially if you watch it when you're stoned because then you just know they're lying to you."

His dad gets the joke, but sometimes it's not funny anymore. Cassidy knows it, too. "Some days I feel pretty burned out," Cassidy admits. "And people say that in the long run, it's gonna fuck me up. My ex-fuckin'-girlfriend wants me to stop smoking pot altogether and my dad and my teachers and my old counselor."

His dad sent him to the counselor when teachers at his public middle school got worried that Cassidy's grades had dropped. Cassidy said that his grades were in his usual trough between report cards and midterms. He was gonna bring them back up. "The teachers saw me hangin' out with the wrong kids, and they found my notebook and for some stupid reason, I had scribbled all sorts of drug things all over it: Stoned, Marijuana. I drew marijuana leaves and little hits of acid. And they said I was doing cocaine—I've never done cocaine, never. I was congested for six months. I had terrible nasal problems, and they blamed that on cocaine. They were just *so sure*. So they told my dad that, and for some reason, I mighta been acting bummed out at that point, and it all kinda added up and my dad said it was time to see a counselor . . . so I could find my happiness."

Cassidy thought the counselor, who had been a druggie himself, was cool. "He told me that I was gonna lose part of myself that I was never gonna get back. But I can't see anything too bad. I feel . . . I still have energy and motivation, nothing too prominent.

"But I told him I'm not gonna quit now. I'm not gonna do drugs for the rest of my life, I'm just absolutely sure. But that I had no intention of quitting anytime soon cause I'm enjoying it."

The phone rings. It's their boss from the construction site. He says he wants Max to work the next morning but not Cassidy because there's not enough work to go around. Cassidy shrugs and blows it off. His birthday is next week, and he's expecting both a mountain bike and a backpack. "See I got my parents divorced," he says slyly. But Max still has married parents. He needs to save up for a new bike. "Cool, bro," Cassidy tells him about the job.

They sack out to watch the *Mary Tyler Moore Show* on Nick at Night. "Cheesy classic American tv," Max says, smacking his lips.

Cassidy flips through *High Times* magazine. "This makes me drool," he says, pointing to pictures of "one big crypto marijuana plant" after another. "Ahhhh," he sighs, "the search for Superbud."

"Superbud"

I t's been this ongoing schtick, even before I laid eyes on him, ever since Kelli and I picked him as one of the kids we might interview: my crush on Cassidy. I jokingly subtitled his chapter "Jane's Crush" on one early draft—all right, it was late-night, me-and-my-Powerbook humor. It was his name partly. And the fact he was a skater with long blond bangs and a best guy friend he spends all his time with. But what I like most about him here is his honesty about what's such a quintessential element of teenage life: drugs. It's also what concerns me about him. "Pot, pot, pot, an ode to pot" is what one seventeen-year-old suggested we title this book, laughing heartily. I guess you have to be high to understand what's so funny, but anyway, he then added, "That sums up teenagers."

I wouldn't go that far, but it is true that after tapering off among teenagers for years, drug use has increased. The rate hasn't been this high since the sixties, and the risks have gone up too because drugs have been tinkered with in labs or are grown in superhybrids. Plus, they're cheaper and more widely available in all parts of the country. After alcohol, pot was and is the biggest drug for teenagers, but now most pot is about ten times more potent than what their parents were doing thirty years ago.

At the same time, they're using more psychedelic drugs, like X&L (a hallucinogenic blend and LSD) which is priced as low as $3 a hit for doses of 20 to 80 micrograms, lower than in the sixties when the range was between 150 and 500 micrograms. What those *reduced doses have done, I think, is to make taking acid not as big a deal as it used to be. I remember a friend in college telling me, "It's called a trip for a reason. You have to plan for it, get all the circumstances right. You can't just take it any old time." Which isn't so true anymore.*

There are new drugs that didn't even exist in the sixties: engineered drugs like GBH, an amino acid that can alter moods at high dosages, and "cat," a drug used in the Soviet Union for depression during the thirties and forties that some University of Michigan students learned to make in 1989 out of asthma medicine, Drano, Epsom salts, and battery acid. When I was writing this in the fall of '94, the most dramatic trend was the growing number of kids using heroin again and how they were spread across social classes. Then it was still more common in LA and New York, still a shock to hear about heroin-addicted kids elsewhere, like this kid I used to babysit for, from North Carolina, who was arrested for embezzling hundreds of thousands of dollars from his job to fund his heroin habit. Another guy I knew got his heroin addiction at Harvard and said heroin was huge there. But by the time this book comes out, probably most kids will know at least one person who does heroin. One reason it spread is because its price came down on the global market, and it's more pure than it used to be, when you had to inject it to get any impact. Now, heroin can be smoked through a rolled-up foil straw, and a lot of people will do that who never would have stuck needles in their arms.

If you weren't even born until sometime after 1975, then the late sixties, when heroin was the leading cause of death among young men in New York, is like ancient history. I know a couple of people my age whose dads died when they were real young from either hepatitis from dirty needles or overdoses. I also remember my mom getting incredibly upset when she read in the paper that Janis Joplin had OD'd. But kids today haven't grown up with those examples. So they're producing their own, like River Phoenix, Hillel Slovak from the Red Hot Chili Peppers, Will Shatter of Flipper, Stefanie Sargent of Seven Year Bitch, Andrew Wood of Mother Love

Bone, Kristen Pfaff of Hole, and like fifty thousand noncelebrity "medical emergencies" involving heroin last year. I had to update this list three times while we were working on this book, and I bet by the time you're reading it, it needs more.

As a rule, I'm the last person to believe these expert theories on why teenagers do what they do. But I think there's some merit to the theory that the trend toward more dangerous drug use can be partly ascribed to "generational forgetting." Since I can remember, drug education has been focused on the dangers of cocaine and its derivative crack and not stuff like heroin or LSD, both of which seemed to have gone way underground. At least they were out of sight enough that everybody figured they weren't threatening schoolkids.

And from what I've seen, if we don't talk about them, drugs get invested with more allure and therefore more power. I grew up knowing about drugs. That was probably part of the reason I got bored with them so quickly. How could drugs ever be some big dark mysterious thing, or a way to rebel against mom and dad, when from the age of five, I remember watching grown-ups at my parents' parties getting stoned and passing around the headphones so they could all listen to Big Brother and the Holding Company? Even years later, after my parents had outgrown drugs themselves, one of my mom's Duke students gave her a marijuana plant as a good-bye present. And mom, who saved even the tiniest portions off our dinner plates, just didn't want to waste it. So she planted it in our backyard garden in between the corn rows. By the end of the summer, the plant was the tallest thing in the garden, and we kids would get nervous and whine "Mo-om" every time a cop car cruised by.

When Hill and his friend started getting high in the ninth grade, the other kid's mother called mom and asked her to talk to them about it. My mom was supposed to know about these things, I guess. So she got them together and told them, "If you get caught, you're on your own. I'm not coming to pick you up at the police station. You're responsible for yourselves."

Of course eventually, at about twelve or thirteen, I got around to trying pot myself. Meanwhile, Mom had dried that huge pot plant she grew and crumbled it into old mayonnaise jars, so I used to sneak and take some to school with me in sandwich bags. I was real popular for that. Later mom found a pot pipe in a down jacket we shared but couldn't bring herself to say anything to me. So she asked Hill to do it. Which just proves that even in families that are more open about drugs, it's still awkward. But anyway, I didn't keep getting high every day for that long because when I was fifteen, I started getting too paranoid whenever I tried. I may have smoked a little, without inhaling too much. I think I did try cocaine at Andover once. Or I told people I did anyway, since a lot of students there did it. Mostly I drank. And I kept drinking when I got to Oberlin.

There were a bunch of nights at Oberlin that I didn't remember the next day—like my eighteenth birthday, where these guys, friends of mine, handcuffed me to a chair and made me drink eighteen shots of Bacardi 151. My freshman year, I also did acid for the first time. I did it probably twelve times in all, and I never really liked it; parts of it were great, but every time I wound up in a little ball on the floor thinking the world was evil. Mostly I don't remember it that much.

Actually, spring break freshman year, five of us in a little two-door Toyota drove straight through from Ohio to Daytona Beach—the drivers taking speed to make it through the night. When we got there, we drove right out onto the beach where we each took a hit or so of acid, and spent the night wandering around in the surf in our clothes and then watched the sun rise over the water. The rest of the week we spent smoking pot, collecting guys' phone numbers in pen on our hands/arms/legs, getting as many free drinks in any way possible, buying what was supposed to be cocaine but turned out to be Tide, and every night sneaking back into the filthy two-person hotel room to crash on the floor. I wouldn't really remember this many details, except I wrote all this embarrassing stuff about it in my journal. Such as "Post-tripping Revelation #231: If

*during a moment of realization, you dig your fingers into the sand
. . . your fingernail polish is chipped the next night when you want
to go and pick up guys." Or this line written in bright turquoise ink
across the same page: "Tripping. Hard to explain. Harder to experience."*

*For the next couple of years, I would pretty much always take
what someone gave me; I liked to be known that way. I took mushrooms, cocaine, speed, and friends teased me by calling me Karen
Ann Quinlan because I liked to drink and take quaaludes at the
same time. I'm sure I would have tried heroin or cat or crack if it
had been around and smokeable.*

*I ran into a group of parents recently who had all done their
share of pot smoking back when. They were interested in my perspective on how much of their pasts they should reveal to their
kids. Some of them admitted they had hidden most of it. But one,
who'd always been really open with her kid, told me about one
night when her seventeen-year-old didn't want to go out drinking
with his friends. He was tired, and anyway, he thought he was kind
of over that, he said, and would it be all right if he lied and said she
wouldn't let him go? He felt he could confide because she'd been
honest with him all along.*

*So I tell parents that when they talk to their kids about drugs, if
they've done them, they should say that. Don't lie to a kid because
when they start wanting the truth, they won't come home, they'll
go to their friends. Parents need to be careful how they throw facts
around too, like telling your kid, "Marijuana is highly physically
addictive and can be fatal." There's still a good chance they'll try it
and see it doesn't kill them and think if that's just some untrue
antidrug propaganda, then what they're hearing about other drugs
must be too, and that all drugs are actually fairly safe.*

*Instead, tell them what you do know. For example, say that even
though marijuana can produce a lot of revelations, it's hard to
translate those thoughts into action, or sometimes even into words,
and some of the most uncommunicative and unmotivated people
you know are people who get high a lot. Say you worry it might*

lower their vigilance about safe sex or guns, or that they might get psychologically dependent on it. That sometimes it's laced with other stuff. And that public service announcement which ends with the father at the graveside of his eleven-year-old drug-casualty son does make a good point: Parents need to talk about drugs with kids way before they themselves needed to know about them. One woman I met recently told me about her eleven-year-old going off to camp, where he larned to smoke through a bong made out of a beer can. "I mean, I did all that stuff too," she says, "but not at that age. And I look at his face, and he's just a baby." *In some ways maybe, but among eighth graders, for instance, marijuana use in 1993 increased by 15 percent and cocaine by 30 percent.*

Not all kids will react the same way, no matter what you say to them. A set of parents I know told their seven-, nine-, eleven- and thirteen-year-old kids one night at the dinner table that experimenting with drugs was fine and something they expected they'd all probably want to do at some point. "But," the oldest kid, now twenty, tells me, "They said that you never know what you might be getting at a party, that kids could buy it off the street and you don't know what it might be laced with, and that I'd be safer if I used the drugs they used. So they said if we ever came to them and asked, that they'd try any drugs that I wanted to try with me and show me how to do them at home." Well, the oldest kid says their tactic worked, that drugs never seemed that alluring, partly because they were something her parents condoned and did themselves. But Mark, who's eighteen now, says he thought it was "majorly uncool" to do drugs with his parents, "so I just did them with my friends and still do and never talked to my parents about any of it. But they know." Jason took them up on their offer when he was eleven, got high with them at home once, then went on to try just about every other drug with his friends at school. Including one night this year where he wound up in the hospital for three days after some friend put a prescription depression medication in his beer at a party when he was already on acid. He's sixteen now and still does plenty of drugs. And the youngest says he knows a lot of people who do drugs, including his parents still, but he has less than no interest himself. In other words, a lot of other factors affect whether your kids will take drugs or not, aside from what you do.

Anyway, drugs are a fact of teenage life. What I always say to kids is just be hyperaware they can be dangerous. I'm certainly not setting myself up as a role model in terms of my past drug use, but in my own control freak way, I was always cautious. As much as I wanted to seem wild and fearless, I was usually scared to try a new drug. So most times I would just take half a hit of something if I didn't know how much I could handle. Even when I was tripping on the weekends, I'd never do it if I had a big test or a dance performance the next day, because I knew I'd be burnt out. One thing I learned is, if you don't want to do drugs but feel dumb about saying that, try using an excuse, like "I'm in ice hockey and my coach would kill me." Also, I would just fake it sometimes, not inhale, for example. It's important to stay focused on yourself and what you want and can tolerate. Remember that having an urge to do drugs may be a way of your avoiding facing some emotionally painful thing, but that's only a temporary solution because unfortunately you will eventually have to face whatever it is. And when you do go ahead and deal with your problems, you'll get that great sense of I got through that so "I can live through anything"—and not just the drug kind of "I can do anything" which isn't true and goes away when the drug wears off.

Then, in some ways, I wasn't careful—mostly because I really didn't know how dangerous some of what I was doing could be, and I was just lucky. Eventually, I stopped liking doing drugs and moved on, which is what I'm hoping will happen to Cassidy and Max. But a lot of kids go the other way—plenty I know from junior high still get high every day, have every day since junior high. Other people who did drugs with me in college are now battling heroin addictions, alcohol addictions, coke habits, some more cleanly than others.

If your craving to do drugs is more intense, if you're doing them *alone in your room a lot or they're messing up other things in your life or if you can't do certain things without being high, you might have a more serious problem and you need to talk to somebody who can help you more than I can. It's not something to be ashamed of. Talk to your parents if you can. Find a friend who's dealt with this. Or call Alcoholics Anonymous or another 12-step program for other addictions. After all, you could always be really radical and good to your body and do what most of my friends and I ended up doing—no drugs at all.*

ANDY LEWIS,
DANE BRANDON,
and
ALEX NEWMAN
(What's Left of Chicken Hawk)

The Hole in the Middle—Called Mack

*A*ndy and Dane met in third grade and played radio-control race cars together. Then Andy moved to England with his architect/computer-whiz dad. Dane went to Germany for a year with his dad, who's a private-school teacher. But then they both came back to Seattle and ended up at Garfield High, where they started running into each other in the hall.

By then, Andy was friends with Mack because they both played in the high school jazz band that was winning all the prizes around Seattle. Andy was also playing the trombone in the marching band, which is where he met Alex, the drummer, who only became a musician in the first place because when he was a freshman he heard that you had to run five miles every morning in the freezing cold for gym class—unless you took band. He figured, how hard could it be to play the drums. He'd fallen asleep all his life to Jimi Hendrix, Steve Miller, etc. He figured music was in his blood.

So when the talent show thing came up, Mack wanted to sing and Andy wanted to play lead guitar and Dane wanted to play rhythm guitar: they'd be like a band. Alex was two years younger than they were, but they figured he'd do for drums. And there was this tall blond guy from Sweden named Humpus who was an exchange student and he could play bass guitar. So he did.

They became Chicken Hawk.

The talent show surprised them. The curtain was still down, the music just a short bass prelude to a song they'd written called "The Groove." But the other kids started getting up and dancing. The guys in the band *never* thought Garfield would go for rock and roll. Garfield is an urban school with about 3,500 students. Rap reigns at Garfield; rock is considered suburban music. But there were the Latinos, the black dudes, even the guys with "G-attitude" (gang leanings), up grooving to Chicken Hawk.

"We're like, *'Cool,'* " Andy recalls. "The energy there was just so much. We'd been practicing, and we'd gotten to the point where, God, I hope we can do this. We're gonna have to concentrate out there. But concentration just disappeared, and we just played."

After that, they gigged at parties and saved money from their grocery-store janitorial jobs to cut a demo. But then Humpus went back to Sweden. And eventually they had a falling out with Mack who had this thing with "crybaby manic depression," which they say was really just "the sorriest, the lamest plea" to get some attention away from his big brother who was touring with a jazz ensemble.

"I mean Mack had the only musical aspect that didn't just click with everybody else," Andy says. "Me and Dane spent hours laboring and Alex helped us out to come up with this nice mellow song. It's a good, happy-sounding song, and the lyrics Mack puts with it are: *Laying here in bed but never do I sleep. Dreams of life and death and world depression sets in deep. Nightmares plague my mind so never shall I reach the point of ecstasy that my body deeply needs.*

Alex starts singing: *"The blood drips from my veins."*

Andy joins in: *"Runs out my wrists. Afraid of life but you know what I like, I'm scared to death. The blood runs out my wrist."*

"It was really hard on us," Andy says, "because we're all taking lessons and we're all spending a lot of our hard-earned money on gear so that we can sound better and so that we can play better and he's spending his money."

The Ego

"The thing to remember," says Andy, "is that I'm always right." Andy Lewis is eighteen. He has blue eyes and blondish curls that stand up longer on top, shorter on the sides. He's great-looking.

Alex laughs giddily at Andy. "At least he knows it," he says. Alex Newman is only sixteen and a little pudgier and more serious-minded. He shows off his new "very professional" drum bag, filled with CDs—Cypress Hill, Red Hot Chili Peppers, James Brown—and a bunch of new drumsticks.

Andy admits that Mack left Chicken Hawk partly because Andy is always right. "We kinda hit heads pretty hard," Andy says. "He's very lax but he's very . . . he thinks of himself as being very right about being lax."

"They're both egomaniacs," Alex puts in.

"Yeah, yeah anyway." Andy cuts him off. "I know it, and I try to use it in a positive way. I try to make the band make good decisions. Just there are a few things I can't stand, like being wrong actually. I hate that."

Alex snickers: "He'll climb himself out of any hole, man."

"I'm always right," says Andy, not joking.

"And he *knows* he's always right," Alex says.

"I know I'm always right," Andy says.

"Even if he's wrong, he knows he's always right."

"But the thing is I'm almost always right."

Alex sputters into laughter. It takes Andy a sec to laugh, but he does finally. They laugh until they snort into their caffeine.

Caffeine

Dane Brandon, who's nineteen, slouches through the door of Surreal Espresso. He's lanky and has a lazy-looking blond ponytail that he grew after he gave up on dreadlocks. There's a tattoo of a wild boar on his shoulder. He sits down with Alex and Andy. Time for caffeine injection. Not the $3 latte kind. The 50-cent black kind. Coffee. Or Mountain Dew. Both are good when you're spending $400 of your parents' money and twenty-two hours a day to record your first demo tape. Both keep you awake so you can riff on all those mixing knobs until you can crawl to Denny's at six on Easter morning and order French dips while families come in for omelettes. Caffeine is "heinous."

"Bring me another Americano," Andy says as Dane heads for the coffee bar near a psychedelic reefer poster. Stuck on top of the ficus by the window is a globe of the world, and Van Morrison's singing, "Yoooouuu, my brown-eyed girl."

Suck and Blow

"We've been up since yesterday morning," Andy yawns, then tries to physically shake off his morning-after-ness. "We went to this party thing last night—it was like an all-night thing." It was a no-alcohol, no-drugs party for the all-city high school band. "I lost my key last night, my car key. "It was just like this long night from hell. There were bodies everywhere. It was pretty cool last night so everybody was huddling up, trying to stay warm so you could easily trip over people. My key was lost in a field over to the side, where we were playing this game called suck and blow."

Alex begins to giggle. "Suck and blow," he says, drawing it out fondly.

Andy describes the technique: "What you do is you take like a playing card and you suck it up to yourself and then you take it to somebody and blow it to them and they suck it and if you drop it, you have to kiss the person. Since I was a freshman, we've been playing this game and I've gotten good enough to the point where I can do cartwheels and stuff while I'm holding the card up to my face and you get points for style. So I was doing cartwheels and flips and somewhere in all that my key fell out of my pocket."

"It's just basically like spin the bottle," Alex says.

Andy adds: "But this takes a lot more skill. See some people drop them on purpose but some people with real style just take the card and set it down. The definitive one depends on how well you know the person and how many style points you want. There are a lot of young people there this year, like a lot of new people in the band this year and watching them play was hilarious."

"They just don't have the suction," Alex says.

Andy agrees: "They just don't have the suction."

From the Inside Out

Dane not only stayed up late; he had to go to work early—busing tables at Finnegan's restaurant. "I got four hours of sleep last night," he says. "Actually watched television, thought about my new underwear."

They all laugh, and Andy says, "He went on a big underwear-and-sock-buying spree."

"Yeah," Dane says, "I got a whole bunch of new cool boxers and stuff like that." He flexes a bicep theatrically and grins. "I'm working from the inside out on my life."

Tonight he's doing the big thing. He's finally moving out of his parents' house and into an apartment with a friend.

"Are you like expecting help with this?" Andy asks, meaning will he have to carry a stereo or anything.

"Not really," Dane says. "I'm just gonna move like my bed and my radio."

"Are you gonna be staying at the new place tonight?"

Dane nods.

Andy: "You know what that means, don't you?"

"More beer," Dane says.

Beer

To be poetic about it, beer is more than a cold can of Schmidt; it's an attitude instilled in them by their old Swedish bass-player, Humpus.

It started at one of their first party gigs: "We all had just got done playing our set. And we're all sitting around drinking and first Humpus grabbed me and he's like, '*Alex, you need more beer.*' And he took every single one of us back into the keg room and he gave us the same speech."

"*YOU NEED MORE BEER!!!*" they say in unison.

"He made us take tap heads," Alex says.

Andy explains, "He was like, '*Lay down.*' And he put the tap in our mouth and goes *glubglubglub.*" As Andy makes drowning sounds, Dane goes: "And then Andy just got totally blitzed, and he face-plants in the corner of this bedroom—like his face was actually all *smashed up* in the corner of the room. And then the people said, '*Hey guys, these guys out here we're tired of listening to them. We want you to come out and play again.*'

"We're like, '*We played it all.*' And they said, '*That's okay. We liked it. Play everything, just play all your stuff again.*' And I said, '*Oh, man.*' Because we're all just totally blitzed."

"We're all just blotto," Andy confirms.

Dane says: "I just go back, and I grab Andy, '*Dude, you gotta get up. We're s'posed to play again,*' and Andy's like *aaarrghhhh.*"

Says Andy, "I got up, and I went out to play. I sit down, and I forget why I sat down, and I was just like watching the room go by."

Dane smirks. "And it was just a rippin good time. We've mellowed out a little bit."

"A little bit?" Andy says, like *who are you kidding?* "We're just busy doing so much else that we find it hard to go out and drink. We try to make time in order to just go out and drink, *lots.*"

"We *always* make time," Dane says.

Alex says: "It's kinda sad that the youth of America . . ."

His buddies start laughing 'cause they've heard this heavy opinion stuff from him before.

"It is," he continues earnestly, "I mean 'cause . . . because there are so many kids that are alcoholics and drug addicts and everything. It's because major cities, any city, doesn't give anything for kids to do."

"Exactly," Andy concedes.

"What can a kid do on a Friday night that's fun?" Alex asks. "Go to a party. Get drunk. Go out with your friends. Get high. Get drunk. All the clubs are twenty-one and older."

"There's like two or three like really lame dance clubs that play techno music that are underage but those places, underage clubs are just swarmed with drugs," Dane says.

"The only time people go to the clubs is to usually buy drugs," Alex says. "And I mean like—shut up, Andy—I mean the Okay Hotel, which used to be a very big underage club where a lot of really good bands would go and play but the city like upped their insurance rates because some kid got injured in a mosh pit."

How Chicken Hawk Got Its Name

Andy gets a vanilla milkshake. Alex and Dane move to another table to smoke, because it bothers Andy. They keep their conversation going the whole time, just sort of yelling back and forth. "We were comin' up with all of these stupid things. Psychedelic Brainwaves. Anything." Dane goes on, recalling the study hall when they named the band: "We'd go, *That's kinda cool.* Then, *No it's not.* That kind of thing. So we get totally desperate, and I ran over to an English class and I grabbed a dictionary and I'm flippin' through it and I saw like a Falconhawk or something and then I thought, *Wait a minute,* what about that little cartoon character, the Chicken Hawk, from the Foghorn Leghorn cartoon? He's rad. He's that little dude and he always goes up and says, 'I'm a chicken hawk and You're a chicken, I'm gonna eat you.' "

"So I just said, Dude, we'll be Chicken Hawk. You know we can eat the audience." Dane roughens his voice into his stage scream: "We're Chickenhawk," he yells. "We're gonna eat you."

They all laugh. "We thought that was the raddest shit. So that was our name."

"And then later we discovered there are *other* meanings for it," Andy says, raising one eyebrow.

Dane groans and says: "How'd that start? Somebody comes up and says what's the name of your band, and we said Chicken Hawk and they said, So it's a gay thing? And we're like *what?*"

Andy continues: "And apparently, we looked into it, and it's also a term to describe like old guys that chase after little boys."

"See it's a chicken hawk like after the little chicken. And we're just like, *It's really sick,*" Dane says. "So we went through this big phase where we're like, We can't do this. That's *bad.*"

"And one night we were in Dane's bedroom for like a couple of hours and we just got so heinously drunk and like we just did shots of vodka for like . . ." Alex says.

"That's when he was in his vodka days," Andy says, nodding at Dane, who laughs: "Vodka days, yeah!"

Alex continues, "And we just came up with the dumbest names like all night, like . . ."

"Any stupid name you could think of," Dane says.

"But it just got to the point where our name was our name. It's who we were. We were the little guy who eats chickens. We don't pick up on little guys. We eat chickens. Big chicken hawks," Andy says. He flexes his biceps humorously and grins.

Dane says: "The people who are gonna listen to our music will more immediately identify with the cartoon character and know that's what it is and not that. . . . I mean do we look like a bunch of stinking perverts?"

"Come here little boy," Andy says fake-hoarsely.

"Fuck this," Dane says. "We're Chicken Hawk."

Censorship?

As the coffee kicks in, Alex sits up straighter and starts striking the table with the palm of his hand everytime he makes a point about what gets on his nerves, like that certain forces out there would like to tell kids what they can and can't listen to. He says, "My policy is if you're old enough to pick it up off the shelf, then you're old enough to listen to it and make your own judgment."

Andy groans.

"That's the way I feel," Alex says, "because if you know what you're picking off the shelf . . ."

"There's some pretty trashy shit out there," Dane reminds him. "I could understand why they wouldn't want kids to listen to it and stuff."

"Yeah but you're a pretty fucked-up individual if you're gonna listen to a song and just, say, do the whole cop killer thing," Alex says defiantly.

Dane nods. "If you're so unstable that you're gonna listen to that and go out and kill cops, then you're gonna commit it anyway. You're gonna flip anyway."

But Andy continues: "It makes sense to a point. I can see like PG13 or something for kids who don't really understand what they're buying: *'Oh my big brother has this tape. I wanna go buy this tape. I'm gonna get this.'* And you've got your allowance saved up and you go buy this tape. You don't really know what you're buying and you become exposed to something that may or may not be good music."

Alex tries to say something, but Andy keeps going: "I mean, I don't have the right to say what is good music or not, but there is some really trashy stuff that you can get your hands on and if you don't understand, if you're not able to comprehend that it is that trashy. . . . It's trash because . . . stuff like N.W.A you know, it's fun to rap to. I've got some of their tapes, and it's fun to listen to, but I don't relate with what they do and I never could. I could never relate to that lifestyle and I understand that and I know that but I mean I could see at some point being young enough to listen to this and start relating to it. I mean at some point, at some age."

Alex says, "I agree with what you're saying."

Andy adds: "But I mean the question is: Whose right is it to choose?"

"I don't think it should be up to the government to say what kids should be listening to and what they shouldn't," Alex says. "It should be the parents."

"Yeah," Andy says firmly. "It should be the parents."

Parents

"It's just like I'm in a good situation," Alex says. "My dad likes a lot of the music that I listen to. It is hilarious actually but . . . My dad was at this cafe and this lady, his waitress, had a Cypress Hill [band] hat on and he's like, *'Oh, Cypress Hill. You like 'em?'* And she goes, *'Yeah.'* He goes, *'I guess that's good, if you like that foul-mouth marijuana-loving shit.'* " Alex laughs and adds, "My dad's the typical ex-hippie."

"Yeahyeahyeahyeah," Andy sing-songs.

"But I mean he's not a flake though," Alex adds quickly. "He's a really good parent."

"He's a good guy," Andy affirms. "He's not like the renegade bearded hippies who still wear tiedye. He's survived the generation. He learned his lessons."

Alex says, "He's a tough country boy turned hippie turned father."

Andy says: "My dad had just gotten out of the navy when Vietnam got going. So he was off pursuing a graduate degree in architecture and he didn't get caught up in any of that stuff. He was passive. He's a little more reserved when it comes to being a father."

Alex does a little more bragging. "My dad was in architectural school at the U. Like him and his friends led all these peace rallies."

"Really?" Andy asks, impressed.

"Yeah," Alex says. "They led a rally cause when we were gonna invade Cambodia or something like that, they led this big march. And my dad and his friend like made all these shirts, like thin denim shirts with this hand touching a peace symbol. And I have the original. My dad took off his shirt and tried it once to see if it worked and I have the original shirt. It's not worth a damn thing. But I wear it with pride."

"Yeehaw," Andy jokes, adding: "My dad is fiftysomething."

Alex says. "My dad is fortysomething. Forty-two to forty-seven. I lose track. He's old."

"They're getting there," Andy says. "They're gettin' up there."

Dane says, "My folks are a little older too. They're both over fifty. Anyways they're up there and they were kind of around the hippie generation, but they just kinda missed the whole thing. They were totally straight. My dad went to school. He studied to be a minister for like four years, to be a Presbyterian minister at Winston seminary and that's how he avoided going to Vietnam. I don't think he did it with that in mind."

"My dad took the Dan Quayle route," Alex says. "National Guard."

Dane continues: "My mom dropped out of college her freshman year and got married to this guy who she divorced like two years later."

"Really?" Andy says, amazed.

Dane nods and says, "So my mom is basically just a housewife. She married my dad somewhere along the line. But my parents are pretty mellow. They're real trusting and stuff. I like my parents pretty well. I don't really have any problems with them at all. They're pretty supportive whatever I do. But they're pretty oblivious to teenage life and stuff." Like the drinking, the pot-smoking.

"My parents, since they don't really know, they've just been fed the government/media stuff about [drugs], and they just totally think it's all bad and stuff," Dane says, illustrating: "Like a couple of years ago they're like, *'It's okay to experiment and stuff, but it's really bad stuff if you get into it.'* And they're like the other thing is, *'We can always tell, you know. You can't get away with this stuff.'* And I'm just like thinking to myself, *I've been drinking and smoking for like three years now and this is the first time I've ever been caught, you know. So you guys just don't have a clue."*

Andy nods. "My parents are really against it, but they've come to the conclusion that there's really not too much that they can do about it. Because we're gonna go out and play music and then go drink Schmidt. They've grounded me so many times." He remembers a good example: "They left town for a week, and over that course of the week, my girlfriend came over, and I was out partying and stuff, and I just took off from school and went skiing, and all this kind of stuff. And I was supposed to be grounded while they were gone—for grades—but then they came back."

Dane snorts. "What a ridiculous idea—grounded while your parents are out of town."

"I know," Andy says, "they shoulda figured that out. It was a big fiasco. I was grounded for like five months. It cut me down a little bit, but there were all these excuses to go out: *I'm going to the library, I've got a paper due.* But you'd go out and see your friends. Then my neighbors were out of town one time and they had this hot tub you know. I didn't think they'd mind if I went and used it. So this girl and I went and used their hot tub, and I got grounded for three months for that. And then I passed out in front of my mom and my sister one time. I got grounded."

"Because you were so wasted?" Dane says.

"Yeah, 'cause I was just plowed. Alex was over as a matter of fact, dude." Andy elbows Alex: "The time with my mom and my sister and my oooopppp . . ." He makes a sound like a falling tree. They all laugh. "That was hilarious. Anyway, I got grounded for a weekend for that. And then I disappeared for a couple of days once, and I only got a warning so like the punishment has . . . They've come to the conclusion that I'm gonna go out and do crazy things, and I've survived so far, you know, and there's not really much they can do to stop me."

Bootleggin'

"Bootleggin' is one way [we get beer]," Dane says. "We don't have to do that so much anymore—where you just go out to a grocery store. You just sit out in front waiting for some . . ."

"Cool looking person," Andy puts in.

"To come by and you say, *'Hey, man, you wanna do us a favor?'* And he says, *'Sure man,'* and you say, *'You wanna buy us some beer?'* and he says, *'Okay.'* And so he buys us beer, and we like buy him an import or something like that."

Drinking and Driving

"Another way to get beer is just to go to find a kegger somewhere," Andy says.

"Which always get busted most of the time," Dane adds.

"Yeah," Andy says. "But if you're lucky you can drink a whole bunch of really cheap beer, really fast."

Dane laughs. "Pound it down and get the hell out of there. Go drive around."

They look at each other because it's admitting to drinking and driving. Then Andy says, "I don't." He points to Alex. "He doesn't." They both look at Dane, who says: "Well, I'm firmly . . . I strongly believe against it, but there are some instances where you just can't help it. And we've done it enough so that . . ." The other guys grunt.

"Yes, *we* do," Dane reminds them. "But we try not to. But we're good at it, and we know the limit. There are times when you just like *know.*"

Andy agrees, "Yeah, like screw this, and you just fall asleep in the car. We try to avoid [driving drunk]. If we can get somebody else to drive who we know is not going to drink."

Dane elaborates. "But it's never where we'll say, 'I'm not gonna drink cause I'm driving.' It's just never that. It's 'I'll drink and then I'll have two hours to sober up. Two hours and a whole bunch of coffee.' Which doesn't work. Keeps you awake behind the wheel. We're pretty . . . we've driven for like three years."

"Driving's kinda habitual anyway," Andy says. "We don't really pay attention to it."

"We're as responsible as we can be about it, I guess," Dane says. "Well, not really."

"Well, not really," Alex echoes.

"Usually we try to keep the distances down," Andy offers.

Alex says, "If we know that we're gonna have to end up driving home drunk we make sure it's like less than like three miles."

"But it doesn't always work out that way," Dane admits.

"There's been a couple of times where I've had to drive all the way home from Dane's," says Andy.

"There's been hundreds of times," Dane corrects him.

"No," Andy says, "Not from your house, man."

"Well, there've been a lot of times where we've been drinking then you have to take me home and then drive back to your place. Think about it," Dane tells him.

"Yeah," Andy says. "There have been. That's craziness. Wow."

"We're not proud of it," Dane says.

Rehearsing

They are proud of their music. And it's way past time to make some.

"Are we gonna go play?" Dane blurts out impatiently. "Or are we just gonna sit here all day?" So they drain their coffee and squeeze into the cab of Andy's minitruck for the ten-minute drive to Dane's house, where they practice in a basement room heaped with mattresses and board games like Monopoly and a six-foot cutout of a beer bottle.

They show off a Quadroverve amplifier. Andy introduces his guitar, Kylene, a Fender Stratocaster. Dane introduces his guitar, Millie, "custom everything—look at this saddle, vintage fender bass knobs, these are chrome, compared to Andy's."

"But do you have a chrome switch?" Andy counters. "I don't think you've got a chrome switch, so you are slackin', boy."

Dane goes on anyway, pointing to the pegs high on the neck: "Finest tuning pegs money can buy, very custom, very cool."

Alex, who is sitting behind his drum set, adopts a Don Pardo voice: "And notice the strap locks both Andy and Dane are sporting today."

"Shaylor strap locks," Andy emphasizes.

"Shaylor German-made strap locks so that when we swing our guitars around our necks they don't fly off," Dane elaborates.

"Not that we endorse any of this shit," Andy says.

Bootie or No?

For the next hour, Chicken Hawk pounds out a frenetic kind of music that sort of twists together blues, heavy metal, jazz, funk, and classical. The guys are trying to stay keyed into each other as they search for a female lead who can sing down into the alto, even the tenor range, which they think would sound cool.

Andy and Dane are heavy into theory. One of them will say something like, "I'm going from a minor third up to a major third." And the other one will go, "You have to play the sharp nine in there so you have a major third and a minor third sounding at the same time to get that dissonance and stuff."

But then Alex will say, "Fuck dissonance, just play the damn song." He is big into how the music feels. He's always vetoing certain "theoretically beautiful" passages because they don't "move" him. "It's bootie," he'll say, which is some made-up phrase that means really bad. On the other hand, if it works for him emotionally, he'll immediately give the okay: "That's rippin', dudes."

When they take a break, Alex says: "A friend of mine, he's a trombone player, he's a great trombone player. He's like theory has its place, theory has its dominant place in music but you can limit yourself. The one important thing about theory is, you can learn theory till you die but it's gotta have that soul. If it ain't got that thing."

"But there's a flip side," Andy says. "You've gotta learn the rules to break them."

"Exactly, exactly," Alex admits. "But you cannot let that hold you down."

"And we don't," Andy concludes. "We do some crazy nondiatonic stuff."

Dane wants to get back to playing. He says, "From the last bar whatever to the bridge."

Alex counts: "One-two-three, you-know-what-to-do."

They play together. Dane growls appreciatively: "Heinous, man. I really dig when I'm playing my little dominant thing, one of those mass thick heavy descending chords, dude."

Mortal Kombat

"Dude, my ears are just going . . . grrrrrr . . . ," Dane snarls sort of like an angry animal.

Andy says, "Let's take a break, go up to 7-Eleven."

They walk up the block to the convenience store. They say they used to be "really religious about pinball." They still go out every rehearsal. Dane got sixty-four million on his first Terminator 2 ball ever.

As they come into the store, Andy says urgently, "Is it turned off?"

Dane groans, "Dude, it's *not* broken? NOOOOOO!"

They both shake the machine.

"Dead, dude," Andy says, after asking the clerk.

Dane shakes his head. "That's tragic."

They're not in the mood for Mortal Kombat, a video game where you could die a "brutal graphic way." Dane says, "He reaches in and he grabs your head and rips it up and there's a head with a spinal cord dangling."

They walk back to rehearse some more because they feel like they have a lot of work to do still. They have one demo tape, which they sell to friends for $5 but which they say is basically a moot point because it was recorded with Mack before he left. They can't gig until they find another singer. But they still get together on Wednesdays and Sundays to practice. "It's like we're a family almost," Dane says. "I always describe playing in a band like the relationship of it is like being married probably must be 'cause I mean it's such a . . . we spend so much time together it's just ridiculous. Basically, my life consists of I play with this band, I go to school, and I work my ass off, and that's all I do. And it's such an intimate relationship. We spend all this time together and we get in all kinds of fights and butt heads about what we're gonna play and we're all . . . it makes us all feel I guess you could say *secure*. It's sort of like our security blanket. We're all part of this thing. We always will have this and each other."

"Homies"

Back to what I was saying earlier about teenagers not readily talking about their parents. Well, try to get them to stop talking about their friends. When a teenager starts a sentence with "Scotto told me that . . .", or "Well, I don't know, but Maria thinks . . ." it's more than just an alternative to like, that teenage term I overuse myself as an excuse for not taking full responsibility for whatever it is I'm about to say. As one girl explained it to me, "I read somewhere about a girl saying she didn't know which parts of herself were experiences she'd really had and which were things she'd read in books. But that's like me and my friends. I don't know which of my opinions are really theirs and which are mine. It's wild, but great too."

I have a bunch of photo albums I never bother to update; they just pile up the way I originally put them together, whenever that was. While I was packing them up to move recently, I procrastinated by looking through them and noticed that sometime around my thirteenth birthday, my family just sort of disappears. That was about the time I made a point of walking separately from my parents at amusement parks. Up until the photographs taken at my college graduation, it's just me and my friends—all crammed into a photo booth at Myrtle Beach, artsy shots with too much eyeliner from the year we thought we were real photographers, yearbook pictures of not only my boyfriends but of the guy my best friend had a crush on.

Teenagers have always been maligned. From that ancient Greek quote about teenagers signaling the end of civilization to the "juvenile delinquency" era of the '50s. Today talk-radio callers vilify teenagers using statistics about everything from crime to unsafe sex, and more and more towns impose eight or nine o'clock curfews for anyone under eighteen or they ban all teenagers from malls. Or pipe in classical music and alter their lighting to really highlight acne, so kids won't even want to hang out there.

So kids turn to each other. Not just because they want somebody else's opinion when they pick out a sweatshirt, but because they need support on big issues—whether to move in with their boyfriend, what they should study in college, or whether to go to California with dad and stepmom. In a world where they're blamed for a lot of the problems, they can support each other. They also feel stronger about who they are by being in sync with their friends on everything from which beer to drink to which presidential candidate to vote for. Together, they come up with their own morals and values.

Yes, I said morals and values. I think a lot of ex-teenagers are surprised to hear kids have moral codes. But as more families split up, even alliances that are decried in the media, like gangs, often are founded on the characteristics families were supposed to be about when TV had Father Knows Best: love, affirmation, predictability, security. For a lot of these kids, their homeboys and homegirls are the only home they feel they have. A kid from an Oakland gang told me, "What's the big deal about gangs? Kids always had gangs," he claimed. "What did people think the Little Rascals were?" Friendships also provide discipline for kids who don't get much of that. One fifteen-year-old who was trying to quit smoking pot, something her parents don't know she ever did, told me, "My friends are like my family. They support me. They even punish me when I go off and don't follow my own rules."

Max, who's eighteen, became a member of the Akron, Ohio, gang called the Folks when he was sixteen.

Basically, I joined for the power, the respect, the money you get from selling drugs, the girls. 'Cause you have a choice of being a victim of one or a part of one. But you learn when you're in a gang that it's really about the friends. The friends you get in your gang are number one because they'll always be loyal. What I'm saying is, you know they'll be loyal 'cause they'll get beat up or killed if they're not. So you've got your code in your gang and you can depend on the code.

Max left the gang recently when his family moved to Florida, partly to get Max away from the gang.

I wasn't sorry to leave. I mean, there are bad things, bad drugs, cops fucking with you, other gangs, worrying about being shot at. I've been shot at a lot of times. Me and my little brother and my girl got our car attacked by [a rival gang] one night. They threw bricks at the car, pulled us out, beat us with baseball bats so bad my girl needed brain surgery, broke my hand. I don't miss all that. I miss the friends, though. Loyal friends are hard to find. They're everything. They're true. More than your family.

Partly because gang culture and drug culture are so intertwined, another kid, Mike, feels like they are going out of style. "They're all just turning into droopy drug dealers," he says. "And I know a lot of kids who used to think you got respect from being in gangs are realizing that you get more respect by standing out on your own." Trevor, who's fourteen, agrees with him. "Gangs are just for people who can't take care of themselves," he says.

And you just always wind up in jail. But friends are the most important thing. You are what your friends are. Like when I used to play on the soccer team, I became just like all those guys, just like a dumb jock rating girls' bodies and stuff. And then when I got to my new school and got smart friends I got more into studying and I care about where I'm going to college even though it's a few years away. Who you spend time around definitely rubs off on you.

And since the majority of teenagers say they haven't had more than a ten-minute conversation with at least one of their parents in the last month, that means their friends.

June 14, 1977

I woke up this morning and the song on the radio made me sentimental for my best friend and I didn't know who it was. Was it the kid I played with on the merry-go-round or the one I talked to last night before falling asleep? Or both and all in between? Having good understanding friends makes all the difference in the world. On days like this when everything's bad, or on days like yesterday when I was so happy I felt like crying all the time, or on nothing days you make into something somehow (how Mary Tyler Moore). You'd die for them. You'd live for them.

GABRIEL'S CORNER

Gabriel is crouching on a curb in Oakland. It's sunset, and everything is peaceful: Houses that are turquoise and aquamarine and rose-colored seem to cling to the steep hills, and cypress trees rise like spires against the summer sky. It's the time of day when the colors are their most vivid but your eyes don't distinguish dimensions well—everything gets kind of flattened. Gabriel seems wary. He doesn't settle. The small muscles in his face and along one arm twitch, making him look tensed to spring and leave. His eyes keep touching base over where his Mexican-American homeboys are hanging out on the corner. They drink beer out of brown bottles and glance over at Gabriel protectively. "If not for the hard time, life wouldn't have no good time. And right here, I get a little bit of both," he says slowly. He tracks the customized cars as they pass, the boys on their fluorescent bikes, a mother pushing a stroller with a toddler sucking hard candy that runs down his chin in purple streaks. "There's no other place I'd rather have that done than here. Everybody knows me. I got love. I got *love*, you know what I'm saying? The homeboys *love* me.

"I could probably hang out on the corner and fuckin' you'd be trippin' out because I bet I'd probably know nine out of every ten cars that go by. I bet you I wave to them and they wave back, 'cause they know me. Everybody knows me. That's just the kinda community we have. Everybody knows one another. You gots to. You gonna be a neighborhood, you gots to know who lives in it, who's in it, what they're about. Because you don't wanna shoot nobody on accident."

* * *

Gabriel stands and runs his clean fingernails along the pleat down his way-way-oversized pants that looks like it could cut you. His T-shirt is white, blinding white. He has tawny skin soft as a child's and a whispery voice that sort of rubs all the hard edges off of words. He doesn't smile, and he has a ragged scar down one cheek, and his right arm is withered against his side from a gunshot wound. He has been shot more than once and stabbed. "I got stabbed and shit," he says, dismissing it with a flick of his hand. "You just gotta clean it up and go on. This is my way of dealing with it, just like you people have your way of dealing with it. Something has traumatized your life, something has happened major in your life, you can't sit around and cry about it and pout about it. You just gotta pick up the pieces and go on. You can't let nobody get you down. It's just a way of life, just the way it is."

His mother is a cook in a hospital raising two sons alone because her husband left when the kids were little. She doesn't want Gabriel in the gang. Gabriel really does understand what concerns her. But it's his life. "In the beginning, it was hard," Gabriel recalls. "My mom said, 'I don't want big pants in my house, that's *cholo*, low life. I don't want that in my house, blah, blah, blah.' To be true to the gang, then well, you've gotta deal with it whether or not you've gotta get kicked out of your house. If your family loves you, they're gonna take you back. It's just a matter of them willing to accept it."

"If that's what you wanna be and that's what you wanna do, well then there's nobody that can tell you that you can't. If you want it, that's what we're gonna do." He shrugs. "It's not because somebody else is pushing you behind your back, pushing: *get in, get in, get in.* You don't have to. Nobody's gonna pressure you into getting into a gang—if they do, well, that isn't the gang for you. That's what makes up the love here. You know what? How you gonna get love from a person if they're fuckin' pushin' you, if they're constantly on your ass—*get in, get in, get in.*" He pushes the growing summer dusk with his good arm.

To get into the gang, you have to be jumped in: the "gangsters" beat up the new guy. When he was thirteen, Gabriel decided he wanted "into the neighborhood" because he thought it would just make his life easier. "I hung around with them. I dressed like them. I was down for it, and if I could get beat for it, then why not get in it. Even though I wasn't from it, people would say, 'Oh, you live in that neighborhood.' So I got a lot of static, you know. And I said, 'Fuck all this. If I'm gonna get jumped for something, this better be for real.' So I just got into the neighborhood, and said, fuck it."

Since the night two years ago when his homeboys pounded him until he bled, Gabriel says he has known who he is: he is one of the neighborhood. As he looks up and down the streets and into the alleyways, he seems hyperaware of everything that is happening. It is not just a backdrop for what happens to him; it *is* what happens to him. He watches who goes into the doughnut shop, who comes out and when. He counts heads in every car. It's part of what he calls "our program," trying to keep the streets respectable and respectful of who his homeboys are: "I'm not saying that we're gonna look for trouble," he says. "We don't look for it, we deal with it. If somebody disrespects us then we have to deal with that problem. But we don't go lookin' for it and say, 'we're bad.' We're No. 1, of course. But we don't go and emphasize that and push it on people and make problems for ourselves."

He looks up and down the street as if for a quick example of what he means. When he finds nothing, he explains: "Disrespect comes in all different shapes and forms. One way: You could be walking down the street with your mother and another guy could fuckin' come up to you and hit you up and ask you where you're from. And that's in front of your mom, and you have to deal with that. Maybe not then and there because of the respect that you have for your mother. But it's like 'I've got you on the rebound. I see your face. I know who you are, and I'm gonna getcha.'

"Another way: When you have a baby. I have a six-month, beautiful little girl." He stops his story and reaches into his pocket. Then he smiles for the first time as he pulls out a picture of a baby with a frilly band around her dark hair, a ribbon on the crown of her head. He holds the picture as he continues: "You may be pushin' the baby around and people mad dog you [give you a dirty look]. That ain't right when it's not necessary, just because you're a gangster. I'm pushing the baby so I let it go, let it ride. There'll be another day.

"And there's some people that show me disrespect by taking something of mine or breaking into somebody else's house that I know and trying to take their shit. Well that's their problem too, but if they ask me, 'I need some help, so-and-so did this,' I'm there for them. Because you know there's gonna be a day when I might need their help. It's all about you scratch my back, I'll scratch yours.

"You got to give love here. Everybody wants love and that's what it is you know. Homeboys get you in and out of their pads and shit—if your moms can't deal with the way you live. That's where the love comes in—because you can go to your homeboys' house and you know they're gonna hook you up with a nice fresh bar of soap, some running water, and they'll kick you down some clothes. It's goin' on, man. Snag a toothbrush from the store. It's all. It's all, you know." He giggles.

*　*　*

He says he knows that some people might be shocked to hear him talking about love. That makes him so mad. "If they get surprised, then that goes to show what kind of person they are," he says, striking his knee sharply. As if by radar, his homeboys sense his agitation and all stop moving and just stand and look at Gabriel. They don't come over; they just watch steadily. "That ain't all it. A lot of people got this bad image of a gang. I'll help an old lady across the street in a minute. But it's just like when I try to, they look at me and because of my appearance, they don't know whether I'm gonna rob 'em or help 'em. But I say, 'Hey, lady, relax. I'm here to help you. I'll help you get your cart across. I'll help.' I'll help her out.

"We all do it. That's just the kind of people we are. We don't try to be something that we're not. We're out there with a lot of respect and a lot of love."

Suddenly, Gabriel stands up and walks out into the street. He squeezes his eyes into slits and scrutinizes a car cruising around the corner. He watches it until it disappears. Then he sits back down, a ferocity in his eyes. He won't say what's up.

His homeboys have started shifting around on the corner, restless. Gabriel stays, but he's watching them as though he'd really rather get back to them now. "I've just gotta survive, man," he says, "whatever comes up. There's not much really that I can do. I just keep dealing with the hard times day after day. What isn't the hard times? Just because you look a certain way, you can't walk up the street in peace, especially if you're in somebody else's neighborhood. If you're in your own, it's okay, but you still have to deal with the hard time. You've gotta deal with the police who wanna pull you over and harass you, fuck with you. You gotta deal with the people fuckin' comin' up to you in your neighborhood, laughin' at you. You gotta deal with one big merry-go-round, you know what I'm sayin'? One big merry-go-round."

Gabriel looks at the picture of his baby he's still holding. Gabriel feels responsibility. He loves her, he says often. He knows what he needs is a job. But jobs are hard to find. He has looked, he says. No one's hiring. At least no one is hiring him. He doesn't have many choices, and his voice is bitter when he speaks of them. It's filled with bitter consequences: "People are gonna do what they have to do. Not because they want to and not because it's fun. Because it's a part of reality, and it's a part of life. They have to do what they have to do. If they have babies, the way they make their money is the way they make their money. Because nobody is gonna come and give you fuckin' money and opportunity. Nobody's gonna come knockin' at your door and say, 'Here, here's the money for your Pampers.' Nobody really expects anybody else to do that. But the homeboys might, you know. We do it amongst ourselves because you know that's just the way we are. We give each other love. If we know somebody's out and down in the dumps, we help 'em out. Not because we have to. Because we want to. That's love." But his voice doesn't hold much love in it just now.

"I'll tell you right now, if there were more people out there willing to give out jobs and shit, more people willing to set up programs like youth clubs and YMCAs here in the neighborhood, there would be less people out there gang banging—because the homeboys always get together and play ball. We're not lazy and shit. We're not dirty dudes. We're clean-cut. We're all healthy. We're all in good spirits, *up,* you know. And we're healthy. We need more places like that, gyms, you know, for homeboys to go and box. Because that's one way of taking out anger. Instead of going up and beating up a dude on the street we can go to a punching bag and go to a gym."

Gabriel calls over one of his homeboys standing nearby, drinking beer. His friend is a big guy with a deep voice who works with computers in a government-sponsored program that pays $5 an hour. Gabriel listens to his friend describe it. "I went in to try and to apply for those jobs," Gabriel interrupts, his voice speeding with urgency. "My mom is a cook, and she makes good money. But that's *her* money. What do I do for myself? She's got bills, you know. It's like, if you're under eighteen and you go in there to apply for a job, because you're under the care of your parents, it's like, 'Oh, your parents make good enough money. You don't need a job.' And that sucks. My mom's got bills and shit. She's my mom, and that's her job and everything. But she's got a house to hold up.

"But they look at you and they see the way you are. They see you're a gangster, and they see how much your mom makes and it's like, *Next.* We want somebody who's down in the dumps. Which is cool and everything. But, hey, what about us? We're our own person, equal opportunity." They both shake their heads wearily.

"If we work, then we wouldn't be out in the streets. Our parents are working, and they're not out on the streets. They're working for us, and we're out on the streets. What about all us people who are on the street who wanna work to get outta the street? You know what I'm saying?" He shakes his head again. His voice seems, suddenly, tired as an old man's, but it is too dark now to see his face.

"Since they didn't hire me, that's when I start selling this shit, selling drugs and shit, anything that makes a buck. That's where crime comes in. You've gotta make money.

"We wanna make our own money. We wanna make a portrait of ourselves, for ourselves and not have our parents mold us. We like to have our own character. We like to have a sense of our own responsibility. As long as you're under Mama's wing, then you ain't gonna have no sense of responsibility. And that's when you get all the fuckin' knuckleheads out there that are doin' what they're doin'. 'Cause if I had a job, well maybe then a lot of things that happened to me wouldn't have happened. But, then again, maybe they would.

" 'Cause maybe that day that it happened . . . see if I were working that day maybe I would've been too tired to come out that night and party with the homeboys. And I wouldn't have even been there."

But Gabriel was there the night he got shot, the night he won't talk about more than that. He was in the neighborhood. And he's still there.

"AK-47$_2$"

The violence in this story is nothing compared to what Gabriel, and so many teenagers, live with every day. But I'm telling it for a reason.

It was lunchtime five years ago, and I was on the corner of 86th Street and York in Manhattan. Plenty of people were around. I was at a phone booth talking to my assistant at Sassy when a guy came up to me from behind, shoved something into my back, and said loud in my ear, "I've got a gun. Give me your wallet or I'll blow your head off." I didn't bother correcting him that his placement of the weapon was off if he in fact planned to blow my head off. And for some reason I didn't believe it was a gun and, stupidly I know, didn't just hand over my wallet. Instead, I started yelling at people to get the police. No one did, though a woman whose face I will never forget did stop to cross her arms and watch. Meanwhile I turned around and saw it was actually a knife, not a gun. I fought him for my wallet and got a cut across one hand and puncture wounds from his fingernails in the other hand. We both dropped the wallet, and he ran. Some firemen who were driving by sped up and tackled him a couple of blocks away.

After the police came (and high-fived each other over the fact that a mugger had actually been apprehended: "We caught a mugger! Can you believe it?!"), they made me identify the guy. Then we went in separate police cars to the police station so they could book him, bandage up my hand, and get some more information from *me. When they pulled his record, they told me he was sixteen and had been arrested many times before for robbery and also for selling drugs. And they said he'd been in and out of foster homes his whole life.*

Maybe that's part of the reason it was so hard for me to say, yes, that's the guy, when the police walked him up a few feet away from me out on the street. Partly because he looked so young, and so much more vulnerable with his hands cuffed behind his back. But mostly because of a deep sad aloneness in his face, not just alone because he was without the friend who'd been keeping watch while he pulled the knife on me but who'd run off in the other direction and managed to get away from the firemen. This looked like a life sentence kind of aloneness. Now maybe that was just him manipulating me so I wouldn't turn him in. Or maybe I'm reading way too much in.

Either way, this guy was not born to steal or do drugs or hurt people. And I don't know who I'd be if I'd never had a family that lasted more than a few months. What I do know is this: We need to stop blaming teenagers for being so violent and start solving the real problems: poverty, racism, abuse, unemployment, drugs. We need to get guns away from kids. We need to get automatic weapons off the streets. We need conflict resolution taught in schools to show kids other ways to deal with conflict, whether it be that someone takes your pencil in study hall or someone tries to get your kid brother to sell crack. We need better schools for all kids, especially ones where teachers help instill values like tolerance and respect for life. We need summer job programs and midnight basketball. We need to recognize that violence isn't just adolescent; it's cultural, and everyone gets hurt by it, especially kids. Here are the reasons why we really have no choice:

• Violent crimes against teens are up 23 percent since 1987. And 1 in 13 teenagers is a victim of violent crime.

—a 1994 study

• *Today's teenager runs roughly twice the risk of being murdered or becoming a victim of suicide compared with teens during most years of the turbulent 1960s.*

—Rolling Stone, *December 9, 1993*

• *"The idea that we become violent because we watch violence on TV or in music videos or movies is just ridiculous. We don't need to watch TV or movies to see it—we see violence every time we go to the mall. Somebody will have a gun; others have baseball bats or knives. There's always some kind of trouble."*

—*a teenager in Arizona*

• *For every violent or sex crime committed by someone under 18, there are three like crimes committed by adults against teenagers or children.*

—Extra! *March/April 1994*

• *"Guns, fights, someone blew up the bathroom a few days ago with some TNT. They haven't caught him yet. You get kinda numb from all the violence, and it doesn't bother you much once you've seen it for a while."*

—*a fourteen-year-old in Texas*

• *Thomas Jefferson High is a stolid red-orange-brick block of building set down in an East New York neighborhood of boarded-up row houses. In the past four years, 70 students have been killed, shot, stabbed or permanently injured on the school grounds. According to a report prepared for the New York state assembly and quoted by the New York* Daily News, *50 percent of the 1,900 students have some kind of puncture wound on their body at any given time. "T.J." has a "grieving room," where the students can seek peace and quiet and counseling when these things happen. The school maintains a burial fund to help families with the expenses.*

—Time, *March 9, 1992*

• *"I go to a private school in New York City and usually there are very few problems regarding violence. We have security guards 24 hours a day."*
—*a middle school girl on the Upper East Side of Manhattan*

• *"Some kid was shot right in front of the school as I was walking to my car at the end of the day . . . and I remember all the kids running and gathering around where it happened. The school has already taken all the precautions, not like it's done much good. We have see-through backpacks, metal detectors, video cameras in all the hallways, security guards, and police officers there at all times, especially after school when all the biggest violence tends to happen. And the school itself is a mess, gang graffiti everywhere, bathroom stalls torn off, windows broken and TVs and VCRs stolen."*
—*an eighteen-year-old in Florida*

• The average age of the more than half-a-million teenagers and children who have been raped in this country is 10. The rapists' average age is 27.
—*The* Rape in America *report*

• *"Violence is not a major problem at our school. Ours is the only high school in the district. It is a school where no ethnic group has a majority. It is a school of 3,789 students. And we have had only one death on campus because of violence."*
—*a sophomore in the Midwest*

• Three hundred and fifty thousand children and teenagers are victims of violence every year at the hands of adults.
—*The National Center on Child Abuse and Neglect, May 1993*

• *L.I. Boy Accused of Fatally Shooting His Brother*
Tortured by sibling rivalry and angry about a guidance coun-

selor's reprimand, a 15-year-old boy went home from school on Wednesday morning and killed his napping 19-year-old brother with their father's licensed .38-caliber revolver, police officials said today.

—New York Times, *June 10, 1994*

• *"In Rego Park, Queens, there isn't a lot of gun action. One time, though, I was getting off the bus and there were gunshots. Then I saw the gun: in the hands of a boy who looked about fourteen. He then started shooting again at the kid who had gotten off the bus before me. People started screaming, and my knees buckled. My first instinct was to run, but the guy who was getting off behind me threw me down to the ground and threw himself next to me. I was freaking out because we were on the ground in the middle of traffic."*

—Jennifer Parris, an eighteen-year-old college freshman

• *"Violence is every day of life . . . I had so many people I know killed, shot. About everybody here is down with somebody and if you're not strapped you'll probably get smoked."*

—a Bronx sophomore

• *Fifty-nine percent of high school students say they know where they could get a gun if they needed it.*

—1993 Harris nationwide poll

• *One hundred thousand kids carry a gun to school.*

—National Education Association

• *Homicide is now the second-leading cause of death for fifteen-to-nineteen-year-olds, behind car accidents, and the leading cause of death for African-American males between fifteen and twenty-four.*

—Rock the Vote's Rock the System *manual*

• *"If you have a gun, you have power. Guns are just a part of growing up these days."*
> —*an Omaha, Nebraska, sixteen-year-old, quoted in* Time, *August 2, 1993*

• *"I looked right into his eyes and it looked like he was trying to say something. There was snow on the ground and the blood from the back of his head was spreading all over it. Another buddy tried to lift his head but the back of it was gone. He had a small hole right in the middle of his forehead. And then he was gone. He died. That was my buddy. We were real tight."*
> —*a nineteen-year-old Detroit gang member who started carrying a gun at age nine and who has spent two years in jail, quoted in* Newsweek, *August 2, 1993*

• *Gabriel*

JESSICA MILLER
GOES BEAR HUNTING

*J*essica Miller is thirteen years old and tracking a grizzly along a tributary of a glacial river in Alaska. She has identified him by his five toes and claw gouges. "There he goes," she says, though there is no bear in sight. She follows the paw prints through the rushes, the silt sucking loudly at her bare feet.

"Look," she points to different tracks that are sort of teepee-shaped hoof marks. "Moose," she says. "Maybe the bear was chasing the moose." She watches her dog, Willow, sniff the tracks. Willow is half-malamute, half-husky, and her grandmother ran the Iditarod Trail sled race, so Jessica trusts the dog's instincts.

But abruptly Jessica looks up and throws her hands into the air. She starts to run. "I can't believe I'm tracking a bear without bear spray," she yells from her canoe where she left the orange canister of hot pepper spray. It's like the Alaskan version of mace, and the only thing besides a shotgun proven to make a bear keel over. "That's one of the stupidest things I've ever done," she says holding up the canister. *"Chasing* a bear without bear spray."

When it comes to grizzlies, Jessica knows stupid. She was born in Alaska and lived first in a reviving ghost town called McCarthy (pop. 26), where her parents, Jerry and Judy Miller, owned a lodge. By the time she was two years old, her father says, "the politics got to the point where we had to move." They sold the lodge and moved to what Alaskans call the bush. They took over an old homestead that was isolated by the river and a mile away from the nearest her-mit. In the summer, the only way out was by plane, but in the sub-zero cold of winter you could run your dog team over the frozen river and into McCarthy. The homestead had a sagging log cabin and a barn on the verge of caving in. They propped everything up, added a greenhouse onto the cabin, installed a solar energy system, and planted big gardens of vegetables that win blue ribbons at the state fair every August. Her parents sleep in a long main room, which is also the kitchen and living room. There is a woodstove and a shotgun hanging over the bed. Jessica's room is also the pantry. It has bunk beds in the center and all around the walls are shelves with canned goods and batteries and boardgames and books. In the summer, she can also sleep out in a loft over the barn.

The Millers work constantly to keep this place going. They have to store replacement parts for the all-terrain vehicles and the snow-mobiles, plus haul in gasoline to keep them running. They have to shoo bears away from their fabric-covered airplane and make sure that there's enough flour and yeast or sourdough starter for making bread. They have to peel fallen trees in the autumn while they're green, drag them home by snowmobile in the spring snow, mill the logs into lumber in summer when the solar power is most plentiful. "You have to really gear your life around the seasons. You can't fight nature," Judy says.

But Judy Miller sings as she bakes banana bread in the wood stove, and Jerry Miller goes around his place whistling and stacking logs. Jerry, Judy, and Jessica eat most every meal on a big home-made picnic table outside where they can watch the clouds float among the peaks of the jade and cobalt mountains. Sometimes, Jerry will interrupt himself in the middle of a sentence and look up at the ridges and say something like, *"Why* would *any*one live *any*where else?"

* * *

Back on the sandy river bank, Jessica is explaining what the procedure is if you do find a bear. "If you have to shoot bear spray, you have to go downwind because if you go upwind [the spray's] gonna get on *you*. And it's gonna knock *you* out, and the bear's still gonna be just fine. And then the bear's gonna end up eating you anyway *so* . . ." she says matter-of-factly. "If they're stalking you, they always come from downwind. Like a grizzly. Now a black bear won't stalk you so you don't have to worry about a black bear. But it's nice if they come from downwind if they're gonna come 'cause then you don't have to worry about circling around."

Bears or no, Jessica misses home every time the family has to leave. In fact, when she's down in "the Lower 48" visiting her grandparents, she gets ticked off because people say annoying things: "They say, 'Oh, do you see eskimos up there, and do you live in an igloo?' And I *ab-so-lute-ly* hate it when people think Alaska is nothing but snow and ice all year round. Or a foreign country. And there's polar bears roaming around and all you eat is whale fat or something. No one would ever dream that you could have one hunded degree summers up here. They think it's like it never gets above zero, all year round and all this stuff. It just drives me *ab-so-lute-ly* crazy, especially like in my schoolbooks and stuff when they have these maps and stuff and they call this like subarctic or something and okay, what if it is subarctic? But then they have to go and have like these crazy temperatures that are totally unrealistic. Or a population of like zero you know. Uninhabited."

Jessica sort of stamps her foot in the sand at the river's edge as though to prove it is not *uninhabited*. "It's really fun 'cause there are just so many things we can do. A lot of people ask us, like in town, *How do you keep from getting bored?*" Jessica says, then cocks her head to one side and adds comically, "Okay, let's see, how do I explain this?"

She takes care of the six sled dogs. She mushes her dog team fourteen miles round trip to catch the mail plane twice a week in winter. She watches all the changes as the wildflowers go from windflowers in April to the wild roses and the purple monkshoods and the Siberian astors to Jacob's Ladders in August. In the winter, she helps keep the fire going for heat and for baking and for cooking the dog food, which is a smelly mix of barley and meat powder. This summer, Jessica's major project was to dig a hole for the new out-house—nine feet deep, five feet square. She was also in charge of the three big vegetable gardens and for putting up the bright purple and red jars of berry jams. And, since her parents' birthdays come in the warm months when it's often too hot for a wood fire, she made birthday cakes in the microwave that runs off a solar-energy system converted to 110 volts.

Jessica does not have a telephone or television reception. But in the winter, she can sit and read in the hot tub, which is in the greenhouse and is heated by a woodstove submerged into it. In the summer, friends from other parts of Alaska come out for a few weeks at a time. They canoe to this strip of riverbank that Jessica calls "the beach" and swim in the warm branch, then lie in the sun and get "boiling hot" and then jump into the "cold, cold, cold, swiftly moving" side of the stream. Lately, Jessica's been amused by watching moose swim across the lake outside their cabin.

As long as she's here in the bush, Jessica has a mission of one kind or another. But for the past six winters, the Millers have spent part of the season in Anchorage because of her parents' work. Judy Miller coordinated the animal rescue by aircraft after the *Exxon Valdez* oil spill in 1989 and ever since then she has had to spend some time in Anchorage and go down to the Lower 48 occasionally to do consulting work for other oil companies. And Jerry has to do research to sustain their bush life. But for Jessica, getting out into the part of the world that has MTV is no compensation for leaving behind her dogs.

Last year, she begged her parents to at least have Christmas at home before they went into town. So they stayed and had a Christmas tree lighted up in the yard and another in the cabin. Jessica gave her father a battery-operated "mosquito chaser awayer" and her mother some red cashmere socks. Afterward, Judy left for Anchorage. Jessica and her dad were planning to follow her shortly, but then, abruptly, Jessica's dad had to get to town because of an emergency. But they couldn't both just desert the place. So he had to leave Jessica, then twelve, to care for the dogs and to train a young caretaker whom they had recruited long-distance. Jessica waited two days for the caretaker to make his way out so she could teach him how to run the dogs and how to cook the dog food and make sure that the solar water pump system was operating and how to work with the firewood.

The days were short, as little as three hours of daylight. And at night, Jessica had to get out of bed every couple of hours to keep the woodstove going. But one night she just lay in her parents' bed shivering instead, and the next morning, she saw by the outdoor thermometer that it was sixty below. She had never seen sixty below in her life. The new caretaker showed up late that day, but that was worse. They worked outside together. "It was harder cause this guy, he had absolutely no idea what was going on. So it's like, babying this guy along: *'This is how you do this and this is how you do this,'* " she says. "He was from Oregon," she adds, by way of explanation. "He had on these lousy boots. We thought he had frostbite. I'm like, *frostbite* and I'm out here *alone.*"

*   *   *

The grizzly tracks have disappeared into the river, and Jessica is bored with the search anyway. He might have been here a week ago, for all she can tell. So she wades in shallow riffles and then sits in the sand to catch some warm rays of the high five o'clock August sun. In a week or two, she's going to get the big white boxes filled with schoolbooks and she can't wait. Her mother is her home teacher. In Juneau, teachers make the assignments for each of her courses, things like science, two kinds of English, math.

She's only been to school twice in her life—both times in fifth grade when her mother was working in Anchorage. The experience unnerved Jessica about as much as running into a bear drunk on a bellyfull of fermented dandelions.

The first school was private and Catholic, like the ones where her parents had gone when they were growing up in the Lower 48. They thought it would be easier for her. "I bopped in in November so it was already like the middle of the school year anyway, and it was a lot harder than if I had come at the beginning of the year," Jessica says. "I ended up getting pretty rotten deals on schools anyway. The teacher had her own problem like she had a brain tumor so we had substitutes all the time and stuff like that. So it was really hard. They were just like totally unprepared for new kids. And to make it even worse, the kids were, they were totally, I mean they had been together since first grade, and they thought that they were so important because they went to this private school and they thought they were really special and so any new kid who came in there immediately got picked on 'cause you're not one of the group—whereas in a normal public school you'd have more new kids. It was *horrible*.

"During Christmas vacation, I said, 'I'm not going back,' and I never have been back there since the first day of Christmas vacation. I didn't even get my stuff out. They were horribly mean. They punched me in the stomach so hard I was sick for three days. And the hardest part is that when they do something like that, nothing happens to them, nothing happens at all. When he did that, he had to apologize, that's it. *Apologize.*

"Even if someone's not hitting me or doing something like that, it's still hard just to be picked on all the time, people always calling me names and doing nasty stuff. Just stupid little things. It wasn't because I've never been to school before. I've always been like taller than most of my friends and stuff and in fifth grade of course, I was taller than everyone. I was the tallest kid in the class by about an eighth of an inch, and Ned, the kid who punched me so hard, he used to be the tallest kid in the class. And he's a boy and now I'm the tallest and I'm just a smidge taller than him and it drove him crazy. He couldn't stand the thought that a girl was taller than him."

As she talks about school, Jessica's hands pull at the grass. She's subdued. You can tell by the way her voice gets tight that her confidence with bear spray and sled dogs and solar-energy panels are no help when she gets around certain other kids. So she and her parents are talking about the possibility that a year from now, they might move into Anchorage for nine months so Jessica could start high school with other ninth graders and spend a complete year going to school instead of studying by correspondence course. "How could we deny her that?" her mother asks.

Jessica herself has mixed feelings about the plan. If she does go, she's insisting that all six sled dogs and the cat go as well.

*   *   *

As she climbs back into the canoe to paddle across the lake and home, Jessica shakes her head again, still shocked that she would go chasing after a bear without her bear spray. Now that she's out in the water that seems almost fluorescent because it's reflecting so much green, with Willow swimming alongside, now that she's safe, she tells bear stories.

Once, when Jessica was even younger, her father went down to "shoo away" the bear who had been biting their fabric airplane, which they leave on a landing strip about a mile from their homestead. He took Jessica along to shoot a video of him firing the gun and scaring away the bear. But what they didn't know was that there was another bear around. It got between Jessica and her dad, just started going after Jessica, just walking toward her grunting and snorting like a pig. "He was just a little black bear," Jessica says. "But I mean plenty big enough to eat you." Jerry had to shoot him and Jessica didn't get any of it on videotape because she was shaking too much. But they had plenty of bear meat to make burritos for a while.

Her parents still worry about whether or not she's prepared enough to deal with a bear. At lunch, while they were eating a taco salad that they kept fresh with the rest of their food in the "cold hole" under a tarp on the north side of the cabin, they told a story about a bear coming in a cabin window, chasing a woman to the roof, and then eating her. They told the story the way people in

Los Angeles talk about drive-bys. It's grim. But it's part of life.

So as she paddles toward home, Jessica thinks she won't mention to her parents that she went bear-tracking without spray. It wouldn't amuse. "At least it wasn't a mama with cubs," she says. "That would have been *really* stupid."

JOHN ROBERT HUNT'S LIST OF WHAT IT TAKES TO BE A COWBOY ON THE VERGE OF THE 21st CENTURY

1) A tough backside

John Robert Hunt is built like a rope—skinny and long and sturdy and rough. He wears brown cowboy boots and Wrangler's. His face is two-tone—rusty as the Arizona land from his eyebrows down, but pale in a band just under his buzzed hair because he wears a dusty black ten-gallon hat year round. The widest thing about John Robert is his grin. It seems as wide as he is tall.

He's grinning now, even though it's July and hot enough to make the arid land waver like water. He got up just after five while the stars were still out to ride a horse named Chipper, rounding up cattle and driving them to a far pasture where the "feed" is better. His two younger sisters helped. When the three of them finally rode back coated with sienna-colored grit, John Robert got off Chipper and went into the round corral, where he worked for a couple of hours on breaking a colt. Then his dad said he could have the rest of the day off. It's almost suppertime.

John Robert swears he's not saddle sore. He's tough where it counts for a cowboy: "From the time I was two and a half to seven, I probably had an average of three whippin's a day," he says, stretching out the easy grin that shows the little gaps between his teeth.

"But I'm beyond getting whipped-beyond-all-belief. I guess I don't need it or they're too tired to give it to me."

2) A dad with a little outfit

Cow-punching and horse-breaking and fence-building take a lot of time on the L O Ranch, even though it's a little outfit (Arizona-speak for ranch). John Robert's parents maintain the 40 square miles of brushy range themselves, with the help of the three kids. Their father, John Hunt, is the kind of man who's happy to have his son along hunting mountain lions but also expects him to help out with branding or butchering cattle. His mother, Mary, knows how to use her muscles and marshal her kids. John Robert loves her, but sometimes she would like to know more than her son would like to tell her. The little sisters are teenagers too. John Robert brushes them off like flies or teases them like hound pups that amuse him. "They're okay," he says. The family is easy together. They do chores like a choreographed dance. They have had lots of practice being together.

Farflung neighbors trail dust along the road, a kind of smoke-signal announcement that they might be about to drop by for coffee. The forest service guys stop to chat—when they're not galloping their all-terrain vehicles through the Hunt land, part of which is actually public land that the family has grazing permits to use. But mainly, it's just the family, some horses, some cattle, some dogs, some chickens, and some hummingbirds. "Don't say farm," John Robert insists. "I don't live on a farm. I live on a ranch."

At eighteen, John Robert gets $850 a summer month to be a cowboy. It's more money than the hired hands make over on the ORO or the Diamond A, but it's a different kind of work. "They're horseback every day," John Robert says wistfully. "Sometimes I have to sacrifice and do dog work on this little outfit: I have to haul wood and fix this and some of the stuff that they don't have to do because they're hired on."

But there *are* advantages to working for his own dad. For

instance, he's made it into town—Prescott, Arizona—three times in the past month. He knows other cowboys who were lucky to make it in just once because the boss expected them to work straight through the weekend.

3) Wheels

"Livin' out here is all right," John Robert says as he paws the dust with the tip of his roughed-up boots. "But you durn sure wanna go to town and see people besides your family once in a while." Town is forty miles away, about twenty of those on a dirt road. It takes an hour and a half on the school bus, 50 minutes by pickup. John Robert's record is 35 minutes, and he thinks he could make it in 30 minutes in his dad's truck. But for now he's stuck with his old Ford, which he's kinda fond of despite himself.

He walks over to a battered red pickup that is parked with all the other ranch vehicles outside the fence that surrounds the family's rock and cedar house. "That's my truck, the very special truck," he says in a mock-boast that's not all mock. "If I'm on the highway where I don't think I'll hit a cow or something, I'll put it on the floor. I've only got a six-cylinder, and on the floor I've got a top speed of about 85. I can get 90 to 95 if I've got a little bit of a down-hill." He runs a hand along its "thrashed" flank where the metal is crunched looking. It has 150,000 miles, several huge dents, and a sign hanging below its license plate that reads "VERY SPECIAL!!!"

This truck is his freedom, his favorite ride (sorry Chipper). "Prescott's a big enough town for me," he says of the 26,455 population place. "Not everybody knows me. But everybody knows my truck. Half the town's been hit by it," he laughs and adds: "I've only had three collisions with other vehicles, and only two of 'em have been my fault."

The worst wreck didn't go ahead and happen when it could've. Last year, some buddies talked John Robert into trying to jump a cattle guard with the Very Special truck. "They told me I could jump," John Robert says. "I could go real fast and I could catch some air." He laughs nervously. "We did catch air, and when we landed we were kinda sideways, and I threw a big sand rooster tail. We went across the road several times but I got her . . . I got that truck slowed down and we got back under control."

That kind of accident could've cost him big, and it's what scared him into always wearing his seatbelt since then. Even as it was, the accidents that did happen cost him about $400 dollars a wham. They were chrome-benders—two of them in parking lots when John Robert was more intent on cruising the strip of Gurley between Woody's gas station and the church on the other end of town.

4) A bedroll

Cruising means partying. He's been cruising hard for the past seventeen weeks, which is how long he's been broken up with his girlfriend. He races into town prepared to party—cash, ice chest, bedroll. "I can hard-core party for three days," he says. "Then I need some sleep."

Take the Fourth of July. He rolled into town, hooked up with friends, saw his ex with her new boyfriend, got a case of beer from some guy for $5, and then headed out to Thumb Butte to "kill the case." On the way out of town, after about two and a half beers, which is about one and a half past where John Robert can think straight, the cops stopped him at a water balloon checkpoint. They were trying to round up a bunch of water-balloon hurlers who were ambushing strolling tourists along Prescott's historic square.

As the cop approached, John Robert popped a piece of gum into his mouth and followed his number one motto, which is "Remain calm." (Motto number two is "No fat chicks.") The officer inquired if John Robert had any balloons. "No," John Robert said calmly, then grinned: "You got any to give me? I've been gettin' bombarded here, buddy, and I need some ammo." The cop waved him through with a smile and never discovered the case of beer. (John Robert got a kick out of telling that one to his dad.)

After the water-balloon checkpoint, his memory of the holiday weekend gets kinda bleary. "There's stuff I'm not sure what went on," he says as he walks along Walnut Creek back of his house. "I know that someone on Ruth Street isn't real happy with me 'cause I puked in their yard. And then we went to this girl's house—I call her the Party Angel because she's only seventeen and she can buy beer anywhere in town pretty much and she always helps me when I'm drunk. Anyway, we went to her house, and we were gonna see if she was there, and it was like three-thirty in the morning. And we went around a corner kinda fast goin' up to her house, and I got sick there too. They opened the door, and I fell out on the lava rocks. I dry-heaved there for a while."

At some point, he and his very special truck got to a motel in Prescott, where he and his friends were spending the night. His ex was inside the motel, so he climbed into the bed of his truck with his bedroll. "I remember feelin' pretty bad over the side of my truck," he says. "And then I woke up the next morning cause the sun was on me, and I got too hot, and I had to get out. I remember dry-heavin' then too."

"I'm a lightweight," John Robert admits gamely. "Into my second beer, I'm gone. And when I'm in party mode and fully operational, I usually don't eat too much. It takes even less to get drunk that way. And it doesn't taste real bad when you puke either."

He shakes his head, amazed at, even proud of his own hard-earned reputation: "They call me the Power Heaver. I might not be able to drink very much or hold very much, but I can throw up better than anybody. The Party Angel has been to a lot of parties, and she says I can puke better than anybody she's ever seen. I can chuck it to that tree over there." He points to a pine some yards away. "It's all in the stance. I never get it on my shoes and I hardly ever have to wipe my mouth."

5) At least occasional access to MTV

That Fourth of July morning-after, John Robert didn't have to go home and run a tractor (as he did once in a morning-after daze that almost got him killed because he knocked the wrong lever on the machinery). Instead, John Robert just crawled into the motel room to indulge in one of his favorite forms of hangover healing: MTV, a rare treat. He's into "heavy metal and some rap," he says: Metallica, Ozzie Osbourne, 2LiveCrew, Ice T. He's especially into "Liquid TV." He just can't get all that on the three channels at home.

Don't even mention country music to him. "I'm not into that hick music, even though I might live here," he says. "If Garth Brooks woulda never been born, I'da been happy enough."

6) A good aim

Back home on the ranch, he spends a lot of time with his rifle. He polishes it. He loads it. He shoots it.

"I started shooting a .22 when I was like twelve," he says. "I was too little to work all the time, but I was big enough to where I didn't wanna just sit around in the yard. So I'd spend hours at a time goin' around and shootin' things. But I never shot anybody or any property that I wasn't supposed to."

Once, that year he was twelve, he saved himself with a gun. "The time I 'bout got ate," he calls it. He and his father were out hunting mountain lion on Juniper Mountain. "We had this lion up in the rocks, and he crawled in a hole. We had the whole pack of dogs, and my dad left his Thompson Center Contender pistol with me and he left me holdin' these two dogs because he was gonna go to the house and get a flashlight and a rifle so he could crawl in the hole and shoot this lion.

"But before he got back, these two dogs got to lunging real crazy. And they started dragging me down the hole, so I had to let go of 'em because I didn't wanna go in the hole. Then, I could hear 'em barkin' out on the other side, and I figured they must have this lion out there. I got around, and it's a younger lion—it wasn't like a kitten, but it was a younger kinda lion. And it was sittin' there on the ledge, and then there was a big dog fight goin' on, and I had to kick the dogs apart and beat them up for a while. Then the dogs started crawling around on the ledges, and they jerked this lion off.

"This lion was fightin' with 'em, and I was worried that the lion was gonna kill one of these dogs. So I was gonna shoot the lion in the head. But you have to be careful because there's been a lot of dogs killed by people that were too ignorant. I was just young and ignorant. Well, I still am young, still ignorant. I was younger and more dumber and somehow this lion got ahold of my foot. I started trying to jerk away, and his head was on there, but he bit hard enough that he bruised my toe right there by the toenail.

"I finally got the lion kicked off my foot and the pistol down there. He reached up and snapped at the end of the barrel. His mouth was on the end of the barrel, and I just pulled the trigger."

John Robert chews on his fingernail. "That was the third one I killed. The fun part's not killin' 'em. The challenge isn't shooting the animal. That's real easy. The fun part is watchin' the dogs hunt, tryin' to get 'em. When you get 'em in a hole or something, and they just jump out of a tree and run to another tree. That's what's fun."

7) A good barbecue recipe

The skin of the lion may go on the front room wall. The meat goes into a big barbecue pit down by Walnut Creek. Friends come from all over. Kids catch tadpoles. People play volleyball. And everybody eats too much.

You start with hot coals in a pit. "There's lion, and there's pork and beef and turkey," John Robert explains. "And you just put it all in that pit and leave it overnight. You get that meat and you put it in one of those oven bags that you put turkey in and then you wrap it in wet burlap and get it in the pit. Then you cover it over so no air can get into it and cause it to catch fire. Then it just cooks in there overnight, and then you dig it up the next day about noon. And it's great."

8) A way with words

People come from ranches all over for the barbecue, and they all compete with their "Wild West stories, usually featuring themselves," John Robert says. He's in training with the storytelling. He dishes up adjectives that leave no doubt about his opinions. Kids who wear tie-dye are "granola bunny huggers." Hondas and Toyotas are "rice grinders." The Forest Service, which dictates when his dad moves his cattle where, are "wood pigs." And when he parties, even though most people (including himself) think of him as a lightweight, he likes to have enough alcohol to "kill three bull elephants."

9) A thick hide

John Robert didn't use to require enough alcohol to kill three bull elephants. That caliber of thirst started four months ago today—exactly. He's kept track. That's the day his girlfriend abruptly dumped him in the school cafeteria. John Robert has had a broken kneecap, a broken wrist, a broken arm, and maybe a broken toe. But this broken heart thing is the one he still can't handle.

He used to go to her house every Friday night. He stopped bronc riding to go to her house every Friday night. They went to movies with her brother. Just the two of them played Nintendo—or didn't play Nintendo—down in a cabin on her property. He imagines he was in love with her.

They saw each other every day at the public school where all the kids from ranches around Prescott go. And then there was that day that started like every other day and ended everything, it seems to John Robert, in the cafeteria. He asked his girlfriend if she wanted what was left of his Mountain Dew and she said, "Can we see other people?"

"I go, *Why don't you just tell me what you mean?* And she was all, *Well I like other people.* And I'm all, *Who?* She said a guy, and this guy's a dweeb, a real geek. I like him but he's a geek. She's like all, *We can still be friends.* I was like, *Yeah sure.*

"She just walked off, and I was left staring into the bottom of my Mountain Dew can."

He shakes his head glumly and says what he still can't believe: "She crawled into another guy's bedroll three days after she dumped me."

When he's out roundin' up the cattle, he thinks of her, "the chick from Lonesome Gulch." He shudders, as though he could throw off her memory. "Today makes four months," John Robert says. "My friends tell me that I am the most wrecked guy that any of my friends ever seen. I just can't move on. I talk about it way too much. Actually, it makes it worse cause it's just aggravating to everybody, even me."

He's not sure what he wanted from his ex ultimately. He wants to punch cows after high school, not get married. His dad has offered to pay for college. But John Robert's not sure yet what he'll do. He looks around the ranch that he rides in snow and wavering heat. "My granddad grew up here, and my dad grew up here, and I'm growin' up here. Don't ask me how much longer we'll be here. But I guess as long as the forest service doesn't run us off."

The hunting dogs are baying, anxious for John Robert to feed them. He himself is ready to take off his hat and tuck into his barbecued steak and potatoes. As the stars start coming out on this end of his long day, he starts home along the fenceline that runs behind the house. There are stiff cowhides draped over the wire, flapping in the hot wind. Every time the Hunts butcher a cow, they throw the hide over the fence, where they dry to a ragged tenacity. "That's some thick hide," John Robert says, pointing to them. He looks at them every time he saddles up and rides by. He says those hides will last a long long time, maybe even longer than a broken heart.

KATHLEEN DOXEY'S
BOYFRIEND MARK

Wherever she looks, Kathleen Doxey sees a guy named Mark. Kathleen's been in love with Mark since she was twelve years old. Now, he's almost a senior; she's about to be a sophomore. And when he's out on the football field trying to win a game for Marshall Academy, that's Kathleen on the sidelines in the red pleated skirt and white Reeboks cheering: "ONE TWO THREE FOUR Y-E-L-L!!!! WHO ARE YOU YELLIN' FOR?"

And the other cheerleaders may scream out "MARSHALL PATRIOTS," but in her heart Kathleen Doxey is only cheering "MARK, MARK, MARK." Tall Mark with his Cherokee heritage and his long arms and his tan skin over big muscles.

Kathleen has jewel-blue eyes and long hair that she just dyed "champagne" blond because the sun streaks it so unevenly when she "lays out"—either in her backyard or the tanning bed at the beauty salon. Just before school let out for the summer, she won second alternate in her school's Beauty Review. In eighth grade, the first time she competed in the school-sponsored beauty pageant, she won first alternate. This time her mama says she would have won the whole thing if only she had had a full-sequin dress like the other girls. "We don't really have a lot of money to go and spend on that stuff," Kathleen says. Also, she thinks she should have curled her hair. She wore it straight in the casual segment of the beauty pageant because she wanted to wear it French-braided in the formal part.

Soon after the Beauty Review, Kathleen got Miss Junior High, which is not a beauty contest. "The whole junior high votes on it," she says. "It's like a favorite for the whole junior high. You just get pictures taken and you get put in the annual; this big section of the annual is about you. And I got a letter not too long ago about *Who's Who Among American Students.* I've got a notice to do that."

Now when Kathleen thinks back on that night, she couldn't care less about not winning the Beauty Review. That's because of Mark—partly because she put a snapshot of him over the portrait on her bulletin board that was taken of the winner and all the alternates. What Kathleen remembers is that she competed in the same long dress—black satin with blue sequins on the top—that she later wore to Prom with Mark. So if she thinks of that night, she thinks of the dress, and she ends up imagining Prom night in the cafeteria when she danced in Mark's arms to a band called Three.

* * *

It's June now, and Kathleen is driving her mama's Cadillac to cheerleading practice. She is fifteen, Mississippi's legal driving age, and the car is gray and unwieldy and bigger than anything Kathleen has ever driven. Her feet, in clean white Keds, look too small to work the pedals, and her manicured hands keep a white-knuckle grip on the steering wheel. "This is the first time I've ever driven this thing," she says, with a nervous laugh. She's waiting for her daddy to fix up an old car that he has saved for her. She's been waiting since her birthday ten months ago. But it's okay because anyway she likes riding with Mark better.

At the cheerleader sponsor's house, set high on a swell of golfing-quality lawn, Kathleen joins the other cheerleaders for practice. Not everybody's here but all together there are eleven. They are practicing a choreographed dance that they will compete with in July at camp down in Oxford at Ole Miss. Kathleen, who won Outstanding Junior High Cheerleader this spring, moves fluidly, her hair swinging around her like curtains of water as she kneels and jumps and waves. She's in sync with the other girls as they kick and bounce under the carport. You'd never know it, but she says she feels out of place at cheerleading practice. She doesn't know why. Her family is as old as any in Holly Springs. She belongs as much as anyone.

The town, forty-five minutes south of Memphis, is famous for having survived the Civil War so well. Its good luck was that General Ulysses S. Grant lived there with his wife when the Union held that part of Mississippi. When the Confederacy reclaimed it, the Southern general ordered that Mrs. Grant, alone at the time in Holly Springs, not be harmed. She wasn't, and when Grant's forces rode victoriously back into Holly Springs the general thanked him by sparing the town. Now, the town of 8,000 has more antebellum houses than any other in the South, and lots of tourists who come to see them.

Kathleen is not sure how many generations of her family have lived in Holly Springs, but "we go back," she says. She does know that three generations of her family have practiced law down on the old-style square, where you can buy a sixpenny nail or a cup of coffee. Her dad, a wide-shouldered guy with a generous handshake, still practices there, on the second floor above the pizza place. His granddaddy, Wall Doxey Sr., was a U.S. Senator, and a state park down the road is named after him. But her great-great uncle on her daddy's side, Robert Holt Hindman, is the most famous because he was killed over in Tippah County in 1849 by William Faulkner's great-granddaddy.

So Kathleen has no really dramatic reason to feel different from the other cheerleaders. She just does. It's not about money. "We're better off than some people but not as good off as other people," she says. Maybe the way she feel just comes down to Mark. "My friends, I don't know, they think I'm stupid because I only spend like most of my time with Mark. They try to make me go out just with them and everything. When I'm not with him, they go back and tell him that Kathleen did this and this and this, stuff she wasn't supposed to do. See I don't drink and smoke and stuff like that. And they do."

She just *feels* more like Mark. Mark's family is newer here. He went for a while to the public school, he knows black kids. Kathleen doesn't know any black teenagers, and she thinks it's nice the way Mark speaks to them by name.

Kathleen just generally admires Mark. And she feels like he's a good influence on her. When he took the ACT test this past weekend, she took it with him. Her family couldn't believe it; her two older sisters didn't take it until they had to. Even Kathleen knows she's young to be taking it, but she wanted to practice. Someday, she hopes to do well enough on the test to get out of Holly Springs, to choose any college she wants. She gets As and Bs, and Mark helps her with math, and she understands it better now.

Mark needed at least a score of 25 on the ACT so that he can get into the Air Force and move up to Colorado. Kathleen says she loves the mountains and thinks it might be nice to go to a college "up there," even though she has never been north of Virginia in her life. "I want to get away and get something bigger instead of just stayin' here," she says. "[My family] thinks I'm stayin' here for the rest of my life, but I don't know, I guess it'll be a shock."

*   *   *

When she walks into the house after cheerleading practice, Kathleen goes right to her room. She spends most of her time there. She got the pastel comforter from her parents for her birthday, and all the deflated foil balloons and dead bouquets of flowers are from Mark. The room is spotless.

"Every day, I have to clean our house and wash clothes and just keep the house up. And my brother does the outside," Kathleen says. She's good about doing her chores, including the laundry and ironing her father's shirts, but when *Family Feud* comes on before supper that night and the question is "What do most men take for granted from their wives?" Kathleen yells, "Housework!" Which turns out to be the number one answer. "I just won $11,000," she tells her mother, who guessed laundry and wouldn't have won anything.

Supper is leftovers from her parents' latest barbecue contest. They go around the South with their team of cooks competing against other teams. The idea is to have the cleanest fingernails, the whitest shirts, the most tender pork—so that the shank bone just slides right out with no meat clinging to it. There's a real strategy to a barbecue cookoff, with attention to details like giving the judges a palate-tainting piece of chocolate before they advance to the next team's pork. Kathleen's parents have been putting a lot of their time and money and energy into barbecue contests, and there's a running bet with the cafe downtown about whose team will come out on top each time. So her daddy, Ralph, is real proud when his kids compliment his cooking.

Mark wins big points because he comes over and eats a ton of the leftovers. Kathleen keeps loading up his plate. He grins, doesn't say much, and eats. He's wearing a purple muscle shirt, a gold chain necklace and Teva sandals. The family boils around him as though he were just another one of them. He almost is. He shows up most every night. Sometimes, he and Kathleen go fishing down in a pond behind the house. Sometimes they watch TV or a video. Once in a while, they'll go downtown and sit behind Fitch's gas station with all their friends or just ride around. But if they do go out, there are strict rules: "We can go out, and you have to be in by ten thirty and you can't leave before seven and you have to know exactly where you're going and if you change your plans, you have to call," Kathleen recites.

Kathleen's parents are more strict with her than her two older sisters. "Everything that both my sisters got to do, I had to wait a year or two afterward to do it. At the age they got to do it, I didn't get to do it. Like in seventh or eighth grade, I didn't even get to go to one dance. So I didn't get to go to dances till this year. They just said, We think it's better if you don't go. So that made me sit at home while all my friends went."

At least Mark would sit at home with her (if it was in one of the phases when they weren't broken up). Or she would stay in her room alone, rearranging the dried blooms of all the flowers Mark has ever given her. Or she'd sit on her bed, reading his poems. She has framed the poetry he's written for her—it's about angels and all their time together.

He gave her a poem for their first anniversary; they sat in his parents' Ford Taurus on a dirt road between her house and his, and he lighted a candle and read his five-page poem by its light. He even toasted her with champagne but neither of them liked the way it tasted so he ended up giving it to his parents instead.

Even though they do go parking, Kathleen quickly explains that as far as sex, she and Mark "have decided that we'll know when." But "This is a secret I haven't told anybody," Kathleen confides eagerly, her face flushing. "But the other day he, uh, we kinda got engaged cause he's leavin' when he graduates."

That happened last Friday. She and Mark went to the town of Olive Branch with her parents, who were tending the big barbecue pit with their team. The cookoff was a big fair with lots of smoked meat and beer and merry-go-rounds for the kids. They were walking around through all the crowd, when Mark blurted out that he wanted to marry her. He'd have to go away after he graduated but he wanted to make sure they'd be together after that. He slipped a pop tab on her finger, which is going to do until he can save up enough money from digging golf holes at a new course outside town. She's keeping it in a special drawer until he can buy her a diamond.

Until then, it's a secret they're keeping just between themselves, this big Presbyterian Church wedding they're planning for two years from next May. Kathleen is sure it's the right thing to do. "It's just kinda like a feeling that you get," she says. "He lets me do what I wanna do. He lets me express myself the way I want to, and he doesn't tell me I have to do this and I have to do that. A lot of stuff is what I wanna do and not just what he wants to do."

They think about what they want to happen in the future when they sit on the hood of his car and look up at the night sky. Mark has picked out a star for them. It's whatever star is brightest on that night. And when he's away in Jackson for Boys' State or at basketball camp, she can look up at the same sky and see the same star. Then Kathleen says she doesn't have to feel lonely, she sees Mark in the sky.

October 7, 1981

Judgment of the Moon and Stars
(For B)

She looks at the stars.
Then she looks up at him
and proclaims them to be
splinters of the moon.

He looks down at her
and laughs.

He knows.

He hurdles his rational suns of knowledge at her.

but he does not know
that the last time he looked at the stars was long ago, when
*   he was closer to the ground and further from the stars*
and he, like her, had to bend way back to see them all.

and he does not know
for he cannot see
that his scorching suns
are bouncing off of her
and are splintering in the sky.

And she, knowing, does not hear his words.

She looks at his stars.

LYNN THOMAS'S BABY

*L*ynn Thomas has just worked eight hours at Hardee's, where every couple of minutes she says, "May I take your order please?" and then gets people their fried chicken or grilled chicken or fries. She has to wear gray pants, a red polyester Hardee's smock, and a hat that smooshes her short black hair. She started at eight in the morning and at four her mother came and picked her up and dropped her off at the trailer. Lynn's blue trailer, left over from about 1973, sits in a cramped trailer park out on an edge of Champaign, Illinois, where the train tracks cross under the interstate highway. Lynn, seventeen, moved out of her mother's house and now halves expenses with her twenty-one-year-old cousin, Tammi, who has a toddler just ten days younger than Lynn's son.

Cameron Antaious Mosley is eighteen months old and wired. He has a big open grin and a razor-attachment haircut that accentuates his ears, which are still too big for him and poke out a little. He's racing around the room pushing, then dragging a plastic lawnmower that's bigger than he is. Tom Brokaw is roaring on a large color television at one end of the living room. A sheet hangs over the doorway of the hall that leads to the bedrooms. The red clock on the microwave glows out of the dim kitchen.

Lynn has changed into blue jean shorts and a gold tank top with a scalloped neckline. Her feet are bare, her toenails painted a matte red. She is talking—her words dodging around Cameron's screaming—about being a skinny little girl who found out she was pregnant: "It took me a long time," she says. "I didn't find out until I was like four and a half months. We thought there was something wrong with my pills, me and my mom. So we went to get my pills checked and found out I was pregnant. So that was kind of a shock, and my mom was there. And I was going to have an abortion, but my mom is Catholic so she was . . . It was a hard thing, and it was worse to have an abortion than it was to be pregnant.

"I wasn't ready at all, cause I sorta wasn't a girl who wanted to grow up and have kids. I didn't wanna have kids," she says, as her son throws himself against the screen door.

That night she found out she was pregnant, she called her boyfriend, Kenny. He came over. They had always gone to school together and had started hanging with the same bunch of kids and had finally gotten together earlier that year. She liked him because he was funny and brought her roses. When he found out she was pregnant, "He felt that it was up to me what I wanted to do because like it was my body—whatever you know I wanted to do was okay with him. But then his parents found out, and his mom wanted us to have the baby, too. They're Baptist, I guess."

Cameron comes over and takes a pillow from her lap and screams, "Mine."

"Ouch," she says, as he pulls it from her grasp. *"Let go,"* she says.

"Mine," he insists. She goes to get him a drink. He won't take it. *"You wanna toy?"* she asks him, presenting him with a plastic car. He zooms it around the floor.

"It seemed like I was pregnant forever," she continues. It was summer when she found out and that fall she went back to Urbana High School. They had a prenatal class for pregnant students taught by a social worker. She was one of about fifteen pregnant girls in the 1,200-student school. The class taught them about taking care of a baby, and the social worker also interceded if there was trouble with students or teachers in any of their other classes—like once when a guy teacher told a girl who needed frequent permission to go to the bathroom that she should have thought of that before she got pregnant.

Lynn didn't have any trouble, though. She could have opted for the Homebound program when she was seven months pregnant, but she decided to stay in school because as a class officer she had duties for homecoming and prom. The other students were supportive. In English, some even brainstormed about names for her baby, which she didn't need because she liked the name Cameron— for Kirk Cameron who she'd had a crush on when she was a *Growing Pains* fan in seventh grade. Then she just had to convince Kenny that as mother *her* choice got to be the first name and *his* choice, Antaious ("the kid would never be able to spell it") could only be the middle name.

After school, she and Kenny went to Lamaze classes, and they waited for their January baby. She ate more; the pizza man got to know who she was when she called every night at nine to order a large pepperoni. Kenny got used to riding his bike to Rally's to get her seasoned fries. "I ballooned up," she says, laughing. "And I had bad backaches and stuff. When the baby moves at first, it feels like a tickling sensation, and then when it starts kicking, you can really feel like a baby's kicking. And you can see them moving around inside of you and stuff—if you look at your stomach when the baby's moving. You can see your baby moving."

Then the baby came early. "I was in labor for like three days. I went to a basketball game like that Friday night 'cause he wasn't due until like January 3. My stomach started hurting. I was joking around saying maybe I was goin' into labor. I went to bed. I woke up and my showing came during the night, a little blood. So I called my doctor's service. As soon as you see the blood you know to call immediately—

"Cam-Cam come sit up here," she hoists the toddler onto the couch beside her. He squirms and wriggles free.

"So they told me to go to the hospital, and I was having contractions really far apart. They weren't hard or anything. They just felt like menstrual cramps and . . . *Cam-Cam stop. I'm gonna take that from you.* And so well, they kept me all of Saturday because his heart was beating irregularly. *You come up on this couch. That's bad. Yes, that's bad. No, no."*

Cameron is crying. He has developed a fascination with the whirring fan by the couch. He wants to go back over to it.

"And, um, he was having irregular heartbeats so they just wanted to check it to make sure, but they decided it was just because he was in labor. *Cam-Cam, that is bad. Come sit here. NO.*

"So they let me go that Sunday morning and they told me I probably wouldn't be havin' my baby until like Monday because my contractions were a long way apart," she says as Cameron begins howling. She has a stiff arm between him and the fan.

At five that evening, her mom took her back to the hospital, her contractions fifteen minutes apart. But she wasn't dilated enough for them to call Kenny away from the line at the Kraft factory. He had already been up with Lynn all night, missing work. She had already bitten him once when he leaned in close to her during a contraction. They didn't want to call him away until it was time.

"And then when they had come and checked me at like nine, nine thirty, I went from being dilated four inches to being dilated seven. I started pushing, and they told me to call Kenny hurry up because I was about to have the baby."

Cameron jolts out a piercing scream, straining toward the fan.

"So Kenny got there in time. The doctor I went to doesn't really like to use drugs because any drugs they give you they're giving to the baby. And so, she really only gives it to you if you're really, really, really in pain. It wasn't that bad. The only shot they gave me was before they cut me, before they gave me the episiotomy."

Lynn sees movement out the door. *"Cam-Cam,"* she yells. *"Here comes Daddy."*

"Dad-dy, dad-dy, dad-dy," Cameron sings from the couch. Outside, a long old-looking brown car has pulled up. Cameron races to the screen door and stands with his palms flat against it. His daddy leaves the car running and makes his long-legged way up to the door, grinning at the baby. Kenny ran track in high school and has that kind of build. He's wearing jean shorts, ankle-high hiking-type boots, and a muscle shirt that says Illinois on it, and his muscles look tightly twisted together where his arms attach to his shoulders. Kenny grins at Lynn, then dives onto the floor and tussles with his boy. "Tell Dad how bad you're being," Lynn tells Cameron.

"Whaddya doin'?" Kenny asks Cameron, who giggles.

"He's bein' trouble," Lynn says. She watches as Kenny rubs his nose against Cameron's round belly. "Is he staying at your house tonight?" she asks.

Over Cameron's laughter, Kenny says he's just gonna take him for a while.

"Oh," Lynn says, " 'cause my mom said something about your mom saying that she wants him."

Kenny loops Cameron under one arm and then loads him into a heavy-duty car seat and carries him that way out to the car. He straps Cam into the back seat, opens the front passenger door and crawls through to the driver's side.

Kenny and Lynn have never lived together. But Lynn says her baby is lucky to have a daddy who is involved. When Cameron was tinier, Kenny would come over every night and put him to sleep. Now, he takes the toddler to his parents' house two or three nights a week. "I have one friend who can like call her baby's daddy and say that her baby needs Pampers at like two o'clock in the afternoon," she says. "It might be eight o'clock at night before he comes."

But Kenny's not perfect either. "He gets on my nerves," she shrugs. She also knows she got on his nerves during her pregnancy. "I was not very nice to get along with actually. He told me I was mean when I was pregnant. Like if I wanted him to do something, and he didn't do it, I would get mean and I would yell at him and stuff. Just little things would make me mad.

"We have a weird relationship," Lynn explains. "Everyone's sorta like, *'Don't you guys go together?'* And I like say, 'No, we don't go together.' *'But you're together all the time?'* We are together all the time, and we do things with the baby together all the time. And we go out on dates, but we just like officially don't go together."

"I don't see myself getting married anytime soon," she says. "When we still were going together, he wanted . . . we wanted to get married."

The trailer seems bleak without Cameron. But now, she can talk. The first thing she volunteers about her own parents is that her mom is white and her dad, who died four years ago, was black. "When I was little I never got teased or anything like that," she says. "I think it's more now that so many black boys date white girls that mixed relationships have gotten a badder name. I just date black boys. I grew up in a black neighborhood, and so all my friends are black. If I have to pick, like when you take surveys and you can only mark one thing, then I usually mark black."

She says she was her daddy's little girl. She was named after him: He was Jesse; she is Jessica Lynn. He died of a stroke at age forty, she says because he wasn't taking his high blood pressure medicine. "I always wish I woulda told him I loved him," she says, "because that's not something that usually comes up in everyday conversation with your parents when you're a teenager."

Now, she's paying her $175 half of the rent and utilities from her father's Social Security payment to her, which expires in September when she turns eighteen. By then, she'll be attending a local community college with the help of government financial aid for single mothers. She's always liked school. She enjoyed reading *The Scarlet Letter* almost as much as she likes the romance novels she reads one of a week. She graduated from high school and her grades didn't even drop when she was pregnant her junior year, or a mother this year, and even though she was suspended once for fighting in the hall over some rumor she can't remember now. ("I just told that girl to keep my name out of her mouth. When she got smart with me, I just swung at her.") She hopes someday she'll be a real estate agent.

Kenny brings the baby home after a couple of hours. Lynn goes outside to meet him. Kenny runs a finger under her chin playfully. She says she dates other guys, went to the prom with another guy. But in her narrow bedroom there are only four pictures on the wall.

All of them show her with Kenny, except for one baby picture of Cam.

When she comes back in, she asks Cameron if he wants a drink. He runs to the couch and looks outside for puppies that are sometimes there, runs to the other couch, looks outside for the train. She smiles at him, proudly. She says she's been shocked by motherhood, by how it makes her feel. "It's kinda weird, I mean, because most teenagers are—and I am too—most teenagers are pretty shallow. And I used to be pretty shallow. It seems weird now that you think of somebody else before you think of yourself." Yes, sometimes she's disappointed when she can't go out with her friends because her mom or Kenny's parents can't babysit. But when she got $100 for graduation, she spent $30 of it on a pair of Air Jordan tennis shoes for her baby.

Cameron throws his juice and she threatens not to give it to him again unless he really drinks it. He fakes taking a drink only to hurl the juice away, spewing purple sweet stuff all over Lynn. Then, he surprises himself by unplugging the fan; he watches it spin down, making the connection. She slaps his hand, but he sneaks back over there. "The fan's hot," she tells him. "Hot," he repeats, heading for it again.

He hears a train. He bounds over to the window as it vibrates past. Lynn pulls Cam down from the window and into her lap. She holds him on her knees as though he were still the tiny infant that she says she never put down because she loved holding him so much. She rubs noses with him, and he giggles. He is still looking up at her. "I love you," she whispers. "I love you," she tells him. He giggles.

"I keep hoping he'll learn to say I love you," she says as Cameron squirms free, grabs his juice cup, and shakes it until it squirts a fountain of grape Juicy Juice.

"Condoms"

I've gotten into a lot of trouble for talking to teenagers about sex. A few angry parents and at least one newsletter have accused me of being obsessed by sex, journalistically at least. But can I please explain? First of all, most teenagers, if they're going to tell you the truth about it, will say that sex is one of their major obsessions. It's a hormonal thing. It's a bonding thing with their friends. It's all over movies and cable and magazines and CD-ROMs and billboards. Somebody just surveyed teenage girls about their top five concerns. The answers were stress, sexuality, sexual assault, suicide, and pregnancy. Well, three of the five are directly sex related, and I bet in most cases the stress is coming partly from sexual issues too.

This is no big nineties teenagers' revelation. Sex was important to teenagers in 1982 when I was one, and I'm sure it was in 1952. I remember when I was fifteen, I was desperate to sleep with someone. Who didn't matter. But I also remember it wasn't as much about sex drive. It was part of the same fixation that made me and Claire from down the street decapitate all our Barbies and then bike down to the park to choke through our first cigarettes, the very sophisticated-looking More Menthol 120s in the brown paper. It was about acting what I thought was grown up. But much more important, it was about seeming grown up to my friends. When people talk about peer pressure, there's this idea, I think, that kids sit around urging, "Oh, come on, Joey, try it (meaning marijuana, *intercourse, heroin, jumping off a bridge, whatever), you'll like it. When actually, I've never seen that kind of peer pressure. (I mentally keep putting "peer pressure" in quotes because it's a term I've never used). The pressure that adds to kids' wanting to try all these things is much more internally generated, I believe. It's anticipating and attempting to live up to whatever image you and your friends think you should have at this advanced age.*

Then in high school, I got lucky. I made out with this guy at a party, and the next day, he told some of his friends we'd slept together, also mentioning I was "good" (why, thank you). And after that every guy who walked me home from a dance didn't want to be the only one who hadn't slept with me. So I was a virgin with this wild reputation that I loved. But I still felt pressure with girl-friends who knew the truth. After graduation, my fellow-unintentional-virgin-friend Kathy and I made a plan to pick up two guys at a bar and just get it over with. We were under a little bit of a time constraint, since I was only staying at her house for a week, and it didn't work out right. Then, to make matters worse, she lost her virginity later that summer, and I didn't. So you can imagine why one month into my freshman year at college, in the dorm room of a guy who didn't know if this was my first time or not, while his three roommates continued drinking in the adjoining room, all I could think about was getting back to a phone to call Kathy and tell her I wasn't a virgin anymore. I was elated. That night, I started a list in my journal so I wouldn't forget any conquests.

The difference between the sex I had as a teenager and having sex now is, of course, that sex today is more dangerous. When I had intercourse that first time, we didn't use a condom. I'm not proud of that, and it's another of those cases where I'm definitely no role model. But because teenagers didn't know much about STDs, the concern centered around whether you were pregnant. Either way, there's no excuse. And I know any advice I give will be like one of those quintessential do-as-I-say-not-as-I-did lines adults use with teenagers when teenagers find out that, wait a minute, mom's telling me not to have sex before marriage, but my six-

*teenth birthday was just six months after their sixteenth wedding
anniversary, so wait a minute . . .*

*What's more important than my example is the information I've
tried to give kids, starting with the first issue of* Sassy *in March
1988: detailed facts, in straightforward language, that they can use
to make educated decisions. The premier issue had a cover line that
said, "Think you're ready for sex? Read this first" and an article
with a lot of information about birth control and AIDS prevention.
Well, after the controversy that caused, I had to go without even
mentioning the word* sex *in the magazine for two years, two vital
years in which I was reading in the newspapers about how quickly
AIDS was spreading among teenagers in particular and about how
teenage pregnancy rates were escalating even past statistics that
already put the United States way ahead of other industrialized
countries. I agreed with people who said it was the parents' job to
talk to their kids about sex. So why weren't they? A poll at the time
showed that most kids said they learned about sex from their
friends; second from the media (my guess is they must have meant
music videos and* Playboy, *obviously both more titillation than
information); a distant third said from school (though one high
schooler told me his bio teacher's idea of sex education was "one
day showing us pictures of apes"); and a way distant fourth learned
from parents.*

*It's easy to understand why parents find it difficult to talk about
sex with their kids. One sixteen-year-old guy told me his dad left
pamphlets under his bedroom door that looked like they were written in the fifties, with titles like* How to Talk to Your Teen About
Sex; *he and his friends got a good laugh out of them at school the
next day. I heard about a commune where the parents took groups
of kids down to the barn to watch the pigs make love. My parents,
both painters, drew detailed pictures for us when we were kids to
explain sex and reproduction. Then when I was sixteen my mom
asked me what I wanted to know about birth control while she
parked the car outside an electronics store. (Fortunately, I could
answer that my friend Kara and I had gone to the school clinic and*

gotten ourselves diaphragms, although it would be a year before either of us used them.) And when my dad was putting me on a bus to go see my college boyfriend, he said something like, I hope you guys are careful, which made me want to throw up, the idea my dad could even think of me in that context.

But at least all these parents were trying, which is totally laudable. Somebody has to do the talking. Information is essential, now more than ever because of AIDS (which I'm going to come back to later because there's so much to say on it) and because teenage birthrates have risen sharply since the mid-eighties. In Akron, Ohio, which has one of the highest teen pregnancy rates in the country, Misha tells me, "Every girl's goal is to be pregnant by fifteen. It's like life's a party, and it's her initiation to the party. If you don't, you're out of it." Two of Misha's fifteen-year-old friends got married this year when the girl got pregnant. "That's really good for them, 'cause they stayed part of the party scene, but they've got their baby," she says, not explaining that the couple lives with the boy's mother, who takes care of the baby for them a lot of the time. When I asked Misha whether she'd ever been pregnant, she said yeah, when she was fourteen, but that she'd had an abortion. "A lot of girls get abortions, too. It's just getting pregnant that's the thing. So you can say you did. You don't have to have the baby." Altogether, more than a million American teenage girls get pregnant every year and 500,000 have the babies. That's ten times the average number of teenage pregnancies in countries with mandatory sex education in their schools. These are girls whose bodies are still growing, who are not financially secure, whose chances of getting a good education are ridiculously low once they've got a kid to deal with.

All of this just makes it so clear to me that we need not only sex education in schools, but we need it taught in early grades. One teenage girl laughed when she told me that by the time her school bio teacher got to teach "human reproduction" in the ninth grade, four of the girls in her class already had babies. Also, as lots of teenagers have brought up with me, we ought to make contracep-

tives available in schools. Ahmad, who's a sophomore at Pinecrest High School in North Carolina, says,

And they need to be given to us free. The whole problem is the awkwardness factor. They're awkward to buy, plus who's got the money? It shouldn't be based on your age or what type of school you go to. I mean, kids know about sex and condoms from like age seven now. Plus they're awkward to bring up with girls, but if schools were giving them out, it would just be that much more common to have them on you and you know, if they were like an open condoned thing at school, it'd probably be easier to talk about when you really need to talk about them. At that big moment.

It's been a personal crusade of mine to work for sex education—and for abortion rights, especially for young women. A lot of clinics have been shut down, and there are fewer doctors who perform abortions, partly due to lack of funding, partly due to threats and harassment and now murders by antiabortion protesters. The people this hurts most are poor women who can't travel the distances often required to get to a clinic, and young women who in some states have to deal with parental consent laws that require teenagers to get their parents' consent—both parents. How many teenagers even know where both parents are and have good enough relationships with them to talk about this? Raise your hands. Or go before a judge. This is not the way to encourage communication between parents and teenagers. It just punishes the girls who already have abusive or uncommunicative parents.

But the point is, if kids had more information, it might never come to that. And parents are still my first, though old-fashioned, choice for who should provide it. What I tell people who ask about how to talk to their kids (or who ask me to do it for them) is first of all start discussing the basics three years before you think you need to. Kids are more accelerated sexually these days: The average age for girls to start having intercourse is fifteen and a half and for boys fifteen. And there's plenty of sexual stuff besides intercourse happening before, if you remember back to Amber's version of sex-as-baseball. Also, the number of partners they have is increasing. An average teenager sleeps with five people before he or she turns twenty. And they don't necessarily do it with the amount of consideration you might hope they'd give it, and their partner, beforehand. By the way, based on the teenagers I know, that whole Spur Posse one-point-per-girl tally system incident was much more shocking to adults than it was to them. It was hard for a lot of teenagers to see why the media made such a big deal out of these guys' attitudes toward sex, when they live with that all the time. One guy, when I asked what he thought of the whole thing, said, "I can't believe it. One of those guys only had sex with like 12 girls, and he got on Geraldo!"

So when you've picked your moment to talk to your kid, it's all right to start by just being up front that this is not comfortable for you either. Be cool about whatever questions they have or whatever shocking statements they make. Don't freak out if your kid says she might be gay or bi or that he has already had oral sex. Support her and be glad she feels she can confide in you because what you want to do is establish a mutual ease about talking about sex. The bad news is you can't just get by with one explanation about reproduction. It's an ongoing process; there are always new forms of birth control being developed, new diseases, and also new terminology and new media role models. Your kids may hear about these things way before you do, so they also need to feel they can bring questions about all of it to you. And if you don't have all the answers, just say that and then offer to find them. Try Planned Parenthood or a local organization. That's all you can do.

It's been said a million times, but it's true that nobody else is going to be there in that moment to make the decision for them. They're going to decide who to have sex with, when, and whether or not to use a condom. You can hope whatever religious and ethical values they've picked up from you and others up until now are strong. And that they've also picked up some good sense. But all *you can really do is give them the information they need to make their own decisions. It could save them from having to make another really difficult choice. It could also save their lives.*

November 9, 1980

Is this why they call it "losing it"?
Sometimes I see things happening that are not me at all
I lose my voice even.
Like being on trial and expected to enjoy yourself and
expected to want the sentence, and meanwhile not being
able to differentiate between jail and the free world. But it
can be the opposite. When something is so physical and tan-
gible, it can run even deeper on the less tangible plane. The
thing that distresses me most is the amount by which I am
controlled by other people, for if it hadn't been for others'
opinions of me, I wouldn't have been so eager. Not that peo-
ple make you, but that I make myself based on what I think
they think. From now on, no to saying yes because it
upholds my image of me. And don't dare think of yourself
as a concept.
I miss my self.
It is something or I would not always feel this way the next
    day,
ex post facto.
Truth or consequences.

WHAT DARITH JAMES LEARNED ABOUT AIDS

In searching for a topic for my sophomore English term paper, I decided to choose something that I felt was important. I chose to write about sexually active teenagers and sexually transmitted diseases. My choice was based on my own age and on my opinion that there isn't enough emphasis on educating teenagers about sex and everything that comes with it.

I was sixteen when I wrote the paper and scared by the actions of some of my own friends. Like most teenagers, a lot of the time when they'd talk of sex it was sex that was acted upon because of desires and lust. So it was done frequently without protection. I heard this often from friends: They slept with whomever just because he/she was good-looking, but they didn't use protection because they didn't feel they needed it or it took away from the moment. I knew people who had slept with someone and then stayed awake at night contemplating whether they should get an AIDS test. One of my friends came to me upset because he had slept with a girl who had a reputation for having sex with a lot of guys. My friend really regretted his actions and wanted me to take him to the testing center in a nearby town. This made me wonder how educated we are about AIDS.

I have grown up in a family where strong morals and values are taught. The carelessness of teenagers about sex always surprised me. I never understood how friends, acquaintances, or anyone else could ignore the consequences of having sex. Then, a few years ago, one of my cousins died. We were not close and had probably only seen each other at a few family gatherings, but he was part of my family. His death had an impact on me and on this paper and on the way I view sex. My cousin died of AIDS.

The facts in this paper are scary, but they are true and can hopefully be a reminder to everyone. Whether it be from this paper or from some other resource, I hope teenagers can learn the importance of being educated on all the aspects of having sex.

SEXUALLY ACTIVE TEENAGERS AND BIRTH CONTROL

Darith James
Composition
Term Paper

THESIS

No form of birth control is 100 percent effective, but 52 percent of all teenagers are sexually active, and while 65 percent (females) and 55 percent (males) rely on different forms of contraceptives for protection, another 28 percent don't use any protection at all. These are the facts and we as a society should put all ignorance aside so that we may face them. "We have to put aside our endless arguments about what we wish adolescents would do and instead deal with what they are doing." (Wigfall Williams p. 326). The 90's have become host to a new generation. A generation that is being raised in a society where the media and their peers have taught them to accept sex and has exposed them at an early age. This exposure has led to a much more sexually active generation. No matter who teaches kids and whether they teach abstinence or safe sex and no matter where they have sex or why they choose to, all individuals deserve the right to make their own educated decision and the right to be protected.

CONTRACEPTIVES

Birth control is a term that includes all methods used to regulate or prevent the birth of children. One of the most widely used forms of birth control is the condom. The condom is the oldest and most commonly used method. There are many other forms of birth control. Some forms are more dangerous for teens than others and some are more effective than others. Teenagers should be aware of all the options of birth control. They should also know which methods are best for them.

A condom is a thin sheath worn over the penis. Condoms provide a mechanical barrier which prevents direct contact with semen, genital discharge, genital lesions, and infectious secretions. Condoms are 90 percent effective used alone (when used consistently and correctly).

Forty-seven percent of females and 55 percent of males report using condoms the first time that they have intercourse. A recent study shows that only 31 percent of sexually active teens always use condoms, 32 percent said sometimes, and 37 percent said they never use condoms.

When properly used, latex condoms are the most effective method for preventing infection with HIV and other STDs. Latex condoms are a continuous, impervious barrier that can be used with barriers such as dental or rubber dams, lubricants or non-oxynol 9. Latex condoms can protect against gonorrhea, ureaplasma infection, herpes simplex virus infection and also HIV.

Skin condoms have small pores which can allow the passage of HIV. Condom failure is due to no use, incorrect use, breakage, or leakage. The typical failure rate, as a contraceptive, is 10–20 percent. Some of this failure is due to incorrect use. Breakage and slippage of a condom can be avoided with proper use. Oil-based lubricants can weaken the latex. Prelubed condoms do last longer, but all condoms should be kept away from heat to decrease the risk of them cracking. Manufacturing defects are quite uncommon. Each condom is individually tested for pinholes or areas of thinning. Condoms have no side effects or health hazards.

Another form of commonly used contraception is the birth control pill. The pill is 99 percent effective against pregnancy, when taken correctly. The pill copies the effects of being pregnant by keeping the levels of estrogen and progesterone high. This in turn tells the ovaries not to produce ripe eggs. The sperm will not be able to find any eggs to fertilize in the fallopian tubes.

There are many down sides to being on the pill. Being on the pill can cause tender breasts, nausea feeling, tiredness, water retention, headaches, depression, vitamin and mineral deficiencies. Long time use of the pill can cause blood clots, epilepsy, heart attacks, sterility, liver problems, and gall bladder disease. Combined with heavy smoking, the pill can cause cancer. The pill does not provide any protection against STDs and is not recommended for teenagers.

Other kinds of birth control are the diaphragm, foam, sponge, cervical cap, IUD, and natural birth control.

Abstinence is the only 100 percent effective method against pregnancy and STDs. A common misconception of today is that abstinence means abstaining from any sexual activity. In actuality, the term abstinence means "no intercourse."

American teenagers today who choose to have sex should also have the knowledge to practice safe sex. While there are no 100 percent risk-free ways to have sex, if adolescents are able to arm themselves against pregnancy, STDs and AIDS, they will be much better off.

HEALTH RISKS

Choosing to be sexually active automatically puts you and your partner(s) at risk for AIDS, STDs, and pregnancy. If not treated, some STDs can be deadly and AIDS is almost certainly fatal. Despite this knowledge the rate for AIDS, STDs, and pregnancies among teenagers continues to rise.

Three quarters of all unintended adolescent pregnancies are a result of no contraception being used. Teenagers are more likely to have difficult pregnancies and deliveries. Along with that comes the startling fact that girls who become pregnant try to commit suicide seven times more than all other girls. Becoming pregnant can hamper a girl's life forever, especially when less than half the girls who become pregnant finish high school.

The figure of one million teenagers becoming pregnant each year is minimal when compared with the two and a half million teenagers that become infected with a sexually transmitted disease each year. In 1990 alone, three million teens were infected with an STD. One in every four teens will have an STD before graduating high school. These frightening statistics could be drastically reduced by sexually active adolescents consistently and correctly protecting themselves.

Gonorrhea, syphilis, chlamydia, and herpes have reached epidemic levels for teens. Syphilis and gonorrhea have increased 300 percent since 1956. From 1960–1988, gonorrhea has increased 170 percent for people ages 15–19 years old. At this time, the most prevalent STD is chlamydia.

Chlamydia infects four million people each year. It infects one in every seven girls and one in every ten boys (each year). Chlamydia is a disease that accounts for 20–40 percent of all female infertility. About 75 percent of the people who contract this disease will not have symptoms and may not know they have it for years.

Two of the most harmful STDs are hepatitis and syphilis. Hepatitis can infect a person's liver and do serious damage. Syphilis, if not treated, can lead to death. The most deadly disease of all is AIDS.

AIDS is a sexually transmitted disease that can kill you. AIDS destroys your immune system, leaving you with no

power to fight off even a common cold. It is caused by the
virus HIV, a virus that can live in your body without visible
symptoms for years. Everyone who is sexually active is at
risk for AIDS and there is no cure.

Over one fifth of the people with AIDS are in their 20's. 1.2
percent of the AIDS population is made up by adolescents, but
this mere percentage doubles every fourteen months. In February of 1991, there were 659 reported AIDS cases of adolescents ages 13–19 years old. In 1992, the estimated HIV
infection for teens was one in every one hundred adolescents.

Regardless of the fact that teens are sexually active and that
it should be their responsibility to protect themselves, we as a
society, [including] school and parents, should work together
to prevent these deaths and unwanted children. . . .

CONCLUSION

Young people, as they pass through puberty, will begin to
explore the sexual part of their lives and relationships.
Teenagers are having sex and all ignorance needs to be set
aside in order to prevent unwanted pregnancies and to prevent the deaths of teens. There are many safe and effective
methods of birth control. The only way that contraceptives are
reliable is if they are used consistently and correctly. The only
method that is 100 percent failure-free is abstinence. However, simply preaching abstinence to adolescents is unfair.
They need to be well-educated in all areas involving sexuality.
The education that teenagers receive is imperative. Teens
should already know the basic facts about sex by the time
they reach high school. Studies have proven that sex education is effective in increasing the knowledge and understanding of sexuality issues. Adolescents should also be knowledge-
able enough that they are able to arm themselves against
peer pressure. Teens have the right to make their own decisions and these choices should be made regardless of what
their peers are doing. In this day and age, it is necessary that

adolescents are able to protect themselves against pregnancies, diseases, and infections. With the number of teenage
pregnancies, cases of STDs, and AIDS climbing each year, we
as a society need to work at putting an end to these epi-
demics. The United States Constitution states the legalization of
minors purchasing contraception. Teens have the right legally
but they need the education to go along with it. "Adolescents
are going to make the decision to have sex or not have sex,
whether you like it or not." (Wigfall Williams, p. 39). No matter who teaches kids and whether they teach abstinence or
safe sex, and no matter where they have sex or why they
choose to, all individuals deserve the right to make their own
educated decision and the right to be protected.

JON'S OWN APARTMENT

"*I* was a good boy."

Jon is talking about growing up in an affluent Dallas suburb. "I wasn't a good boy gradewise, but I was a good boy. I didn't go out late at night. I was always at home. I was the doting child, goddammit. *I ran the area babysitting service,"* he says.

"How many sixteen-year-olds do you know who have a brand-new Mercedes convertible?"

* * *

Jon is now eighteen, living alone in a single room, a third floor walkup. He has a mattress on the floor, no sheets. He has a foam couch, an exercise bicycle, and caller ID on his telephone. Today a friend got him in free to a swimming pool, and Jon snagged a roll of toilet paper from the men's room. So now he has one roll of toilet paper.

He is sprawled out on the mattress ticking, wearing loose faded jeans and a white shirt. He has brassy blond hair that used to be "Madonna blond" and then "pretty red" and then "strawberry blond." He says, "It was darker this morning, but then I went swimming." He is trendy lean with long, defined muscles, a few hickies on his neck, and fierce amber eyes. He turns over on the bed and stares up at the ceiling.

His story starts at the dinner table, Thanksgiving Day, 1991. Jon is sixteen. His mother gives thanks, then his father, his brother, his grandfather. Jon goes last. He says: "Thanks for the car, the CD player, giving me parents who will love and understand me when I tell them I'm gay, the great house, all the great friends, rubadub-dubdub, thanks for the grub. Yea, Lord. Let's eat."

Dead silence.

Finally, his grandfather says, "Pass the corn."

* * *

In his Dallas apartment, Jon calls Pizza Hut to deliver two six-packs—one of Crystal Pepsi, one of Mountain Dew—and two Big Foot pizzas, one pineapple, one pepperoni. It's sort of like grocery shopping to him; he'll eat tonight and keep the leftovers in the refrigerator. He's already made out a check to Pizza Hut for $30. It's his last check, almost his last money.

* * *

At age fifteen, Jon was used to dancing alone in his room. Then, he made "instant eye contact" with a male flight attendant on a family vacation. "I noticed blond hair done up like Morrissey you know, sideburns, very 90210 Beverly Hills," Jon recalls. "I was like, yummy, *very* pretty boyish. He kept on serving me food. He kept on *dropp*ing things in my lap.

"So *he took me there*. I went to the bathroom, and he took the hint, and he followed, and *off we went. Sex,* honey."

After that, Jon says: "I was *un*stoppable. I got off that plane, I'm like *Wahwah*. Had sex in the bathroom on the airport on our way home. I got home, and I had sex with *every*thing. I plugged into those free phone sex lines. Started meeting people, older men, not *old* older men, just older men between twenty-five and thirty-five usually. Meet them in back of the supermarket, like alleys, go home with them sometimes. I was going through my I-am-alone-there-fore-I'll-be-a-slut mode."

How was he keeping it from his parents?

"I tell my parents, I'm going to downtown Dallas to be artsy. I got real artsy," he says archly. "I was like Amy Fisher, leading two double lives." He pauses and looks at the bare wall by the door. "That's what I need," he says. "I need a really big picture of Amy Fisher, right there," he points. "I dig her so much. Uh *huh*. Amy Fisher is my hero, god*dam*mit. She had the balls to do what very few seventeen-year-old girls would do. She stood up to Joey Buttafuoco."

* * *

Jon says he was still way in the closet at age sixteen when he was at the mall one day, and his eyes met another boy's. They followed each other down the corridors, flirted in the bathroom. "God, it was obvious," Jon says. It was the first time he had met another gay teenager. The two became friends, helped each other out of the closet.

Jon first came out at high school, which he describes as the kind of school that makes Gap have "lines out the door," the kind of school where a diversity task force consists of "three cheerleaders, an Italian, and a Jew." It was the beginning of his junior year ("and the beginning of the end of my junior year"). It was at a mandatory all-school assembly on discrimination. "They had every minority represented except gays," Jon says. "So I went up there and grabbed the microphone away from my principal and said, *I have one thing to say*. And *off* I went on my tangent. So I outed myself in front of two thousand people in one fell swoop.

"After I walked off the stage, I was like, *Good-Ness* what have I *done?*

"I kinda picked up from a walk to a real quick jog and then lost control in the coming-out process. Taking the mike, I was still kinda in control there, but it got to the point where I could not control what people were thinking or saying type thing. And my image was getting out of hand, to where I was no longer Jon; I was just that gay guy, what's his name? I hated that."

* * *

Then came Thanksgiving. That night after dinner, he sat down with his parents—his father, an aeronautics expert, and his mother, who Jon describes as "shopping and bitching" for a living.

It wasn't like it was the first time Jon had made it clear to his parents. They later admitted that he had started coming out at age two, then at four, six, eight. But his parents never acknowledged it, even though as a little boy he openly got crushes on the teenage boys who came with their parents for neighborhood barbecues.

This was the first time they were acknowledging it. "At first, it started out very civil, very, *okay, let's go from here,"* Jon says. "Then my mother cried and cried and my father turned and said 'Shut up, woman.'

"And I said, 'Oh, good.' I said, *'Finally.* I've been dying to say that to her for years.'"

Anyway, his parents weren't the answer to his Thanksgiving prayers. He remembers: "My mother wouldn't let me touch her for like three days afterwards," he says. And instead of being supportive, his parents sent him to priests to "cure" him. "The priests were all gay," Jon says. "They told me to ignore my parents." He snorts, "You try."

Things only got worse. At school, he was being harassed. "Don't make me take you there," he says with the exaggerated feyness he uses whenever he's talking about the really painful things. "I had crosses burned on my front lawn. I couldn't walk through the hall-way. I would wait till class was like . . . the bell would ring for the classes to end and I would wait the four minutes passing period and when the late bell rang, I would get up and leave when the hallways were all but empty. So I'd always be like four minutes late to a class. I'd always carry like all my books for the day with me so I wouldn't have to go back to my locker where I was a sitting target. I never graduated, I never *got* to graduate."

Then he really lost control: "I had like run away and blahblah-blah and stuff like that. I had bought a stolen car, I had been in jail. I wasn't going to school because you can't go to a school where you're harassed. It just wasn't workin'. The support was just not happenin' at home.

"I bought a stolen car, right down the street here. I had papers and stuff, but for a sixteen-year-old boy from the 'burbs, it was, 'Sounds like a good deal to me, $100 bucks for a car? Sure.' It was a little car, early eighties, and so off I was cruisin' in this thing. I was pulled over, showed 'em all the papers, and they said, 'This car's stolen.' And I said, 'No it's not, I paid money for it.' And so first they put me in like a group home cause they thought *Good-ness* this is obviously a mistake. And my parents wouldn't pick me up so I ran from that.

"I ran away several times, and I was eventually put into a detention center. It's gangs, and it's juvenile hall basically. I was there for the first time about two months. My parents refused to post bond or anything, even when [the authorities] brought the bond down to nothing, where my parents just had to *sign* me out. They still wouldn't. I was like, 'Oh.' I sat there. And then my parents admitted me to a psych hospital. For a month, at eight hundred dollars a day, and now they're trying to take the money out of my trust fund. You know, this is cute.

"The doctor calls my mother [from the psych hospital] one day with me sitting there and says, 'Your son is gay. He is not crazy. Come and pick him up.'

"So I went from jail to psych hospital to freedom and then I came home one day and the door was locked."

He was ten minutes late for curfew. But the alarm system was on alert. "There was a cute little note on the door from my parents that said, *'Your faggot ass is late. Your stuff's by the back door. Social services number is blah blah. Go to hell.'* "

He went to the "streets" and often stayed with older men he slept with. He began to sell his body for $200 to $300 a night, though a pimp took 70 percent of the money he earned. "I played really stupid 'cause to me it was money, and I was living the gay scene." After two months, he called his parents. He had missed a court hearing, so there was a warrant out for his arrest. "So my parents were like, 'Well, come home, you can take a shower, clean up, eat, then we'll turn you in.' "

"I took a shower. [My parents] left to go to the pool down the street, and I took their car and all my stuff and *off* I went, and I was arrested on July 9th for grand theft auto *again* 'cause I got in a very bad wreck with the car. There was no way I could escape. Drunk driver plowed into the back of me, totally destroying that car. Everything was in the car. Everything." Now he was homeless and most everything he owned was destroyed.

After that, Jon lived in a couple of foster homes "with pregnant 13-year-olds" and finally got involved with a gay and lesbian community center in Dallas, where he began to crusade for gay youth by heading fundraisers and talking to city leaders. He began spending nearly every day at the center, joining committees, talking in schools, giving interviews to reporters. He became a nanny for a lesbian couple's little boy. He found himself the one-room apartment. He also found a couple of lawyers, who defended him in lawsuits against his parents, and then sent the bill to them.

His mother sued over the car that he wrecked. She wanted $3,000 for the damage and $10,000 for something else that Jon says he can't remember. He can remember the day in court, though. He says: "My lawyers told me that she might do this, not to be surprised, but I was shocked: *She dressed like a bum.* It was like she hadn't showered. She looked all scraggly. 'Cause they were after money.

"She hopped in the BMW and drove away right afterward though."

Jon lost and was ordered to pay $3,000 damages. He was so distraught over the judgment that his best friend had to "carry me out in hysterics."

"I had a public appearance that night," he says. "It was a benefit concert. We were putting on a little skit, like the new *Leave It to Beaver* with two moms and a drag queen as a son, and Wally had to come out as being heterosexual. And I got up there, and I did my thing, and I got off and I said, *'I'm going home, Goodbye.'* I ended up going to a dance club and getting very drunk, but it's almost like,

Good God, it's amazing that you got up there and did that and just fooled like all those people. They thought you were just a cute little happy homosexual youth."

In fact, it was a worse time in his life than anyone knew. See, losing in court came as a "double whammy." He had just tested HIV positive. His first test a few months earlier had come back negative. But this one was positive. "I was like, Fuck this life," he says.

Jon didn't tell his parents about testing positive. "They read it in the paper," he says. "I did an interview. One of my brother's friends' brother read it. So my brother found out, then my mother found out. She went out and bought the paper. It was *most irritating,* and she gave me this big old spiel: 'We *warned* you about this. *How typical. BAH bah bah.'* It was like *Good-Ness.* 'How typical,' yeah. She said, 'All you guys get it.' So finally, I said, 'Listen, woman.' I said, 'This is no time for you and *dedudedu.'* I said, I don't need this. Either you're supportive, or you step aside permanently.'

"Shut her up real fast."

Jon thinks about his parents a lot. He says he wonders why his mother doesn't look at him and see the little boy he was. But then when he looks at her, he doesn't see the mom who brought him up, and says his dad is not the same either: "Those months when we were battling took years out of both of us. I look at my parents now, they are so old, so old, for their age. They are so old. My father has a full head of gray hair. He had lost weight but he's gained the weight back and looks like hell. They've almost, I kinda look at them as like Bette Davises, they've locked themselves up in the house, up in their separate lives."

* * *

Jon is antsy about his pizza. Where the hell is it? The phone rings. He looks at the caller ID then answers by saying, "You're at a pay phone aren't you?"

It's the delivery boy. It turns out central dispatch gave the order to the wrong restaurant. He's trying to deliver the pizza in the another part of town. "I'm one ill bitch," Jon says, rolling his eyes, as he dials the central pizza switchboard. The phone is ringing. He says, "You are about to see a gay youth throw attitude." Someone answers. He throws attitude.

* * *

Jon puts in a RuPaul CD. He turns it up almost all the way as he flips through the clothes in his closet. He's going out to a dance club. "Now the dilemma that a fag faces," he says through stagily gritted teeth. "What to wear?" He pulls out his old Madonna jacket, which he wore in London when he went backstage to see Madonna dance on a table in boxers and a bra. "What was it with gay men and Madonna?" he asks.

Stooping to look at the shoes lined up on the closet floor, he considers the black Doc Martens he was wearing the night his parents kicked him out. He wishes he hadn't loaned out the pink glitter pair. He pulls out the T-shirt he wore last time he had to meet with his dad to ask for money. It says, I Fuck to Come, not Conceive.

Jon strikes a pose and announces: "What I think I'll wear tonight is cutoffs and a big belt and my boots and my fuck-to-come T-shirt and my leather jacket. And my hat backwards, my baseball cap. Big Q, queer."

* * *

The pizza gets here finally. The guy gives it to him free because they were so late. Jon sits on the floor next to a cardboard box filled with dozens of condoms and shoves a slice of pineapple in his mouth.

Last Wednesday, he and his best friend who is twenty and a lesbian, distributed 500 condoms at a local dance club. A newspaper photographer was with them. She's doing a story on Jon, who in the last five months has become so involved with the gay and lesbian community center that he calls its youth director Mother. At a recent schoolboard meeting, he screamed out: "We are killing ourselves in our high schools, gay youth, and you're doing absolutely nothing to stop it." It made the papers. He has a position on the

Mayor's commission on youth, representing gay kids. He and a friend started a support group for HIV-positive kids. Jon says teenagers are invisible even within the gay community because they can't even go to the bars without a fake ID. Jon is working on visibility.

He likes the idea that he may reach kids who are as lost as he was. He may save them from their "slut phase," before they have slept with five hundred men, as he calculates he has, and before they test positive. "I have yet to meet one teenager, one gay teenager, who is either not in his slut period or has not gone through it," Jon says. "I have met gay virgins. I sit them down and tell them a tale, and they're like, I'm never having sex. I try to tell them I'm not saying that, I'm just saying, Chill. Don't do it right away."

It's given his life meaning, he says, his work at the community center. It gives him something to counteract his mother's accusations when she calls to blame him for the fact that she and his father are separating. "My father and my mother say, 'Look what you've put us through, dededede,' " Jon says. "They obviously don't notice that I lived on the streets and I sold my body at one point, so it was not a picnic for me neither. It's not like I woke up one morning and said, 'Let's give up everything I have, a cute preppie little house out here, a surefire education just 'cause of the school I'm going to, a Mercedes convertible.' "

Jon says solemnly: "Like if I lost the center or lost the public recognition that I get—it's nice, I get recognized at the mall and stuff, that's really neat—if I ever lost that, I think I would just lose *it.*"

Jon takes off his shirt and jeans to put on what he hopes will add up to "that haphazard but put together look." He starts with the T-shirt. He cinches his cutoffs with a big buckled belt. Then rolls the shorts up until they can't go any farther. He considers wearing the jacket that his boyfriend Steve left in his apartment, but goes back to the leather instead.

"My boyfriend," he says, giggling. "It still feels good to say that I have one." Steve is the first boyfriend who was willing to stick around after Jon confided that he was HIV positive. Last night, they had sex for the first time. Jon's still a little itchy from it because beforehand Steve shaved him *down there.*

Steve is not Jon's ideal type. For one thing, he doesn't wear a "magnum-size condom," as Jon says he does. "Steve is old with a job," Jon says. "He's not rich. He drives a cheap car. But he's my Steve. I wish he were rich, then he'd be my Steve forever."

* * *

Jon is dressed and ready. He stomps one combat boot and says, "Girl, we're off like a prom dress."

Instead of going straight to the club, he insists on being driven through a nearby park so he can point out where gay kids who can't get fake IDs go. They are dancing in the backs of pickup trucks. Men in cars are cruising them. "They're much older," Jon says of the men, whom he remembers from the days when he was living off prostitution. "I did some great-great-grandfather who was plugged into a respirator in the backseat."

As he turns out of the park, Jon spots a long black car. He says, "There's my pimp."

* * *

Jon gets into the club with his fake ID. It's early, only about nine p.m., for the club to be really "jumping," but Jon stakes out a back table and watches the "earlybirds": *"Oooh,"* he groans as one man strolls by, "I was with her the night I met Steve." A guy in khakis walks by. "OOooh, yummy," Jon says with an exaggerated purring sound.

As he waits for the place to start "jumping," he talks about how he was almost a father once. He and a lesbian friend experimented sexually. She got pregnant and came out to her mother as they were discussing why she wanted an abortion. Jon went with her to the clinic. "We crossed the picket line, and she exercised her choice," he recalls in an even, serious voice. "I heard the baby hit the pan, and I just lost it. I am Catholic. I go to church every Sunday; it's just the queer one. And I've always been pro-life. Still am."

His eyes swivel like a beam among the shifting cliques of men while he confesses: "I regret [the abortion] sometimes. Especially now because I can never have my own biological child. And I always wanted to."

It is the first time all day that he has spoken of any sadness about having the AIDS virus. He will talk about just about anything else easily. Ask him about shaving his crotch, fine. Ask him about getting a blow job in the men's room at a night club, fine. Ask him about what he feels about being eighteen and HIV positive, nothing, except that he has less sex. "It's not free-flowing anymore. It's murder."

But now he goes on to say that he went to the Gay March on Washington in 1993. He and his best friend took a patch to the AIDS quilt. They stayed on the quilt for five hours, crying and holding each other. Somebody from the community center had to pick Jon up and carry him away.

* * *

The music pounds harder. "Oh, Madonna," he says. Colored dots swim over the crowd on the dance floor. "I've gotta cruise," he calls over his shoulder as he begins to dance freely, melding into the writhing crowd. Dancing anything but alone.

"Absolut Queer"

I was worried about Jon being the only kid in the book we know of who is HIV positive because he's also the only openly gay kid. I definitely don't want to give fuel to any of the groups who have used that link for their own propaganda. But Jon doesn't stand for all gay teenagers. In fact, it's not gay teenagers, but heterosexual ones who are the fastest growing AIDS risk group now. And I think Jon explains well the reason it was still so difficult to find gay teenagers who could be totally open in this book. One in 10 is the regularly agreed upon number of kids who are gay, lesbian, or bi. But that doesn't mean we found anywhere near that percentage who felt they could safely cooperate with us. Discrimination is something gay and lesbian teenagers live with to one degree or another every day, which makes it really hard to come out. It also makes the ones who have come out not so eager to make themselves vulnerable to attacks by talking about it in a book. Also, a lot of teenagers don't realize they're gay yet or aren't sure. Even kids who are fairly solid in their sense of who they are often wait until they get to college to come out. "It just seemed safer," this nineteen-year-old told me. "You know, away from mom and dad and the whole thing. Then I dealt with telling them later, after all my friends at school already knew."

As I don't need to tell you again, talking to teenagers about sex is difficult. It's not any easier for them. And probably one of the hardest things a kid will ever have to tell you is that they are gay or *bisexual. But since the goal is for them to tell you, here's what I'd say to make it easier on them (by the way, this would be my policy whether your kids are gay, straight, or bisexual): Show them you're open-minded. Don't deride celebrities for being gay or presumed gay. Talk in a positive way about gay friends you have or gay couples you know or have heard of. Don't stereotype people who aren't heterosexual by saying things like, "Michael's mom shouldn't give him dolls/dance lessons/your favorite stereotypically feminine product or activity here, or he'll turn out to be gay." Don't bug your daughter/son about a lack of boyfriends/girlfriends. And just let them tell you when they tell you.*

When they tell you, first of all know how hard that was for them. Thank them for telling you. Thank them again. Then if you give them any advice, I'd say what my friend's mom told him when he came out to her: That having love with another person and the quality of your relationships are the most important things. Explain that there are problems in all relationships, but being gay does have some different problems that come along with it, mostly due to society's continuing problems in embracing it.

That's also, I think, the major reason why 30 percent of teen suicides every year are gay teenagers and why 80 percent report severe problems with isolation. But it doesn't have to turn into a tragedy. If you're gay and getting teased about it, there are schools you can go to that are specifically geared toward gay teenagers. I know there's the Harvey Milk School in New York, one in San Francisco and one in Boston and other cities. Chances are you don't live in a place with such a school, but there are other schools that do seem to be at least more open-minded toward gay students and more vigilant about teaching tolerance in general. Friends Schools, like the one I went to in North Carolina, seem really good to me in terms of this. These are not public schools, unfortunately, so unless you can afford it or can get a scholarship, you may still be stuck trying to teach tolerance yourself to other kids and your teachers. If so, the best way is just to be your best self. But that won't always work. I know one kid whose parents kept telling her,

"It's the other kids' problems that they can't deal with you being gay." Ultimately, she ran away because no matter whose problem it was, it felt like hers. Now she's back home and out of junior high and into high school, where she's found accepting friends. However, lots of kids like her don't make it home again. Twenty-eight percent of gay teenagers are runaways.

Even the most supportive parents often don't know how to help when their kids are being harassed. Because being gay is still such a taboo in most places, many parents feel alone with this problem. Some ideas for where you can go for support: Join P-FLAG. Contact the Hetrick-Martin Institute in New York City or elsewhere around the country for facts. Also, inform yourselves about the issues facing gays and lesbians now and be able to inform others who make uneducated comments. Most of all, know that having a child who's gay or bisexual has nothing to do with either parent having "done something wrong." Because first of all, it's not wrong.

Fortunately, some things are finally changing for gay, lesbian, and bisexual teenagers. Because of people like Jon who will get out and crusade for visibility and because of more community centers that are sponsoring support groups for kids, more teenagers are able to be open about their sexuality and just lead their lives. Massachusetts recently became the first state to pass a law prohibiting public schools from discriminating against students because of their sexual orientation. A school system in Westchester County just enacted the same rule, which essentially gives students more protection at school than is provided under either state or federal law. And in Westchester there was virtually no opposition to it.

Meanwhile, more and more advertisers are targeting gay consumers. A whole category of magazines are now aimed at a gay audience, which makes me realize how much things have changed in the last six years since Sassy *did a story profiling two young gay couples. Right after that issue came out (not a pun), in July 1988, we were the target of a fundamentalist religious group's boycott, at least partly fueled by that piece, and subsequently lost most of our major advertisers and were pulled from about a third of news-*

stands. Ironically, I just heard from a friend, who knows the two guys in the story, that they weren't even a couple. But no one they knew who was in a young gay couple at the time was willing to be photographed and even though these two were actually just friends, they thought the mainstream exposure was something the gay community shouldn't lose. So it was great to see this year, along with a newspaper story about the guys in Massachusetts who were allowed to go to their prom together, a photo of the two of them with their quote as the caption: "We are not paid actors. We are real homosexuals."

It was also good to learn that in a survey of high schoolers in Massachusetts, 64 percent of all students condemned discrimination against homosexuals. And I keep hearing from gay teenagers that it's become trendier than ever to pretend to be gay or bisexual. (I admit my friend and I did our share of this in high school, thinking we were very cutting edge.) I recently talked to an eighteen-year-old gay support group leader who told me, "A lot of kids get a thrill out of saying they're bisexual. It may just be an experimental thing, but it's better than when the big thing was to slam somebody by calling them a faggot."

Today there are computer networks where gay and lesbian kids sign on to talk about their experiences and post e-mail personal ads. In New York and other cities, high schools have been designed with their needs in mind. Public schools send delegations of students to Gay Pride parades in their cities. I see more and more parents who are so supportive of their gay teenagers but for those kids who don't have that, at least there are now more places to turn. Support groups for gay, lesbian, and bisexual youth are being started across the country, in some smaller towns along with cities (generally listed in the Yellow Pages under Social and Health Services).

But maybe the best measure of how things are starting to change is what we heard when we asked gay kids around the country about their lives, and more than one said, "I don't know if you wanna hear about me. My life is boring." I'm thinking, boring sounds good.

WHY CHANA ABEHSERA DOESN'T WEAR GAP JEANS

*C*hana's brown eyes widen. She can't *believe* it. Her friend Robin is sending her eye signals from across the Grill Express kosher restaurant on Los Angeles's Fairfax Avenue. Even though Chana has her back to the door, she can tell just by looking at Robin's face that HE has just walked in. Chana can't help it; she looks over her shoulder to see for herself. Yes, there HE is, a thirty-something man with a beard and a hat. He nods in greeting, and she turns around and giggles into her plate of eggs, French fries, and Israeli salad.

"He proposed to me," she whispers.

The man seats himself directly behind Chana, where their eyes will have no chance of meeting and making them feel more uncomfortable than they already do.

"He is a friend of my father's," Chana says. Her father, Meir Michel Abehsera, is a famous inspirational author and an expert on macrobiotics, descended from the great Sephardic rabbi, Baba Sali. Meir Abehsera's book, *The Possible Man,* is popular among not only Hasidic Jews, but also among Presbyterians and Catholics and Buddhists. Chana says that HE was infatuated with her father's teachings and so asked to marry his teacher's daughter. Her father declined. "There were like two other offers for me," Chana says. "But like my father said, no. He wants me to grow up more, be more in my mind and everything."

Chana is beautiful. But when she was eleven years old, she was hit by a car. Her face was blue and unrecognizable to her family.

She was unconscious for two hours. The doctors told her parents the only hope for repairing the damage was extensive plastic surgery. But the Lubavitcher rebbe had given Chana's mother a blessing two weeks before in which he said something good would come of something bad. And as Chana lay waiting for surgery, the doctors came in calling, Good news, good news. *"Good news?* I'm lying there like half dead," Chana says. "My jaw was like totally deformed. I couldn't speak, couldn't eat. He told me, 'You're not gonna need plastic surgery. This whole thing has healed, like overnight.' "

Now, her skin is perfectly smooth. She also has masses of walnut curls and brown eyes that laugh even more often than she does. Today, in late July, she is wearing a long sleeve white shirt and a wrap-around bleached-indigo jean skirt (new from the Gap) with bright white canvas sneakers. She has hoops in her ears and clear polish on her nails. She has just arrived in L.A. to help one of her married sisters through her fourth pregnancy. As members of L.A.'s orthodox Jewish community come and go in the crowded restaurant, Chana greets friends she hasn't seen since her last visit. *"Chana,"* they say enthusiastically when they see her. "Chana, what a *surprise.* How nice!"

*   *   *

Chana (pronounced almost like Hannah only with a harder H, as in chutzpah) is a "religious girl." She lives in the tradition that survived from the Jewish shtetls of 17th-century Eastern Europe, survived because of the devotedly orthodox Hasidic movement. Still, she rarely forgets that she is also living in the world of Boyz II Men, Gap jeans, raves, and Snapple Kiwi-Strawberry cocktails.

She attends a Hasidic school for girls in Crown Heights, Brooklyn. She respects and loves the late Lubavitcher rebbe who blessed his people from a brownstone on Eastern Parkway. (He died sometime after this interview.) Chana recites his miracles with the kind of enthusiastic tone a lot of people reserve for good gossip. She wears only skirts, never pants. From sundown Friday to sundown

Saturday, she observes the Sabbath, meaning that she doesn't do any work or drive or use electricity and that she spends time studying religious writings and just being with her family. She fasts on the appropriate holidays and helps prepare the big celebratory meals that break the fasts. She does not touch boys or men; she will not touch a male (other than her father, brothers, and blood uncles) until she takes her husband's hand on her wedding day. And then, after her marriage, she will cover her hair in public, as wives must. "I come from this religious family," Chana says. "So I guess it was instilled in me since I was a little kid. It's my world. And I know that when I grow up, if I'm strong enough, I want to be like my parents."

Her father did not become religious until after he had moved away from Morocco and met his French-Italian-Jewish wife in Paris. He studied medicine in China. After they had their first two daughters and moved to the United States, he met the Lubavitcher rebbe in Brooklyn. As the great-nephew of Baba Sali, Abehsera was religious but "not observant like with the beard," Chana says. But when he met the rebbe, "he was caught by him." He and his wife returned to the traditions of their faith. They became ba'alei teshuvah, those who return, the most holy of Jews, Chana says, because they have tasted the other life and yet have chosen to come back.

"I was *born* religious," she explains, her voice rising. Her cadences are surprising. Sometimes you hear Europe. Sometimes Israel. Sometimes Brooklyn. She speaks three languages, understands four. "For me [the religious tradition is] not that hard," she continues. "I mean it is . . . but it isn't that much. Since I'm a child, they say, 'Do this and do that.' But it's not like all religious homes. They don't enforce it on you, like: *Be Religious.* It's something that I believe in, and something that I wanna be."

She looks up from her French fries and laughs: "Maybe I sound like someone who's preaching, but I'm not." She explains that she is different from other religious girls because she grew up in a Habbad house, where the door is always open: "It's a house where anybody just walks in. Like during the day, anybody would just walk in. Anybody would just walk in and eat and use a prayer book and do anything. My father doesn't force people to be religious. He'll have somebody come into the house who's totally on drugs. He won't bother them at all. People who are in cults, and he won't bother them. He'll just make them feel at home, make them at ease. We had people who weren't Jewish and converted. We had all kinds of people ever since I'm little. I'm like a little child, and I see people walking around who are really different." Understatement. Members of Pink Floyd have come to visit her father's home. Bob Dylan and Jerry Brown are old friends. "So it's like I'm not close-minded. You know you have these religious people who are really close-minded, and they look at you, and they're like, 'Omigod, she's so weird.' I'm not like that. I'm open to anything."

Chana is allowed to sit at her parents' table with unmarried men, something that is not allowed in many Hasidic families. She sometimes wears the color red, which some religious people won't wear because it calls too much attention to them. In the summer, she doesn't wear socks, even though technically, religious girls should be covered at the elbow, neckline, knee, and ankle.

"Our family, we're cool," Chana says. "We just like get it out. If there's a guy at the table, my dad's not gonna say, Get out of the house [to me]. If I go with my brother to the movies, and his friend is with him, I'll go. My father doesn't mind. I'm not gonna do anything. I'm not gonna stay with [the friend] alone. My brother's there. Usually, my brother will be like the separation between me and him. My friends, my other friends, [their parents] won't let them talk to guys, like at all. The mother says to the boy and to the girl, 'Okay, now it's your day to have girls over, and tomorrow's your brother's day to have boys over.' *They can't be in the house at the same time.* This is like mistrust. The girl grows up thinking, *My mother thinks I'm a bad girl. This is what I'm gonna be.*"

Because she has seen more of the secular world, because she has friends in it, Chana gets into trouble with the more religious parents in her community—a community that stretches from Montreal, where her family recently lived, to Los Angeles, where both her married sisters live, to New York, where her parents live, to Israel where one of her brothers studies. Very very religious parents call her a bad girl because she talks about movies, television, and boys. These are the kinds of parents who tear up the magazines their daughters buy for the pinups of the boys of *Beverly Hills 90210*. These are the parents who shred the jeans that their daughters buy not to wear, but "just for fun to have." Chana doesn't blame the parents for their worries. "They think if [their daughters] start talking this way, they'll go farther and farther and farther," Chana says: "And it's very true. Obviously, if you're in a public school, there's a guy in your class. You're gonna sit in his lap, I don't know, shake his hand, give him a kiss on the cheek, then it goes farther and farther until they're pregnant. That's what [religious parents] don't want, and they're one hundred percent right. But there are some kids you need to give them an extra *taste* so they can feel more comfortable.

"The truth is that [my friends] don't have the opportunity to choose. They're like told, 'Okay, you go there.' In my family, it's not like that. My mother lets me see the other side, and she lets me talk to guys who are in our house and everything. But [my friends], I feel bad. They go against their families. They'll go to guys. They'll go to drugs. They'll go and like not keep Shabbat [the Sabbath]. And then later on they become religious, and they have families because they realize what's good. They just need to have that *little*. Me, I had that little taste of the world all through my life.

"Even my friends tell me—some are not virgins and some are and some are virgins but they do other things—I have this friend who goes with her uncle. I *see*. I don't want that. I don't like it. I taste it, and I'm saying: No. Not for me.

"I try to be strongest. I have a friend, this girl. She's not strong. She doesn't have courage. She doesn't know what's going on. But her mother tells me, like when I went there, that she didn't want me to be friendly with her daughter because she said, You talk about boys. But I try to explain to her: *This is normal. I'm sorry.*

*We don't have to go out with them. We don't have to touch them.
We don't have to go on dates. We can talk. We are girls. We can
relate to each other.*

"It's like my father wanted to register me at a religious girls'
school. They told my father, 'Stop having men in your house
because you know it's making your daughter . . . it's gonna make
her not religious.' They weren't Lubavitch. They were a different
kind. They didn't do it in a mean way. They did it like totally open.
They were doing it for my benefit, that I should grow up very clear.
But they don't understand that that's the way my family works. It's
like something that we have to do."

After lunch, Chana goes back to her friend Robin's apartment.
Robin is a director in Hollywood who studies with Chana's brother-
in-law, a Los Angeles rabbi who instructs others in the innovative
and controversial Kabbalistic teachings of the legendary Rebbe
Nachman. Robin's got books by Chana's father, revered Kabbalists,
and Chaim Potok, as well as *Presumed Innocent* and *Bonfire of the
Vanities.* Chana reads off the titles. She's read a lot of them. *"War
and Peace,"* she says. "I remember that."

Unlike most religious teenagers, she gets to really explore pop
culture. Most of it anyway. "My father doesn't like for me to see dirty
movies," Chana says. "Like I told him I went to see *Pretty Woman,*
and he was like 'Omigod, that's such a dirty movie.' But he knows
that I'm mature enough to handle . . . he wasn't . . . he was like
shocked." She hesitates. "I can't say he was shocked. He was like
upset because I saw like something dirty. But on the other hand, he
was like, you know, he didn't take it so bad because it's good that I
learn. But he didn't want to tell that to *me* because as a father he
has a responsibility to hold it back. Everytime I ask him, 'Should I
go see this movie?' He tells me, 'No, don't go see that movie.' And I
don't. *Truth or Dare,* I didn't see it yet. I heard it was a very dirty
movie. I couldn't go. It's really dirty. I heard it's the most gruesome.
Madonna made two new movies, *Truth or Dare* and another one. I
heard they were really bad. That, I will never see."

"He's really great, my father. He's very rabbi and on the other hand my father's like a friend. He's really my friend," she says. "I can tell him anything, anything. You know those crazy thoughts that teenagers have like I wanna do *this*. I go and tell my father. Like one time I wanted . . . I thought maybe I'll be . . . I was eleven and a half. I was into being a model and an actress because I saw TV. You know you're young. You become totally into the TV." She does a singsong voice: *'Dad, okay, I'm running away now. I'm going to be a model and an actress.' "*

Chana says her father's philosophy is "Be happy with yourself. When you have a problem, don't like make it the biggest thing in the world. Don't make minor problems big things. Be cool with it. Just let life go. If you have money problems, let it go."

Take the time she got hooked on an En Vogue song. "You know the song," she says, "life is all about expression: *You only live once and you're not coming back so express yourself.* These girls who are black sing it, and I'm not prejudiced at all so I love that song. And I was always going around the house going like: *Life is all about expression, Daddy.* He goes to me, 'My daughter, it's not.' He kept on saying, 'My daughter has no sense of what the world's about. She doesn't know anything.' He goes, 'Chana, life is not all about expression. Life is full of expression.' I was like 'Okay,' and I asked him to explain it to me. I didn't want to just take it in. I wanna understand something and *then* I'll do it. So he explained to me, 'You don't understand, Chana. People who say life is all about expression are people who only think about themselves: *Oh, I have to express myself. If you don't like what I like, then don't like me.'*

"You should see the video, the girls who sing it. I love them. On the video they're all like . . ." She twists her arm in a sinewy rhythmic way, a sort of brush-off gesture. "So I took that action. My father's like, 'You see them. They're only singing about themselves. If life's all about expression and you only live once and you're not coming back so express yourself—take all the guys you can get, take all the money that you can get.' "

Her father told her: "Chana, don't take that into your life, please." He told her: "Life is not only for yourself. Life is for people, for you to help people, for people to help you, for everybody to be together."

"I was like, okay," Chana says. "I had written it all over my notebook." She giggles, thinking of herself writing, *Life is All About Expression.* "Typical. I write it all over and after my father told me that, I crossed out "about" and I wrote "full." *Life is full of expression.*

* * *

Several nights later, Chana is at her friend Robin's apartment again. Her brother-in-law the rabbi is coming to dinner with eight or so followers. Chana helps the women in the kitchen, every once in a while grimacing about the fact that HE has been invited here tonight. Her sister has told her she must learn to handle it gracefully. It is right that he should be here too.

At dinner, the men sit on one side of the table in their yarmulkes and beards. The rabbi sits at the head of the table. Everyone is turned toward him, anxious to hear whatever he says. He is beloved not only for his wisdom but for his rock-and-roll music, much of it written on Bob Dylan's guitar. He even inspired Dylan's "Man in the Long Black Coat." Chana urges him to try the Snapple kiwi drink she loves. He does. Everyone waits for his judgment, which is noncommittal. He shrugs.

After the dishes are cleared, the rabbi begins to talk about the significance of the day of mourning and fasting that starts the next day, the Ninth of Av. It commemorates the destruction of the Second Temple, as well as the Holocaust. He says that you know a culture by how it treats its women. He says we shall know when the messiah is coming when women's treatment is in balance with men's. Everyone studies his face as he talks. Chana is listening while she plays finger games with the rabbi's toddler, while she holds his infant son over her shoulder. She carries the children easily, as though they were her own. She seems to respond to them naturally. She nuzzles the baby, and whispers to him, "I love you, Natan. And I know you love me."

Babies. She wants babies. But she won't marry until she has found a husband "who knows where he's going." Her brother-in-law asked her just the other day what she is looking for in a prospective husband. "I told him I was looking for a good person," she recalls. "I told him it means funny, charming, nice, has to first of all have a house with people. I cannot stand people who don't like guests. I don't want him to say, 'Not now, not tonight.' If he's *extremely* tired, then I understand. I want him to always be jumping and enthusiastic."

She laughs. "I don't know *where* I'm gonna find him." She knows only that it will be her choice, not her father's.

For her, the prospect of finding him, being courted, and marrying in the Lubavitch way has more romance than she saw in *Pretty Woman.* She may tease her father by saying she would marry a man who wasn't religious. But she's only joking. She believes marriage is a union consecrated by the role God plays in it. And she believes as others of her faith do that when she marries, God looks on her as beginning a different life.

She knows just how her marriage will happen: "It works like this," she begins. "If I see somebody in the street or at my friend's house or somewhere, I don't go up to him and say, 'Hi, my name is Chana.' I don't do that. I tell my father or I tell my friend and say, 'Can you please . . .' " She stops herself. "Actually the truth is, I wouldn't talk to him, do anything. If I liked him, I wouldn't do anything unless it was really like I loved him. But usually, we wait for the guy to say, I like her. Then if you like the guy, then you go out with him. If you don't want to, you just say no.

"It's more modest for the girl to wait for the guy to come to the girl. It's not like a thing where you say the woman *can't.* It's not like that at all. But if I see a guy, and I find him cute, I'm not gonna go and do anything. But I'll just tell my father. I say, I found that guy cute. And he'll tell me again: I know you find him cute, but he doesn't really have the things that you want as a husband, a boyfriend. Because in my family, we're not gonna go out with any guy cause we wanna have fun. It's like if you wanna go out with a guy, you have to be ready to like get married and have a life."

It might happen that her father would have a candidate. "Let's say my father would tell me, I have a great guy for you, and I would say no. He wouldn't pressure. But then I would say I'm interested in this other guy, a certain person, whatever. If I like him and he likes me, we'll go out. Then we go out on a date, like normal people. We go to movies. We go in restaurants, eat together. Then if we like each other for a while, he'll tell me, 'Okay, you know whatever,' and he'll say, 'You wanna get married?' and I'll say, 'Okay, cool.' " She blushes a little.

Then there are engagement parties with all their old traditions and then come the seven days before the wedding when the bride and groom cannot see each other. Finally, the bride, wearing a "perfectly thick" veil over her face, is seated on a "gorgeous" chair with her sisters and friends gathered around her. The men come in, holding the groom by the arms. They all carry candles. The groom lifts the veil to make sure that he is marrying Rachel and not Leah, as Jacob did in the Torah. After seven long days, by the light of only candles, the bride and groom see each other. "It's like the most amazing thing," Chana squeals, remembering her sisters' weddings. "I'm telling you. You see it, and you feel like you're the one that it's happening to." In the ceremony itself, there is a blessing sent by the Lubavitcher rebbe himself. After, they kiss the Torah and walk away holding hands ("for the first time!"), and then they go into a room alone where they can be intimate for a few minutes before joining the reception.

As the women are cleaning up after the dinner, one of them notices that the Snapple strawberry-kiwi drink is not kosher. All the women gather around. Chana says in shocked disbelief, "Snapple's *always* kosher."

Robin gasps: "I should have checked."

They all stare at the bottle, incredulous that they can't find the symbol that means it's okay. Chana realizes that she not only drank it herself, she offered it to her esteemed brother-in-law and he drank it.

"Don't tell," she says to the women, who murmur sympatheti-cally.

This is not Chana's only example of the ways a religious teenager can get tripped up by the mainstream world. There are nightclubs (that her more worldly friends have talked about). There are jeans, which Chana sometimes wears in the privacy of her room, again, "just for fun." There's holding a guy's hand, kissing him, going all the way with him. "Let's say I'm walking in the street, and I see some other people, like you see a whole bunch of guys and girls laughing and talking and everything. You start to . . . you *think* a lit-tle bit. Everybody has this. Every religious girl . . ." She pauses, then corrects herself: "I can't make this directly. It's opinion actually. It's just my opinion, my way of thinking.

"Sometimes I'll start to think that maybe they're having a bet-ter life than me. But I say, 'No, that's just like my bad part wanting that.' It's like, I think, 'No, I'll be strong enough to overcome it,' and that's it. But I know that what I am doing is more important. 'Cause I speak to a lot of teenagers and they say, 'I wish I was like you but I am not, and I am very happy the way I am.' And I say, 'That's very good. Stay the way you are. You do whatever you feel comfortable with.' "

She remembers going to a Sabbath retreat with her father, where he spoke to the gathering. After a meal, a bunch of teenagers gathered around Chana and began to grill her about why she "keeps from touching."

"The whole idea is modesty," she told them.

And they said: "What do you mean modesty? Like what's this thing with modesty? Like who cares, you know? Like God made teenagers to be attracted to each other."

"Yes, you are right," Chana told them. "But God didn't make teenagers to be attracted to each other to *do* what they have to do. When they find the right person, obviously they are gonna do it, what we're made to do. Adam and Eve are both woman and man. But like to waste it and to do it in a bad way, that I wouldn't want."

One of the guys made a proposal. "I would like to go on a date with you," he told Chana, "just to test what it would be like to be with a girl who doesn't touch me."

"No, sorry," Chana said. "I wouldn't go out with you."

Her close friends who are extremely religious sometimes ask Chana to translate the outside world for them. They know her parents have let her see more of it than they have seen. "Chana," they ask, "do you know what it is like to be in the other world?"

She always answers them the way her parents have answered her: "Trust me, trust me. You do not wanna go there because everyone who goes there wants to come back. And then they regret it for the rest of their lives."

Things Kids Told Us About God

This chapter wasn't titled by teenagers as the other theme chapters were, because this topic, religion, did not come up a lot as one of the top ten, or even twenty, things teenagers listed as being important issues on their minds. Which in itself seemed worthy of devoting a section to. Now there certainly are teenagers, like Chana and like Nicole, who are truly religious. But "most of us are pretty areligious," says Rachel, fifteen, whose family is "officially Jewish, but pretty much atheist. Until you ask us about it, religion's not something any of my friends or I even spend time thinking about." "Pretty much atheist" describes most of the kids I did ask about it. "I just can't integrate it into my life. I have no time," said seventeen-year-old Zach. "We're too cynical now to believe that stuff. We know better," explained one fourteen-year-old, "I think you're your own god. You decide your own fate. Religion is a farce. It creates a false sense of stability for insecure people who don't understand death and everything." Hearing all of them talk I can see that Generation Why? label rearing its ugly head. Of the teenagers I talked to who were raised with religion, I could find very few who weren't at least questioning it. Some reject it completely with well-reasoned responses as to why. Others want to maintain parts of it, maybe raise their kids with a strong connection to their heritage but not all the religious rituals. Others find their own, usually less dogmatic, religions, different from their families'.

Like Rachel, most teenagers' families haven't given them a tra-

ditional introduction to religion. For one thing, there was so much intermarrying in the past couple of generations that many kids have parents of two (or more) different religious backgrounds. Yona, who's thirteen and lives in Athens, Georgia, has a dad who is a mostly lapsed Protestant and a mother who's a practicing Muslim, so she did inherit some of the Muslim rituals: "It drives the kids at school crazy that I don't eat pork. They ask me why. I give them the answer that my mom gave me, because it's an unclean animal. And they say, 'Duhhh, we wash it.'" But most kids in mixed-religion homes don't get any religion at all. For some, parents just don't take the time. As one eighteen-year-old told me,

> *I don't know, when my dad and stepmom had a kid—he's Jewish, she's Catholic—the thing was that they were going to raise the kid to know about both Christmas and Hannukah, Easter and seders. But they're totally not doing it. They're lazy about it. I knew they wouldn't, 'cause my dad didn't even do seders with me, just the one or two when we went to my grandpa's.*

So most teenagers in intermarried homes are raised maybe doing Christmas instead of Hannukah because it's more popular with the kids but never going to church, or having Easter egg hunts but not really knowing what Easter's all about. That was my situation too. Having been raised by a mother who I didn't even know was Jewish until I was around thirteen and a father who had been Presbyterian until the church burned down and his family started going to the Baptist one, I only went to church once as a kid— because it was on our corner and Hill and I wanted to see what the inside looked like.

Approximately half of all teenagers do go to church or temple regularly. And some of them are really active and visible about their beliefs. I'm thinking particularly of the movement that's gotten a lot of attention lately where kids get together and support each other's decisions not to lose their virginity before marriage. But for many others, even if they're going to church, they aren't necessarily believing what they're hearing there. Sixteen-year-old Sam, who had a bar mitzvah and went to a conservative Hebrew school, told me, "I go to temple on the high holidays, but like when my family celebrates Hannukah and Passover, I just sit there. I'm really an atheist." David, who's also sixteen, believed in Judaism until he was about fourteen, when his attitude started to change. "I was into the 'Jew thing,' but now I don't really buy it. The problem is I don't believe in it. I'm wrestling with it, but I don't believe in God." Like a lot of teenagers, he sees himself as "spiritual, but organized religion turns me off. I don't like someone presenting me with such a closed system. And most people are just going through the motions anyway. They're just stuck in it—a very negative thing."

"I think it's about control," explained one astute sixteen-year-old girl. "I want to have as much control as possible over my life, my job future, my looks, my beliefs. You don't want your parents telling you what to believe in. But it's bigger than that. You don't even want to give up control to a higher power either—that would feel just the same as putting your life in some authority figure's hands or something. Yuck." Fifteen-year-old Maggie said something along those lines too, that most teenagers she knows basically operate as independent units, separate from their parents in so many ways—that listening to what a priest or minister or rabbi, or even a god, tells you to do, feels like taking steps backward and listening to a parent's rules, which they're way beyond.

Plus, many of the expectations of religion feel very outdated to them. Not being able to be buried in a Jewish cemetery because of a few tattoos, for example. Or "Like I'm supposed to marry someone Catholic because my parents are Catholic," said one girl. "I should say my grandparents, 'cause it's not like my parents ever go to church or anything. I mean, hello? If I met a Jewish guy I wanted to marry, of course I'd marry him. I mean, in this day and age you've seen so many bad marriages and the idea that you're gonna reject a good human being for some ancient reason seems crazy." My favorite family story about trying to fit religious ritual into this time of multiple marriages, changing religions, and inter-

*marrying took place not too long ago when my dad had just con-
verted to Catholicism. He did it so he could marry my stepmom,
who had actually left the church for a while but then returned.
Still, getting married in the Catholic church was a problem since
Dad was divorced. So he asked my mom if she would show the
church proof that she had been married and divorced once already
before their marriage, meaning my parents' marriage never actually existed in the eyes of the church—never mind what that
meant to us kids, but anyway, my mom said fine. But when she
tried to prove she had been married before, they discovered her
first husband had actually been married once before his marriage
to her (are you still with me here?). In the eyes of the church, my
mom's first marriage had never existed; therefore her marriage to
my dad had existed. My dad and mom had to have their thirteen-
year marriage annulled so dad and Debi could have their church
wedding.*

*Many kids are choosing their own religions now, different from
the ones their parents raised them with. "It's the perfect rebellion,"
says one girl. "My mom, who's Methodist, can't believe I'm Bud-
dhist. She tells her friends it's just a phase." And they don't just
choose long-established kinds. "I'm a mystic," said one seventeen-
year-old guy, elaborating,*

*Meaning that I think there's more that happens in our own
minds, and in the universe, that can't be explained. This is
cheezy, but I think there are forces, aspects of existence, that
can't be explained. I think you get a certain intuition over a lifetime about how the world works, glimpses at answers about who
and why we are and why we can rationalize. Science increases
this intuition. The more one studies science, literature, psychology, the more one can understand why the physical world can
be explained by mathematics. I do believe in an animalistic
nature that we play down. Darwinism is religious. Evolution is
this dogma, how the universe was created for the best reasons,
advantageous to man.*

Other kids have chosen to convert to Santeria and African ritual. And at colleges across the country, WICCA, a religion based on witchcraft, has more and more members, mostly young women.

So it seems teenagers' beliefs are more diverse than ever, and when you ask them what they do believe in, you get everything from therapy to astrology to "myself" to fate, superstitions, psychics, tarot cards, and volunteer work. Most of all, friends, sometimes gangs, and sometimes family. Therefore, when I came upon a sixteen-year-old boy who wants to be a priest, I thought maybe I'd found an exception. But when asked, he said he's "not really religious, but I celebrate Christmas and Easter." So why does he want to be a priest? "I've seen society go into a nosedive. I have a very pessimistic view of the world we live in with all the crime, greed, and especially how people treat each other. So I've been able to seek some semblance of order in the world and something to look forward to in prayer—some hope." He's also not sure how he feels about the Bible, because, he says, "Some of the events are questionable." And, like most of the other kids here, he's going against his parents, who he says "aren't very religious." One of the most touching comments I got from a kid who prays regularly was that he does it only because "It's someone to talk to." And Amber says she has used a WICCA manual to concoct a love potion to get involved with a boy she liked.

That's the other thing you get a lot from teenagers when you get them talking about the idea of religion. How much religious sensibility they have has to do with being part of a group of friends or feeling like a family. That's the way Cindy Parrish, who's coming up next, feels about her church.

So it's not that teenagers are so jaded, that their lives are so bleak, that they are without hope and faith and compassion, or even without ritual. It's just that they want to do it their own ways, differently from previous generations, differently from what they perceive to be what they should do, and differently from each other. On that note, here's the only diary entry from all my teenage journals that I, raised without religion, could find:

November 3, 1978

Last night
Lying in bed in a foreign place very late all so quiet
        you hear the inside of your own head
looking up into complete black
feeling completely completely alone,
suddenly time and space compressed
and every other time I had felt so alone
was this same time
so I had myselves there for company
and I was not separate from the space I was looking into
I was part of it
Maybe that's like god.

CINDY PARRISH'S
SHOPPING SPREE

Cindy Parrish is looking at flowy floral dresses on a rack in U.S. Male, a shop that has bell-bottoms, tie-dye, and combat boots in the window. "Do you need help?" a salesperson asks, "or are you just doing the mall thing?"

Cindy, age fifteen, almost sixteen, her birthday is next week, laughs, "I'm just doing the mall thing." She has $10 with her. School is out, and she's got a ton of babysitting jobs set up for the summer, but that's to pay off a $600 phone bill her parents got after her three-week long-distance romance with a boy she met at a Christian-school academic competition. She lives just outside Nashville, and the guy, Robert, lives in western Tennessee. "I went haywire," she admits. "I just talked to him day and night. My parents were like, Who are you talkin' to? *Oh, just a friend.* I'd think to myself, *Cindy, you need to get off this phone now before you get your phone bill any higher,* and I'd just keep on stayin' on. I felt like screamin' when I saw that phone bill. I thought: my mama's gonna be upset. My daddy's gonna be upset. We're not gonna have enough money to pay this off with because we're buyin' everything else—$130 a month for my school and so much for volleyball. We had to buy uniforms for that."

Cindy is the baby of the family, born when her parents were almost forty. Her two older brothers are both married with their own kids. Her daddy, Billy Charles, works at a plastics plant. Her mama, June, babysits, though she could have retired already if she hadn't wanted to send Cindy to a private church school.

Billy Charles and June found the money to pay the phone bill. Now Cindy is paying them back. She has $100 to go. She's been babysitting whenever someone needs her and not buying any video-tapes or cassettes or clothes. She hasn't even been buying gifts for her latest boyfriend, Frankie. (She spent $100 buying Nintendo stuff for the boyfriend just before Robert, whom she went out with for three weeks.)

Today, she only has the $10 bill her mama gave her so she wouldn't have to go to the mall empty-handed. But, with or without money, this mall, thirty minutes drive from home, is her favorite place.

She angles off into Stuart's to touch all their clothes. She crosses the store and flips through a rack of evening stuff. "I love see-through things," she says. "And black is my favorite color to wear." She holds up a sheer black jacket. She waves it around and watches the way it kind of floats. On another rack she finds a sequined vest appliquéd with a wildcat. She runs her fingers like a comb through fringes on some suede-like vests, over the rhinestones sewn onto a denim shirt. "I love things with diamonds and jewels." As she walks out the door finally, she says: "My mama would pitch a fit if she saw what I liked."

"I was raised in the Pentecostal Church," Cindy explains back out in the concourse. "I've sort of broke some of the rules here, proba-bly broke a lot of them. They don't want you to wear pants or shorts or too much makeup or get your hair cut too short. They feel like pants make you look like a boy, and if your hair is short like that too. But I've had my hair cut. I wear shorts. I wear pants sometimes too." She is wearing a beige T-shirt glitter-glued with what are sup-posed to resemble Native American designs, short navy socks, deck shoes, and hemmed black cutoffs that end just above her knees.

She stops into a little jewelry shop. Jewelry is also frowned upon by the church, and her mother won't let Cindy get pierced ears, though she does sometimes let her wear clip-ons. Cindy admires the fake pearls and the loopy Victorian-type necklaces. She looks at a pair of earrings made to look like little mouse traps and observes, "I don't think I'd ever be *caught* wearin' those."

Next, it's Sam Goody. "I used to have these tapes," she says, waving her hand in front of the Bon Jovi section. "I like Eric Clapton, he's good. I used to listen to them—Def Leppard. Hysteria, I had that one. I collected tapes. I had like 250–300 tapes. I spent all my money on tapes." She moves down the rack: "Duran Duran, I had them too. I threw all my tapes away. I just dumped them in the trash can. I just threw them all away. I decided to do that," she says ultra-casually, then goes into how a year ago she got the Holy Ghost one night at a revival meeting. She says that she's not good at passing on the teachings of her church but she'll try: "The way that I've always been taught . . . if you feel the need to, you go to the altar when everyone's praying or something. And you repent of your sins, ask God to forgive you. And then you know you have the Holy Ghost. They want . . . I don't know how to explain this. Our church is the kind that gets up and shouts, you know, stuff like that. My mom don't like our music anymore. She thinks it sounds too modern, like rock and roll or something. Some of the songs, the music to it they kinda up the beat and stuff. That's what most of the young people like."

There are lots of teenagers at her church, Nashville's big First United Pentecostal Church, where Sunday Services draw between five- and six-hundred worshipers. "I was so scared when I first went there," Cindy says. "If you're used to goin' to a smaller church then it's weird to step into a big church. You feel like everyone's starin' at you when you're walkin' right in front of everybody. I was with my friend Lee, and I thought, my goodness, she's not gonna make me sit up there is she? I'm gonna feel bad enough sitting on the back seat. And she was takin' me all the way to the front. I was nervous, I was really shakin'."

But all the kids sat up front, and Cindy made herself get used to it. She started to like the church so much that her parents transferred their memberships to it. People feel the Spirit there, Cindy says: "Sometimes we get a really good service and some people run the aisles and, you know, whatever you feel like doin'. If you feel like jumpin', if you feel like shoutin', if you feel like clappin' your hands, it's just all the same. Running the aisles if you're excited, that's fine."

All that activity still makes Cindy nervous, a little self-conscious, and that was true on the night when she got the Holy Ghost. "All my other friends, they'd been prayin'," she says. "There're some that shouts, gets up every service and raises their hands. And I'd be the only one sittin' down and lookin' around and I'd feel kinda left out, but I was afraid to get up and do what they were doin' because. . . . I wanted to sometimes but I was afraid because I thought, *Oh, man, my mama's gonna see me, somebody's gonna see me.*

"But one night, we were in revival. We had this preacher, his name was Brother Mahaney, I guess. He was really fun. He told jokes but it was about . . . he was against Clinton and stuff like that. He was for Bush, and he'd say stuff about that. Then he'd talk about gay people or something. He would just say things to make people laugh but he would get his point across. Then at the very last night he got down to *business,* and he, you know, he *really* got his point across then. I don't remember what it was. I cannot remember anything. It was just talkin' about livin' for the Lord and servin' Him, and doin' what's right. And he was talkin' about, *'You don't wanna go to hell, you wanna go to heaven.'* So I guess that just touched me.

"Afterwards, I wanted to get up and do something about it, but I was too scared. I was afraid people were watchin' me and stuff.

"My friend Johnny said, *'Why don't you get up and pray tonight?'* I said, *'Well people would watch me.'* He said *'Don't worry about what people think.'* So he called the pastor over there and the preacher too. And they started prayin' for me, and I got the Holy Ghost that night.

"I just felt like a tingling goin' over my body, you know, down your back. I was just askin' the Lord to forgive me of my sins and save me. You feel yourself get this warm feeling, like you're secure or safe, and like it's a real happy feeling that comes over you."

After the service, Cindy and four of her friends were baptized together in the baptistry behind the choir loft. She was "born again out of the water." And she made some changes. One of the changes involved her aforementioned tape collection. "There's this one stage I went through," she says in her flat Southern accent. "The pastor would talk about demons and stuff, and it would scare me to death. I would be scared to death. He would talk about music, rock and roll music. I used to listen to everything." The pastor would bring the records in question to the church. Cindy says, "Then they'd play back the messages in those songs, and it would scare me cause those bad spirits can get off on you or something. They can take control of your body. I liked the songs that I was listenin' to but I was afraid to listen to them because what if something gets off on me?"

She started to listen more closely to the lyrics in her favorite songs. "There was this one song I really liked by Alice in Chains. I loved the beat to the song. I didn't even know the words to it. I started reading the words to it and it was saying, 'Sew God's eyes shut and kill him,' things like that. 'Deny your savior, serve Satan' and things like that. Tellin' you the worst things. And some of the songs had worse things in it than that. That's not right," she says emphatically, as if committing her life all over again at that moment in Sam Goody.

"I was gonna throw it away, but my mom threw it away before I got to it. I said, *Do you know what happened to my tape?* She kept ignoring my question. Finally she said, *Yeah, you'll probably be mad at me but I threw it away because I didn't think it was a good tape.* I said, *That's okay.* And she said, *It is?*"

Cindy works her way down to the *G*'s on the tape rack in the middle of the store. "Green Jelly," she says. "This song I think is good: Three Little Pigs. It's a heavy metal band that screams it out. It's just about the most popular song right now. It's kinda dumb but everybody likes it." To the *M*'s. "Richard Marx. I think he's good." She stops. "Madonna. I think she's a pervert." After she pulls out John Secada, whose love songs she likes, she heads over into the videos next door.

She explains that she hasn't seen a movie in a year—since her last birthday. The church doesn't approve of movies. But she figures videos are different so she buys them three at a time if she's got enough money: She points out ones she owns—*Pretty Woman, Problem Child, Fried Green Tomatoes.* She can't believe her ten dollars won't buy her the *Dying Young* tape she wants.

She leaves the store and gets a white chocolate chunk cookie from the food court instead. As she cruises through the Disney store, she says nonchalantly, "I got in trouble today, my mom found something on my neck."

She points to a roundish red mark just above her collar. "A hickey," she says. See, she was at her new boyfriend Frankie's house watching TV. His parents left the room for a few seconds, and Frankie gave her the hickey. Cindy tried to hide it with a high collar because her mother thinks holding a boy's hand is going too far. The collar didn't work, and June saw it and said she thought Frankie's parents watched them better over there at his house.

June has warned her daughter against kissing. "I want you to stay a nice girl" is what June says anytime they talk about it. Cindy answers, "Mother, it's not a sin, okay?" Now Cindy is worried her mama might change her mind about letting Frankie's family take her to Twitty City tomorrow for her birthday.

Frankie is a good guy, Cindy says, the cousin of a friend from school. He just moved here from Alabama, and she met him when he started coming to basketball games at her school. He's the latest in a long string of boyfriends that have lasted anywhere from three days to three months. She's had so many this year that her volleyball coach asked her if she was collecting boyfriends.

Cindy was psyched about that. Collecting boyfriends is so far from where she was when she still went to the public school in her town. There she says she made "straight *F*s," and the other kids teased her a lot. She is tall for her age (5´8˝) and heavier than most of the girls in the school. She wasn't cool enough for the kids at the public school. "You'd have to dress a certain way—a certain kind of shorts. They would make fun of the way you talked, the way you dressed, the way you acted," she says. "There were these snobby girls. They'd walk by and give you this look and snarl their nose up like, _You don't belong here_ or say, _Don't you wish you looked like me?_ I thought, _Not really._" She shoves her hands into her shorts pockets as she says it, and there's a strain of defiance in her tone.

At the new school, everybody wears the same thing—a jumper with an oxford shirt underneath it. In gym, everyone wears culottes. In class, if you need to go to the bathroom, you raise the Christian flag on your desk. If you need to score your paper, you raise your American flag. You pray before class, before break, before lunch, after class. You memorize Bible verses at the end of every assignment. You observe the six-inch rule—keeping six inches between you and anybody else. At the Pentecostal school, Cindy makes _A_s and _B_s. "You can be accepted by everybody," she says. "Everybody just mainly accepts you for who you are."

Not that some of the rules don't bother her. The principal called her aside at a basketball game for holding hands with a boy. And the pastor did away with the cheerleading squad she was on; even though the skirts were knee length, he said some of the cheers contained vulgar movements. Cindy is coming up with her own rules: "I know what's right and what's wrong for my church, but I usually just go ahead and do it anyway. They don't believe in wearing fingernail polish; I do that. They don't believe in wearing earrings; I do that. I break all the rules. They encourage us to read the Bible every day and pray every day. I hardly ever read it unless I'm in school. I usually don't pray either. Really, I don't even think about any of that stuff. I should, but I'm not into that right now. I have a lot of people that care about me [at the church]," Cindy says. "And I care about them. They're just like a family there." Cindy says she missed that family thing in public schools. Especially since she has no brothers and sisters her age.

She heads down to one of the two-story department stores that sit at either end of the mall. She browses through the swimsuits, complaining that her mother makes her wear a one-piece with a little flounce skirt for modesty's sake. Then she sees the Elizabeth Arden perfume counter in the makeup section. "Oh," she cries. "Red Door perfume. I'm gonna have my mama buy me some of that."

"Mall Rats"

I keep wondering if the teenagers reading this book are skipping over these topical sections, like I used to whenever a story I was reading would start to quote some doctor from some university's medical school or would cite some percentage of teenagers who all feel a certain way about an issue. I'd always scan right down the page to the next teenager's quote or story. Even more than when I was younger, teenagers now, I think, are so tired of being summed up and marketed at, because so many people are trying to sell them things all the time. (Note to teenagers: you may want to skip this part.) Everyone wants to capitalize on the growing number of teenagers, which will break the record of the baby boomers when it peaks in 2010 with 30.8 million thirteen- to nineteen-year-olds. Already these kids influence the economy by more than $200 billion a year. In 1992, teenagers spent $3 billion on sneakers, $2 billion on clothes, $1.5 billion on jeans, and $724 million on beauty and health merchandise. Forty-eight percent of kids age twelve to seventeen live in homes where the income is over $40,000. Their weekly allowances average $15, up from $11 in 1992. They earn $57 billion on their own on top of that. About 1 in 9 high schoolers has a credit card cosigned by a parent. Since they usually don't have anyone else to spend all that money on, teenagers spend an average of $85 a week on themselves. And obviously it's not the teenagers' parents who are picking out which brand of deodorant or jeans or CD-ROM they buy.

Despite all the potential the numbers may suggest, teenagers can be a marketing executive's worst nightmare. And these teenagers in particular. While they still get caught up in trends, those trends spread a lot faster now and die a lot faster too. Now they're buying the same clothes or using the same slang at pretty much the same time in Philadelphia or Tacoma or Joplin, Missouri, because of MTV and more malls with more chain stores than ever. Even by the time this book comes out, the clothes these kids were wearing and the music they were listening to will be hopelessly outdated, and I'm sure they'll let me know all about it. They also question everything, see through marketing ploys better than just about anyone, and they hate when a product screams Buy Me Because You're a Teenager! as if they're not actually individuals.

Maybe that's one of the positive parts of growing up fast, using an ATM when you're ten and knowing about global warming at five. Teenagers feel very capable. They don't see any reason why their age needs to be a barrier to getting something they don't like changed. And they're right. A boycott against a specific company by teenagers can be devastating when their parents are giving them a total of $28 billion just to spend on groceries every year. Whereas in the past teenagers generally dealt with issues in a personal way, becoming vegetarian or maybe joining existing volunteer organizations, now they organize their own. They started as little kids, by asking their parents to stop using disposable anything, from diapers to razors. They got their teachers to start using ceramic cups instead of those foam kind that clog landfills and never disintegrate. And they've gotten the global mega-company that owns Star-Kist to stop catching tuna in a way that harmed dolphins.

When I once told the then-editor of YM that 45 percent of Sassy readers did volunteer work at least weekly, she laughed and said that what teenagers really put time into was their hair and their clothing, and they only did that volunteer work because they were forced to in school. Well, I don't think anyone forced teenagers to start these non-school-based groups: The American Ethnic Coalition (a Long Island, New York, organization one high school girl started to promote understanding between kids of different back-grounds), the National Student Campaign Against Hunger and Homelessness, and Adopt-a-Grandparent (which pairs grandpar-entless teenagers and grandchildrenless older people in surrogate relationships). Those are just a few examples. And by the way, can't you blow-dry your hair and think about helping bomb victims at the same time?

Actually, teenagers these days make me feel really lazy. And sheltered. Most of them are so aware of what's going on politically, socially, economically, ecologically, in all parts of the world, they're always teaching me things I didn't know—about how much electric cars would ease ozone depletion and about why the dollar is down against the yen. So I think the idea of teenagers as lazy mall rats couldn't be more off. Sure plenty of them hang out at the mall, especially if there's nowhere else to go. (Though most won't admit it. "I only came to the mall to get my nose pierced cheap," said one sixteen-year-old San Diego guy. "We go to the mall to kill preppies," said a seventeen-year-old in Detroit.) And sure they spend money while they're there.

Which is why this section is here. On their "top ten things on my mind" lists, many of them wrote down items they wanted to buy, from a $75 bathing suit to a $40,000 car. But when you get into what they're buying and why, you get answers like this four-teen-year-old gave: "I spent $1,799.99 on a Macintosh PowerBook. Plus I got Elastic Reality software, which cost $348.99 and gives me morphing capabilities when I create my sci-fi scenarios. I only got this one package because if I bought any more I'd've been broke." (He also spent more than $200 on two pairs of Reeboks and almost $7 on lunch at Taco Bell.) My point here is not only did he spend what I still consider a ton of money, he also knows a lot more about the technology he bought than most people twice his age. And that's typical. I asked one kid I met on America Online about how he's using all this new technology, and he answered, and I quote, "My mastery of mathematics has enabled me to use Thiele-Small parameters to their maximum advantage in design-

ing subwoofer boxes for the cars of my friends; ditto for under-standing the fundamentals of Ohms Law." No matter how much adults learn about built-in Ethernet and optional PCMCIA mod-ules, most are probably like me in not having worked on computers until high school or college or later, while these kids grew up with this technology. It's in their blood.

So not only do teenagers have big goals for what they want to change in this world, they have personal cellular phones, Visa cards, and internal 320 MB hard drives to do it with, which is a powerful combination. And they know it.

ON THE PHONE WITH ASHLEE LEVITCH

*A*shlee Levitch can catch the phone on the first ring, even if it's three in the morning. She's sixteen and in total sync with a Panasonic cordless. The phone will ring at 4 a.m., at 4:30. It will be her friend West. Does she want to go dancing Thursday at The Roxbury? To Par One? It will be her friend Tony. She wasn't sleeping, was she?

It rings, rings, rings. It drives her dad crazy. It drives her friend Andrew, who lives with her family, crazy. He might be missing important incoming.

The sun comes up. The phone rings. Ashlee stays in bed as late as one in the afternoon doing business: Her agent is calling. Her manager is tracking her. Does she want a tutor when she goes back down to Atlanta to film the finale of *I'll Fly Away?* Which of the tutors she interviewed does she want on the set of her new sitcom, *Family Album?* Ashlee lies in her waterbed and makes these decisions. This is Hollywood. Today is the day she gets her own phone line. At last. Ashlee's not in Kansas anymore.

* * *

It all started with dance lessons when she was three, Ashlee explains as she drives across L.A. to Universal Studios, where she is rehearsing for *The Circus of the Stars*. As a little kid in Leawood, Kansas, she says, she was always moving, so her parents had decided to channel her energy into something constructive. She loved dance, *loved* it. "I went to public school. I was the only one who was going to dancing everywhere from twenty–twenty-eight hours a week. At eight, I started doing theater. The others were doing stuff like soccer and normal kid stuff, but I don't really qualify acting as normal kids' stuff. None of the rest of them got to take off school for a day or two and make a commercial, which to me was just normal. It wasn't like my parents were making me do it," Ashlee says. "I wanted to do it. I was happy."

One of her teachers had her audition for Peter Pan at Kansas City's outdoor professional theater, The Starlight. Ashlee got the role of a little boy. "They put my hair on top of my head in a hat and with this little squeaky voice being eight, it doesn't matter whether you're a boy or a girl," she says. An agent from New York asked her parents to bring her to the East Coast. "He asked permission to talk to me, and he asked me if I wanted to do this and if I liked it. He told me I did a really good job and all that stuff. And I loved it. I had to do it. And so my parents, we agreed that I could get a local agent in Kansas City. And I did that. I made like twelve or thirteen national commercials. I was the Wal-Mart girl, like the toy expert is what they called me because I had so many Wal-Mart commercials," she says. But she still wanted to work in a bigger market. When she was thirteen, her parents let her start making trips to Chicago, where her first time out she landed a six-commercial contract with Illinois Bell. "My parents were like, Wow," she recalls. "I think they were surprised. They thought it was a phase that I'd grow out of."

Up to Chicago and back, and again, and again. Ashlee auditioned for movies and television series. She would be one of three finalists: a girl from New York, a girl from California, and Ashlee. One of the coastal kids always got the role. *Always.*

Finally, her parents said she could do a performing arts summer camp in New York. She met a ton of agents and managers there. "I interviewed all of them," she says. "And my parents said I could pick. It was up to me. So I picked who I felt most comfortable with, Shirley Grant, who's my manager, who's kind of like the Jewish grandmother who I felt at home with. I felt it was a little more personal than just an agent and a talent—the kids are referred to as talent. It wasn't talent; it was like Ash."

Still, her parents made her go back to eighth grade in Kansas. But they flew back and forth with her at least four times to New York that year for auditions. And then she and her mother moved there in time to do auditions for the next season's TV pilots. She immediately got a job dancing Off-Broadway and was rehearsing for it when: "It was the first day of blocking, and I'd been dancing for like three hours, and my mom came in and she was like, 'Hey, you've gotta go to an audition.' It was like seven-thirty at night. I was like, 'Mom, I'm not going now. Look at me. I'm sweaty. My hair's all messed up. I don't feel like leaving and I can't leave.' "

"You came to New York to audition," her mother countered. "Do you want to go back to Kansas?"

So Ashlee got dressed and went to read for the role of Francie in this NBC drama they were starting called *I'll Fly Away:* "I guess they'd been looking for me. I walked in, and they said, 'Are you Ashlee?' And they're like 'Come in here.' It was just weird. And then the next day my agent called me and she was like, 'So, how'd you think it went?'

"And I was like, 'It went fine.' Because my motto's . . . I basically like put it out of my head after it's over. I forget about auditions after I've done them. It's stupid to let them eat at you, and *How did I do?* and that kind of thing is stupid to me. I was like, I did fine. I did good.

"And she's like, 'You have a call back today.' "

Ashlee went and read lines with a Southern accent. They put her on the phone with these two producers in Hollywood, Josh Brand and John Falsey, who did *Northern Exposure.* "I'm like, 'Who are *these* people?' " Ashlee remembers. "I'm sitting on this phone with all these guys listening. And this is the second night of practice I'd missed [for the Off-Broadway production], and my director wasn't happy with me."

The casting guy asked her to step outside, then came out ten minutes later and said the producers loved her.

Ashlee said: "I don't mean to be rude but I have missed four hours of practice due to these two days, and my director is very mad 'cause we start in a couple of weeks, and I haven't learned any of the blocking." She wanted to go back to the theater but the TV guy made her get in a cab home, where he later called and said she might be on the midnight flight to Los Angeles so she could read for the network executives. Then he called again and said, no, actually she would go the next day.

The next morning, her mother ran out to the Screen Actors Guild to sign Ashlee's papers, and while she was gone, the casting guy called and said they were booked to go on the noon flight to L.A. "Pack everything," he told Ashlee, "because if you get the part you're flying straight to Atlanta where they're already filming."

Ashlee remembers: "I was like so excited but I didn't know what to do, so I sat down on the couch and cried." Then she called her best friend in New York, because she knew her friend had been on a series. She had "been to network." "What do I do?" Ashlee started crying.

My friend said: "Call your dad."

"So I was crying," Ashlee says. "I was excited, but I didn't know what to do. I was nervous and called my dad, and I think it was like the day before April Fool's or it was April Fool's, and that's always a big time in our house. I told him: 'Dad, I have to go to L.A. but Mom's not here, and I don't know where the SAG building is. I can't go down there alone. I don't have any money with me.' I go, 'What do I do?' And he said, 'You're a better actress than I thought.' And he hung up on me."

Her mom got back. They made the noon flight. Ashlee read for the executives and got the part—over "two blondes" who also auditioned. The next night, she was in Atlanta, meeting Sam Waterston and the rest of the cast on a show that became a big critical success on NBC that fall.

Right after that, she got to go back to New York to ride a giant turkey float in the Macy's Thanksgiving Day parade while singing "If My Friends Could See Me Now." Her real family—parents and younger sister, Breean—all moved to Georgia to be with her. Plus, she got so close to Waterston, who played her dad, that even after the show was canceled she still calls him on Father's Day. Her older brother from the series, Jeremy London, is the only big brother she'll ever have, she says. She adores her little brother from the show, Aaron.

It was also while she was in Atlanta that she turned sixteen and got two cars: a red 1973 Stingray Corvette, which she and her father restored, and a brand-new, ordered-special black BMW. "I wanted a Mustang," she explains. "My dad said, *'I'm* not buying you a Mustang. *You're* not buying a Mustang. *You are not going to have a Mustang.*" He was a car dealer in Kansas. He hates Fords. He took her to look at Infiniti cars and then suggested that they cross the street and look at BMWs. "Yeah," Ashlee cheered. "I'm getting a BMW!" They brought it home on her sixteenth birthday.

When *I'll Fly Away* got canceled after only two seasons, Ashlee and her dad drove the BMW across the country. It still has its Georgia license plates, which causes her angst. Like now.

As she shifts gears in a crowded L.A. intersection, another car honks. "Shut up, butthead," she mutters in his general direction, then completes a competent turn and adds: "What really frustrates me is I know where I'm going in L.A. I know my way around, and I drive everywhere. My parents have a fit because I have almost 10,000 miles on my car. I drive *every*where. And other drivers see the Georgia tags, and they don't even give me time to slow down before they honk. They think I'm some little country kid who has no idea where she's going. And that's not true. *I know where I'm going.*"

* * *

She gets to rehearsal at a makeshift circus set up on a high concrete lot at Universal Studios. Here, for ten six-day weeks, she is training for the show, which will air sometime around Thanksgiving. She loves working, even though technically this is supposed to be her summer vacation. She has teased her parents that she is going to run away with the circus.

She changes into a leotard and parachute-fabric pants. She ties her thick hair back with a red ribbon. Then, she and Danielle Harris, who sometimes appears as the neighbor girl on *Roseanne,* do a routine with their trainers, Martin Rodriguez, who's from an Australian circus family, and Richie Gaona of the Flying Gaona family.

"We Are Family" plays on an Aiwa walkman with tiny speakers as Ashlee, Danielle and the trainers go through their gymnastics horse routine. Martin jumps on first. Ashlee jumps on his back. Danielle follows them. Martin falls forward, then they go over like dominoes, one toppling the other until they are a pile on the mat. Danielle's elbow bangs Ashlee's front teeth as they are trying to get up. "Ow! ow!" she wails, laughing.

"Hit the sweet spot," the trainers yell, patting the center padding on the horse as Ashlee and Danielle sprint toward it. But it's a bad day. The other two members of the act, Zachery Bryan from *Home Improvement,* and Pablo Irlando from *George,* are on vacation and not here to practice. So finally, they all give up. "You're busted on your butt," Danielle teases Ashlee. They laugh as though that were a completely funny thing to say.

Instead of going home, Ashlee heads over to the trapeze just for fun. An eighth-generation trapeze artist has been teaching her how to swing out over the net gracefully and then how to dismount safely and with style. Ashlee practices it a dozen times. Eventually, she motions for her little sister to come up. Then her friend Andrew comes up too and tries it.

Tourists gather at the fence and look up at them. Somewhere in the studio lot, a karaoke contest is going on and a nonsinger's rendition of "Celebration!" drifts over as Ashlee tries one last time. "I love it up there," Ashlee says after she comes down. "I'm happier up there, more relaxed there than down on the ground. Down on the ground, all this *stuff* is going on."

What she means is: she's dealing with "baby games," as she calls the politics among the stratified ranks of kids in the business. As she steers her BMW toward home, she says her closest friend out here "was like a light that turned off." They don't speak anymore.

She has made all kinds of guy friends, but the other "celebrity" girls aren't into her. "You know, people get jealous very easily here," she says, waving her tanned hand dismissively to say she doesn't really care much.

What really irks her is that everybody knows every move she makes. Gossip. It's enough to make her miss Kansas. "I think of Kansas a little more fondly now than I ever have," she says. "Now I look at it . . . I miss the people, being able to trust people very easily. That, and there's not the games. I mean there is, and in high school of course everybody talks about everybody behind everybody's back. But it's even worse here. It's worse here than like a high school group of kids. *Adults* do it here.

"Did you see that new Porsche?" she asks her sister. From the back seat, Breean sighs: "Wow."

"That was brand new," Ashlee says. "That was a '94. It has an older body style, they brought it back."

* * *

Back at their parents' four-bedroom house in Sherman Oaks, where the two Chinese Sharpeis greet the sisters, Ashlee checks out her new phone and sets up the new answering machine. She's already memorized her new number.

When she's finished, she sits on her waterbed and tells her mom about her day. Debbie is attentive. She misses her big yard and friendly neighbors back home in Kansas, but she wants to be with Ashlee. She and her husband, Julius, rarely spend a day away from their oldest daughter. Today they couldn't go to Ashlee's rehearsal so they sent Andrew instead. They trust Andrew to watch over her. He's an old friend from their Atlanta days. He's a model, and he happened to be moving out to California when the Levitches were, so they offered him a bedroom. Their door is always open to their daughters' friends. They do things like have Passover seders at their house for anyone who needs someplace to go.

"I did my front flips," Ashlee tells her mother. "Richie said we might go to the circus together. But I told him not Friday because I have that awards ceremony for *I'll Fly Away*."

"Just let me know when I'll see you," her mom says, meaning I never see you anymore.

"Yeah, I know," Ashlee breathes out loudly in mock exhaustion. "I have not a clue. They got us ankle braces. I'm hungry."

"If you want to go to CPK, fine. Somewhere else, fine. If not, I'll fix dinner here."

"I have to call Tony because Rick requested my presence there tonight," Ashlee says.

"No," her mom says.

"We're not doing anything. Just watching a movie," Ashlee coaxes.

"Just for a little while." Her mother's tone is firm.

"Why's that? What'd I do?" Ashlee asks with a little pout-tone.

Her mother looks her in the eye, leveling with her. "Well, you've been on the go. It's like constant."

"That's true," Ashlee admits. She shrugs and tries to compromise. "They might come back over here with me."

Mom grins. "That'd be great. I'm gonna make homemade chocolate chip cookies if they'll come over here."

"Don't say that, Mom. Rick'll eat three batches."

"I'll bake a cake for them too if they come over here," Debbie promises, then laughs.

Ashlee laughs too, "I've been gone every night for a month. I think this is like bribery time."

Her mom says it's true, Ashlee has been in a white-heat of activity ever since she got to L.A. She goes to celebrity surfing. She goes to barbecues. She sits in coffeehouses and drinks caffeine.

But tonight she goes to California Pizza Kitchen (CPK) to eat barbecue chicken pizza with her family. Although after she orders, her beeper goes off. "Whose number is that?" she asks herself out loud as she looks at the digital readout on the pocket-size beeper. "911, what's that mean?"

"It means it's an emergency for somebody," her dad says.

"*Who* is it?" she says, racking her brain out loud.

"Go call," her mom tells her. Ashlee dashes off to the pay phone and comes back some minutes later.

"It was Tony," she announces. A good friend. Nobody unusual.

"What did 911 mean?" her dad asks.

"Call me NOW," she answers. "That way I wouldn't wait around for half an hour to call him back." As if she would ever ignore her beeper or her answering machine or any other relative of her phone. He just wanted to know when she would be getting home.

Her parents laugh at her frenzy. Her mother shakes her head affectionately. His father rolls his eyes. Ashlee shrugs: "I'm getting used to having so much stuff going on at once that it doesn't seem like that much to me, seems pretty normal."

At the end of the summer, she'll tape *Circus of the Stars*. Then she'll start going to work 8 to 5 every day on the sitcom. She'll do her junior and senior courses—algebra II, bead-working, government, books for pleasure, psychology and cooking. Her mother worries that her education will suffer now that they've moved to L.A. Ashlee kept her grades up in Kansas. The tutors on *I'll Fly Away* in Atlanta pushed her hard. Her mother notices they're laxer here. Ashlee's a little sensitive about that. "I'm ahead of the kids in Kansas," Ashlee says when her mom brings it up. "High school has been a breeze for me up to now, knock on wood."

"Wait till you get to that SAT," says her mother.

"I don't wanna do that," Ashlee groans.

"College is very important, but it comes later," her dad says. "When she's on a roll, she's gonna stick to her roll. This show could go three to four years."

"I wouldn't bank on that," Ashlee says.

"It's possible," he goes on. "Anything's possible. It could be down tomorrow, but anything's possible." He talks about how Ashlee wants to go to school "in the business field" so she can "get more involved with her money." Ashlee's been making money since she was eight. She has her own checking account and her own credit card. Twenty-five percent of all she makes goes into a trust fund for when she's older. Out of the rest, she pays her manager and her agent.

"I can remember the first Wal-Mart commercial brought in like $6,000," her mother says.

"We thought that was bigtime," her dad laughs. "It *was* back then."

"I set like a goal everytime," Ashlee says. "Like now I want to book a feature [film], make a whole lot of money so I can buy myself a '61 Corvette. Usually it's not been that big. Like I started collecting Disney animation cels. I'd be working and I'd go buy one. Then I'd have to wait a couple more weeks and I'd go buy another one. So I'd always have myself a set goal: Work for a while, keep my grades up, then I'm gonna go buy that."

Her dad teases her: "Then when she landed *I'll Fly Away*, she'd go in and say I want ten of those at one time each week."

She gives him a dirty look. "Just kidding," he smiles at her.

Her mother remembers one of her early goals. "She wanted a Dooney & Bourke bag. We were from a very wealthy neighborhood."

"A very very wealthy neighborhood," her husband interjects "Per capita Kansas City and Johnson County where we lived have more millionaires than anywhere in the U.S. We're not, but we lived there. We were lucky enough. These girls would come in and they'd all have their Dooney & Bourke bags, $198 for the cheapest one."

"One hundred thirty," Ashlee corrects him.

"Okay, I paid $186 for your purse." He also bought her the Corvette and the BMW, so he's promised his younger daughter a Mercedes.

"I have too many goals right now, though," Ashlee says. "I wanna go buy clothes. I want a '61 Corvette, and a Harley-Davidson."

"We're gonna buy that," her dad says of the Harley. "I looked at those today. Brand new they're only fifty-four hundred dollars. Brand spanking new."

"Not bad," Ashlee says. "Pretty cheap actually."

"I keep going and looking at cars," Ashlee's mom says softly.

"Mom, see by the time you decide what car you want, I could've bought *twenty* more cars. I *know* what I want. I want a '61 convertible red with white inlay. That's it. I want white or red interior. I want a black Harley, a sportster. I know what I want. Now, Mom."

"She's the worst shopper," Julius agrees, pretending to elbow his wife.

"It takes her *years* to decide," Ashlee says, then turns to her mother: "I'm going to buy you a car."

"No, you're not going to buy me a car."

"I wanna buy her a car," Ashlee says urgently to her dad.

"Eventually, I'll decide," her mother says calmly.

"I wanna buy you a car," Ashlee insists. "But I want you to decide first what you want." She looks at her father again. "I'll buy her a car with my money."

Her mother answers: "Save your money, honey. Later on you can buy me something very elaborate."

Julius tells Ashlee that her mom wants a Mercedes 580 SEL sedan.

"I can't afford *that,*" Ashlee replies fiercely.

"Well, then don't be talking," her dad kids.

"You think I'd go buy her a 580. I'd go buy myself a 300 SL if I had *that* much money," Ashlee says loudly. "I'd go buy myself a Mercedes. I know what I'm talking about. I'm a car girl."

April around 25, 1978

God. This is really hard in a strange deepseated way I never imagined. Now stop thinking for a minute how you might be perceived. stop. ok—it is depressing and pulling and what is real and people think this and that and some is true and you can't manipulate it all and who is real to you and who do you really have and who understands you and how thick is your skin and how much do you care and who do you connect with and what is connecting when you fake it all day and people know you can fake it so what's real and how are you acting and you might as well be acting 'cause you'd rather be acting and you wish you could just move on to that next step but you have to finish this one first and you love you love something, yourself maybe, but who else does. you're weird. you're hurt. you can't show it. but you never could and it's no harder now, just more pressure but distributed across new years it feels the same, you know. you are open. you are open to it. that's why it hurts. How you're rambling.

"IT'S LIKE THE SHOW": 90210's RASHIDA JONES

Rashida Jones is driving through Beverly Hills in her black 1988 Range Rover on a night out with her best guy friends, Jason and Keith. She's known Jason since first grade. Keith she met in ninth grade because she got a crush on Jason and decided to get closer to him through his best friend, who was Keith. It worked: She and Jason got together. But then it didn't feel right. So later, she dated Keith for half a year until some "bad stuff" started happening. Now they're all "just friends."

Keith, who looks like he could be one of the Baldwin brothers, is riding along in her car when Rashida stops at Jason's house. There is a yard full of giant cacti, and Jason—everybody says he looks like Matthew Modine—is waiting outside on the steps with his new puppy. Rashida squeals and scoops the dog out of Jason's arms: "You are so cute." Both guys watch the way the puppy lights Rashida up. She has the kind of soft features, accented by hazel eyes and tawny skin, that magazines now use on their covers to show their commitment to multiculturalism.

She kisses the puppy. "Hi, Quincy," she whispers into its fur. Quincy, coincidentally as in Quincy Jones, who is Rashida's father.

Rashida nuzzles the little labrador. It nips playfully at her. "Now he's biting my arm," she says.

"It's a black thing," Keith teases her. She glares at him. Playing.

As a mixed-race eighteen-year-old, Rashida is used to black and/or white jokes. In the rarefied reaches of show business America racist comments are somehow more permissible, less potentially harmful—and that's where Rashida has grown up. Her mother is Peggy Lipton, from *Mod Squad* and *Twin Peaks*. Her father is revered not only as a musician, composer, producer (he's won more Grammys than anyone ever), but for breaking down racial barriers to become a powerful force in the entertainment industry, currently as head of QDE Entertainment, a division of Warner Brothers. Rashida's life epitomizes multiculturalism. In her immediate family, she has a background mix of African and Jewish and Irish and Russian. She says because of that she was raised in a colorblind way. "Our parents loved us and taught us we should love ourselves. Our friends just all looked different from us, but we were taught that that's what made us beautiful." She hangs out with both black and white friends. She dates Jewish guys, Mexican guys, whoever she wants. But it isn't racial stuff that affects her the most. It's the fame. "It makes you live under this double standard," she says. "People will use you and also reject you by discrediting your accomplishments." Some people only see Rashida as someone who gets out of school for the Grammys or to go on family vacations with Oprah Winfrey.

The three of them pile into the Rover, leaving Quincy behind. They squabble about where to eat, but finally Rashida heads off toward Jason's suggestion—Brentwood's California Pizza Kitchen (CPK), a hangout popular for its nouveau pizza combinations. Keith complains because the backseat windows only go down halfway, and they pass a poster advertising the Garlic Festival, which was just celebrated in Los Angeles. Jason went and reports it even had garlic ice cream.

"Garlic ice cream," Rashida gags. "That's like . . . Remember, Keith, I told you about this guy who's in this band called Life, Sex & Death on our label?"

"What is it?" Jason interrupts slyly.

"This guy."

"*Whose* label?" Jason asks pointedly, a grin starting at the corners of his mouth.

Rashida finally understands what he's getting at: her father's power. She sighs loudly. "Warner Brothers," she says, cocking an eyebrow at him in the rearview mirror. "It's the label that I work for Jason . . . not . . ."

"CEO?" Jason teases.

She's a summer intern. Enunciating carefully, she puts him in his place. "If you're an employee at a company, Jason, it's part of *your* company. *You* put effort into it." Then she returns to the Life, Sex & Death anecdote that somehow relates to garlic ice cream: "Anyway, okay, so this guy, he's like the grossest. He's so disgusting. He doesn't bathe. He like throws up and pees all over the floor. Everytime he comes [to the office] he just pees on the floor."

Jason: "Whaaaat?"

"And he walks down the hall and you can smell him," Rashida continues, her nose curling at the memory.

"*Who's* this?" Keith asks, snapping out of a daydream.

Rashida goes over it again. "He's this guy in this band. And in the middle of a meeting he peed on the floor."

"If he had more class, he'd do it on the table," Keith says.

Rashida ignores him. "What happened was, the band, they used to all stay together and there was this house like at Palm Springs or something, and he like shit all over the living room floor."

"Shat," Jason says, correcting her grammar.

"Shat, all right," she says.

*   *   *

Rashida swings into CPK's underground parking lot, and a valet comes to whisk away the Rover. There's a wait at the restaurant, so Rashida window-shops at the neighboring boutiques and talks about how when her family was in Switzerland Oprah sneaked up to their room in her pajamas at four in the morning to eat french fries with them. About how her dad and actress Nastassja Kinski took Rashida's suggestion for naming their baby daughter, Kenya. "She's beautiful," Rashida says of her little half sister. She wishes she had a picture of Kenya in her wallet, but all she has are some other family pictures: she and her siblings when they were little, her older sister with her then-fiancé, LL Cool J, and she and her dad torn out of *US* magazine.

* * *

A table is ready. "Tori Spelling is here," Keith whispers as they sit down.

"Where?" Rashida asks.

"Right directly to my right—outside. You see her? See her right out to my right. She's sitting with that blonde . . . across the table from that blonde." Rashida looks, trying to seem like she isn't. When she spots the *Beverly Hills 90210* actress, she simply raises an eyebrow at the guys.

"So I go to Redondo Beach," Jason says, launching into a non sequitur story. "It's not like a nice beach. There was like brothers who could play there. We came out, my brother and I, and they were like, *'You guys* wanna *play?'* and I was like, *'We'll play.'* Of course I think they're gonna beat us—tall black guys—I don't mean to sound racist or anything but I am sometimes I know."

"Yeah," says Rashida, "you are."

"No," Jason says, flaring. *"They* were like racist. They automatically thought they were gonna beat us."

"Yeah, totally," Rashida concedes sincerely.

Jason continues, "So we're playing and these other guys come up like, *'Who has next, who has next?'* And we had just come on . . . but we finished our game. Will and I didn't say a word about like getting snaked out of our game. These guys were huge and they could play."

"So did you get a game?"

"No."

"Good story, Jason," Rashida says sarcastically.

Jason grunts and snorts. Rashida calls him Butthead, and the three of them do a Beavis & Butthead snicker and snort routine until the waitress approaches.

"I'll have an iced tea, please," Rashida says.

* * *

Rashida narrates the menu: "Santa Fe's good. Thai chicken is good, and barbeque chicken is really good. That sounds really gross but it's really really good."

"I have to go for the chicken potato pizza," Jason says.

"Ewww," Rashida says.

"I have to go for the Thai chicken pizza," Keith says.

Rashida doesn't like that choice any better.

She turns to Jason. "But I give you credit, Jason," she says, "because you have like better taste in women."

"No!" Keith protests.

Rashida, Keith, and Jason bicker like sister and brothers. They says it's because they all went to Buckley, a private school in Sherman Oaks with just 350 kids in the upper school. Rashida graduated last month, but Jason and Keith will be seniors next year. Rashida says it's a very small world, a family even: "It's like everybody's gone out with everybody or had a crush on somebody or liked somebody or had incest." Most students' parents work in the Industry or are doctors or lawyers. The parking lot is full of BMWs and Mercedes and Porsches. Tevin Campbell goes there. Some of the "Jackson family offspring" are there too. "We're more like *90210* than Beverly Hills High, *a lot* more like it," Rashida says. *"Totally.* Every situation [on the show] like has happened at our school. They had that whole thing [on *Beverly Hills 90210*] about how they drank at the prom and they got in trouble. The conversations they had were like *déjà vu."*

Déjà vu because in the spring, Rashida and Jason went to Paris with the school choir. Trouble happened, Rashida recalls: "There's no drinking age [in France] so I had a coupla beers, he had a coupla shots. Everybody did their own thing."

"A couple?" Jason snorts.

"But anyway," Rashida races on, "we got in trouble and Jason got sent home after three days. And I had to stay in Paris *in my hotel room."*

"We signed this contract, and the contract said, 'I will not use drugs or abuse alcohol,' " Rashida says.

"Oh," Keith says slyly, "So you can *drink* because you're sixteen but you can't *abuse* it."

"Right," Rashida tells him.

"Either way, it's illegal," Keith says, "because you're an American citizen, even though you're in another country."

"It's not illegal to drink there," Jason jumps in.

"Yeah, but you see you tried to use . . . even though the contract said *abuse* alcohol, they meant you can't *use* it," Keith counters.

"But the thing is," Rashida says, "the school has foreign exchange programs every year, and *they* get drunk with the teachers."

* * *

They have to order. Rashida votes Santa Fe, barbecue chicken pizza, and, begrudgingly, Thai. She tells Keith he has to have Oreo peanut butter pie for dessert, in her honor.

Then she stops and scrutinizes her drink. "There's a fly in my iced tea."

"Just eat it," Keith tells her.

"There's a fly. I'm not gonna eat it."

"It's a fly, Rashida. It's not gonna kill you."

"I'm gonna get another one."

"It's not gonna kill you. It's a fly."

Rashida flags down the waitress and turns over the tainted tea as Keith jokes he's gonna miss all the excitement. Meaning when Rashida goes away to Harvard in the fall. Another friend is staying in LA to attend a small college, Occidental. "Accidental," as Rashida says some people call it.

"She's gonna transfer," Keith says.

"To where?"

"Somewhere."

"Her parents don't want her to go East . . ." Rashida says.

"She'll end up at UCLA," Jason puts in.

"You think?" Rashida asks, surprised.

"[Occidental's] *so* not her. It's a whole bunch of geeks and nerds," Jason says.

"Really," says Rashida. "Maybe you should go there, Keith. You can get in."

"*Ho* ho. Ouch. I could say something harsh, but I'm not going to." Keith arches an eyebrow.

"No, I didn't get in [to Harvard] just because my father's famous and I'm black and I'm a woman," retorts Rashida.

"No, I didn't mean being black and a woman," Keith stammers.

"You're gonna do fine there," Jason assures her.

"I know," she says. "It's like they're not gonna accept you if you can't hold your own . . . even if you are, you know . . . I get pretty good grades."

Keith clears his throat conspicuously, and Rashida narrows her eyes at him.

He says, "No, no, I'm really doin' that 'cause I choked on food . . . I swear to God."

She says, "I mean, I don't have like 5.0 and A's and stuff. But I maintained my grades, and I had a lot of activities and stuff and I'm not *stupid*. Harvard isn't just interested in SATs and GPAs. They don't just want study bugs." She swivels a defiant look between the two guys.

Jason points to Keith. "That's the one you should be looking at. *I'm* defending you."

"I know, Jason," she says. "You're gonna go to a really good school. Oh my god, what did you get on your SAT—12 what?"

"Thirteen twenty."

"Thirteen twenty. Oh my god. That's amazing," she says. "I don't do so well on timed tests."

She catches Keith looking skeptical again. "Keith," she chides. "You are *so* not one to be *even* smiling, *even* looking at me."

"I forgot to order my half Chinese chicken salad," he says sheepishly.

*   *   *

The pizza isn't coming. Keith goes back to *90210* again—a subject that's unlikely to trigger Rashida's temper.

He says, "You know I was thinking about . . . What's his name?"

"Luke Perry," Rashida suggests.

"Yeah, him and Kelly."

"When Keith was cheating on me . . ." Rashida begins, thwarting
his plan to distract her.

"I was not cheating on you . . . I was not *going out* with you."
He sounds exasperated.

"Whatever," she sighs. "Keith was with me, *and* he was with
somebody else. Dylan was with Kelly *and* Brenda. Yes, it was like he
was cheating. They chose Kelly, which would mean that Keith chose
the other girl."

"Nah, Rashida and Shannon [Doherty] are a lot alike—bitchy
snobs," Keith says.

"Shut up."

"I'm just kidding."

"I don't care, okay? I moved onto bigger and better things,"
Rashida taunts him. Bigger and better things means she's been dating an Actor.

"What do you call it when you go test-drive a car for a week?"
Rashida says.

"Trial," Jason says.

"Yeah, trial run," she says.

"Tough word," Keith mutters.

"Yeah, we're on trial. We went out before. We went out for like
three months."

"He's like forty-three," Keith says.

"He's not, he's twenty-eight," Rashida returns, then goes on to
tell how they met. "See we go to our spiritual place. I met him
there. It's sort of a spiritual retreat, and I have a guru, and you learn
how to meditate and chant and like the whole point is to bring you
closer to the God that exists with you and everyone. But it's not a

religion; it's just like a practice. You study everything." Rashida
started going to the ashram with her mother. Then the Actor came
with his sister. She says, "He was married but actually . . ."

Keith tsks. "He left his wife for you."

"No. He's been divorced for two years. He has one son." Rashida
and the Actor broke up while he was in New York doing a play. Then
they didn't see each other for a while, and he dated someone else.
Then they ran into each other again. Rashida says, "We started talking on the phone. We started going out again to dinner and stuff
and then he started telling me he realized like I was the only person
who understood him. He thought no one else was as tolerant."

"How tall is he?" Keith asks.

"Not that tall," Rashida answers. "Five-nine."

* * *

The pizzas arrive, and Rashida presides over the distribution. She
spreads the guacamole all over the Santa Fe pizza. It looks disgusting.

"Cute pizza," Keith tells her.

"Cute face," she bats back.

"Cute comeback."

"Cute interruption."

They eat. They talk about marijuana.

"I don't understand why it's not legal. It makes no sense,"
Rashida says. "First of all, I don't think it's classified as an addictive
drug, is it?"

"It isn't."

"The thing is, you never hear about oh yeah, *Mass murderer on
the loose under the influence of pot.* It's not heroin or that stuff.
They say that the problem is the more you do it, the more you're
prone to do other drugs, which is so stupid. If anything, drinking
does that. I'm never drinking again."

They grin and reminisce about a party where they were drinking
and dancing and having a great time—until Keith got sick. He
threw up. "I had to take him home the next day, and he hadn't even
brushed his teeth," Rashida says. "It was so gross."

"You're the one who curled up with him in bed," Jason reminds her.

"Where was I supposed to sleep, Jason? You guys had all the pillows and all the blankets."

"You curled right up with him and started talking about kitchen utensils."

Rashida starts to laugh. "The spoon," she says, referring to the cuddling position. "You know how to spoon."

"Who knows what she did to me," Keith groans. "I was like passed out. No telling."

"Oh, yeah, I raped you," Rashida rolls her eyes. She tells Jason, "In the middle of the night, Keith was all like, *'I hate throwing up. I hate it. It's so bad.'* And no one's up so he's talking to himself."

"Eat your pizza all right," Keith instructs her.

Rashida: "Cheat on your girlfriend all right."

Keith: "Okay. I didn't cheat on anybody."

"Keith, you lied so bad."

"I lied. I didn't cheat on you though," he says.

"I think that's cheating."

"Cheating?" he says. "You didn't want to be going out."

"No," she says. *"You* didn't want to be going out."

"You did not want to be going out."

"No, you didn't wanna be going out."

This goes back and forth a few more times. Finally Rashida asks pointedly: "You weren't attracted to me and you didn't have feelings for me then?"

Keith: "That's not what I'm saying, I'm saying . . ."

"I'm asking that question," she tells him firmly.

"Well, yeah," he admits.

"Yeah, okay, fine."

* * *

It turns out the restaurant has stopped serving Rashida's favorite peanut butter pie with Oreo cookie crust. She settles for a chocolate ice cream ball, which she shares with Keith and Jason. They split the check evenly. It comes to about $15 each, and as she figures the tip, she asks if they remember this one time a waiter balked at bringing her another cranberry juice with ice.

"You were rude," says Keith, who remembers.

"Whatever," she says. "I'm the customer. Anyway, we were finished eating, and I left like a $1.05 tip, and the guy like comes outside and throws the money at me and says, 'Here, I don't need it.' He was so rude. He charged me $10 because I asked for another cranberry juice."

"He didn't charge you $10."

"$4.50 per drink," she says.

"It was your idea to eat there. I told you I didn't want to eat there. Gross."

As they wait for the valet to return Rashida's car, she says, "There's a certain image that people like see of California and kids who have a lot of money. And that image is all over the country—in the Midwest, the East, and everything. And it's funny to be like living that lifestyle because it's not as glamorous as it seems. You don't appreciate it or hate it any more or less than anybody else does their life. You're just in it. And the more fortunate you are, the more problems develop. I mean, someone in Oregon doesn't have the problem of people using them for tickets to Soul Train." Later, when she's not with her friends anymore, Rashida adds, "Nobody gives you credit for your own accomplishments because you come from a famous family. You have all this exposure to criticism. Most people, when they get into a good school, their friends are happy for them. With me, people are suspicious. Nobody understands. To them, my life just looks artificial and starstruck because I have this talented famous dad. But that stuff changes the dynamic of parenting. My dad was away a lot. We had all the love in the world, but I never saw my dad the way everyone else did. To me, he's this scared little child that I love because I see his vulnerabilities. He's human."

She knows that most other people will always only see the image, though—of her, of her life, of her father. As they climb in the Rover (yes, it is a Range Rover but she worked all summer to buy half of it herself), Rashida and the guys gossip about the kids at school who *really* embody that image, that "90210 snobbiness." Rashida describes kids who when they go to the airport go in limos drinking champagne, the same ones who won't stay in regular Parisian hotels but only suites at the Ritz, because as one of the girls put it once, "It looked like a whore just slept in the bed."

Rashida always suspects that people are talking about her. As she pulls out into the Brentwood traffic, she points out that even Keith and Jason sometimes go a little far: "And we'll be like in the mall, and you guys'll just start going, 'Yeah, Quin-cy Jones, *your father.*' Going off for like an hour."

"That would not be us," Keith scoffs.

"That *would* so be you," she says, rolling her eyes.

JOSEPH NELSON "TRIPP" WINGARD III's GRADUATION

The night before his graduation from Orangeburg Preparatory, Tripp Wingard is darting around town in his mother's 1986 Chevy Cavalier station wagon, which is really his because he's the only one who ever drives it. On this muggy June night in Orangeburg, South Carolina, it has a can of Kodiak chewing tobacco in the glove compartment (which he calls "the bear"), a six-pack of beer in the back, and a tent so he can get drunk on graduation night and camp out in Angie's backyard instead of driving home. There's also a red rose for his girlfriend, Lindsey.

Tripp met Lindsey the Tuesday before at a softball game. He called her on Wednesday, and she said she didn't really think he would and he said why else would he have asked for her phone number. So on Thursday night he took her dancing at the Silver Spur, and on Friday night he went to another prep school and watched her graduate first in her class and then slept in the Cavalier because he got too drunk to drive. On Saturday he went and exchanged senior pictures with her because she was leaving the next day on a celebratory cruise to the Bahamas. After she left, he wrote her a letter and mailed it so it would be waiting for her when she got home, which is supposed to be tonight but he doesn't know what time. He is going to surprise Lindsey by showing up at her house. "I like to surprise girls," he says.

Back home, wearing knee-length jean cutoffs and his red (for Orangeburg Prep) T-shirt, he's getting around to the lawnmower when his orange-for-Clemson-University phone rings. It is Lindsey. She is home, just got home, and she called the number he sent in his letter, even though he told her not to use it because it's long distance. He paces around his room. He has a stocky frame and skin tanned by waterskiing. His hair is buzzed short. He is grinning into the phone receiver, grinning full out. He's so happy to be talking to Lindsey, he blows his surprise and tells her he'll be over, probably around ten. "Thanks for calling," he rushes to tell her just before they hang up.

Before he can leave to drive the fifteen miles from Orangeburg, South Carolina, to Lindsey's town Tripp has to mow the lawn for his mother, who is married to her second husband, a tall unsmiling man whom Tripp and his younger brother and sister call Mr. John. So Tripp doesn't get to Lindsey's until late, and stays just long enough to give her the rose, help her set up her new television/VCR, and get her to promise that she'll come to graduation tomorrow night.

*　*　*

The next day, Tripp comes home for lunch. He's training as a drive-through teller down at the First National Bank, so he's got on his work look: a steel-colored knit tie, a pink-and-gray-striped short-sleeve shirt, and gray slacks. And before he sits down for some of the pork barbecue that his mom picked up at Earl Duke's down by the Pepsi plant, Tripp calls Lindsey. Someone at her house tells him she has gone to see the boyfriend she broke up with after she met Tripp the week before. Tripp hangs up, shrugs nonchalantly, and stabs some stringy pork with his plastic fork.

He spills a little sauce on his tie. He goes to his room to get another from the closet where he carefully hangs all thirty of his custom T-shirts. They are all school-spirit shirts, most of them designed by Tripp at a T-shirt shop downtown to brag about Orangeburg's championship football team. In fact, his school spirit is everywhere in the room. There are trophies for academic awards and for football, his oldest love. His letter jacket is hanging over the back of a chair, with the state champ patches of the football Indians on it. But his room isn't just about his high school glory days; it's filled with mementoes foreshadowing what he hopes are even more glorious days at college. Pictures of tigers (for Clemson) in wild poses hang on the walls. On the double unmade bed, there is a washed but not folded pile of laundry and an orange (for Clemson) pillow that Tripp made in home ec. Just by the door, there is a cross-stitch picture that says Clemson. "See that cross-stitch," Tripp says. "Yours truly made that." In September, he will go away the five hours to Clemson University, where his grandfather went and where his father would have gone if he had chosen to go to college at all. Everyone in Tripp's family is a huge Clemson fan.

But if Tripp had his first choice, he would have been going to the Citadel for college. The Citadel is in North Carolina, and one of Tripp's neighbors describes West Point as "the Citadel of the North." Tripp had hoped to go, had his heart set on going but the school didn't offer him but $1,000 in scholarship money. And tuition was $10,000. He couldn't get the rest. His father, who lives with his new wife and three little children outside of town, didn't have it. His mother, a nurse, couldn't. And his stepdad—who owns an oil company, paid Tripp's Orangeburg prep tuition, and lives in a big white house near the country club golf course—wasn't offering. Still, Tripp hoped that he could at least be in the Marine Reserves. But when he took a physical, he found out that an ear problem he had as a child had left him deaf on his left side. He would not be going to the Citadel. He would not be going into the Marines. He settled for Clemson. Not so bad.

He goes back to work, not knowing if Lindsey will be at graduation now or not.

* * *

That night, Tripp wears red socks to graduation: red for the school's colors. And to be different. He is not like the other kids at his school. He transferred in from public school after his mother married Mr. John. So Tripp describes himself as a "preppy redneck."

He explains it this way: "A preppy's anybody who goes to our school"—"upper class" guys who wear polo shirts—"and the rednecks are the guys who drive a 4×4, wear cutoffs, chew tobacco." He adds, "I'm kinda like an oxymoron, a paradox." Which he revels in. Thus the red socks and all the other ways he's found to stand out.

As president of the senior class, he came up with the novelty of painting the road to the stadium with arrowheads. When everybody else got plain class rings, Tripp got one with an Indian head embossed on it. On the morning after prom, he made sure the other kids left the beach and came with him to a math meet in Charleston. He was known for wearing wild hats to football and track practice. He had a longtime girlfriend but didn't go all the way with her as his friends did with their girlfriends. However he says now that he would like to lose his virginity. "But I can't find a girl who will let me," is what he says.

Anyway, he thinks someone may stop him and send him home to change out of these red socks. This is the kind of graduation where no one yells when a graduate's diploma is conferred. The history teacher has explained in class that such behavior is "trashy." In this graduation ritual, there will be no messages taped on mortarboards, no throwing mortarboards in the air. Orangeburg prep is the one surviving private school in Orangeburg. People around town call it a white flight school. In 1965, two private schools were formed to get around integration. Since then, costs have escalated. To survive, the schools merged in 1988. Tradition survives at OP.

And Tripp mainly loves it. The night before graduation he sat on a bench in Edisto Memorial Gardens and talked about why. "It's like when you see *Gone With the Wind,* that kind of thing," he says, hurrying his slow drawl in his enthusiasm. "The girls always dress pretty. Most people have respect for each other." He pauses, then adds: "We don't have . . . kids don't bring guns and knives to school like they do to public school. I mean at the public school in the sixth grade, kids are bringin' guns to school. The sheriff patrol is always out at the school picking up people. It's just goin' to the pits. Education is just going to the pits."

What does he blame it on?

As he starts to answer, he sees a young black couple nearby being videotaped. Tripp whispers. "I'll tell you about it later." He launches into a description of the junior-senior prom, which had a jungle theme. "The best part," he says, "was a big chicken wire with toilet paper in the shape of a big tiger. I just loved that because Clemson is the Tigers."

Then he notices that the videotaping has moved around a bend in the Edisto River. "Back to the problem with education," he says. "I didn't want to say it around them . . . Afro-Americans. But I-95 runs from New York to Miami, and Orangeburg is approximately the halfway point. It's not but like ten, twenty minutes from 95 to here. And there's a bad drug problem because the drug dealers going from Miami to New York stop here. I think this is how it goes. And they've circulated around, and they're startin' to have families around here. You've got all these crack babies and drug dealers, and all the black people think they got to have guns and sell drugs to live. And that's why guns are gettin' into school. It's migrating into the school system. That's my personal opinion, you make sure you let everybody know that. I mean that's probably not the truth. But that's my opinion."

He says racial tension is not a problem at his school, though.

So is OP racially mixed?

"Oh, hang no. There's like five blacks out of eight hundred students. I think it's good. I don't know. I don't particularly . . . In the South, in the white population, there's blacks and then there's niggers. Niggers are the ones that carry guns. Blacks are the smart intelligent ones that don't bother nobody. Not that I don't mind bein' bothered by them—but they got a little bit of common sense and aren't smart-mouthed and aren't always saying some racial comment. A nigger carries a gun, does drugs, or is really racist toward everything but the black population. There's a lot of racial tension, I mean, people haven't forgotten it. It isn't totally desegregated."

In 1968, during the civil rights movement, three blacks were killed at an Orangeburg bowling alley. Tripp says no one has forgotten that. He himself doesn't have a single black friend. He says it's because he goes to a private school. "There's a lady at work who's black," he notes. "She's nice."

Would he want to come back to live here after college? "I'm really school spirited. I love my school to death," he answers. "I was voted the most spirited senior. I'd like for my kids to go here but I mean it's so racial and everything. It's so tense. There's a lot of racial tension kinds down here. I don't want my kids to be in that kind of environment, but I want them to go to the school I went to."

Does he think anything could be done about the racial tension?

"You can't make people believe what you [believe]," he says. "I mean, I don't hate the total black race. I just hate the sarcastic ones. People know what I'm talking about—the people who make comments about the whites. That's the people I don't like. I guess the only way you're gonna get rid of it is to get rid of groups like the KKK and the NAACP. I mean the NAACP, they aren't like the KKK but it's because of them that some blacks are so sarcastic to whites. They think they're so good. You can't have people thinkin' they're better than other people.

"Of course, the KKK, when they go around, they go, we hate niggers. Couple of weeks ago the KKK marched in Orangeburg, but it didn't cause a scene really. And they're marching somewhere else I heard the other day. Like in Alabama, they still got neo-Nazi people, skinhead groups. I saw it on TV the other day. They're marchin' every now and then, and they were like, 'We're gonna take back Alabama from the blacks and stuff like that.'

"And the NAACP, an example of that would be like Rodney King. In my book, they're blowin' the whole thing out of proportion. It shouldn't . . . I don't know . . . if they can't win a case and then they go off and try them for civil rights, that's just a bunch of bull as far as I'm concerned . . . It's just like a copout sorta. They couldn't get the cops for the real crime so they try somethin' like that and the NAACP is always in the middle of it."

His agitation shows. He runs a hand over the deep pile of his haircut, and crumples the Pepsi can he's holding. "In Orangeburg County," he goes on, "we got districts, and they were redrawn recently. We had to redraw those things three times to satisfy the NAACP. You'll never make me believe there was a reason for that. They want to have a black majority in a district so there'll be black councilmen and all that. That is a bunch of crock as far as I'm concerned, but that's just my opinion. . . . And I can't understand how an organization has the power to do that. That's like a monopoly in the business world, like some beer company or a wood-making corporation might have in a certain town. They're tryin' to make it be [a monopoly in Orangeburg]. Not just in this town but America."

He tells a story about his last year in public school, when he was a fifth grader, and he was playing soccer on the playground. He fell down. "When I got up, there was a circle of about fifteen black guys around me," he says. A new kid from out of state accused Tripp of calling him a nigger. Tripp denied saying anything at all. The kid punched him in the face. They got sent to the office. "There was a big black principal, vice principal, who took care of stuff like that, fights and stuff," Tripp says. "Of course, the black guy got his side first. When I walked in there, they were already through talkin' to him." The principal asked Tripp, "Did you call this boy a nigger?" Tripp said, "No sir, I did not." The principal said, "He's got friends that'll tell you you did."

Tripp sighs. "All his friends were black. I was outnumbered. I never saw this guy in my life. I never called him a nigger. And we both got the discipline, which was two spanks, two paddles with a wooden paddle."

And earlier this year, he says, he took some freshmen buddies out for chicken wings and pinball—only to get hassled at a pinball machine by a couple of black twelve- or thirteen-year-olds "lookin' to fight." He says they were trying to take over the pinball machine. They cursed and yelled, and finally they followed Tripp and his buddies into the restaurant and heckled them. Tripp slaps his knee. "They just wanted somethin' to do that Friday night."

What bugs him so much about the whole racist thing is that it doesn't fit with how he sees himself. "I'm just a good ole boy," he says. "I'd do anything for anybody really—except for the people I don't have any respect for, which is people who don't respect other people. Say this Friday night at a party somebody asks me for a beer. I won't be a dickhead . . ." He stops, mortified to have said that. "Excuse me," he says, starting over. "I won't be a jerk. I'll be friendly. That's the *Gone With the Wind,* Southern part of me, to be polite and nice."

Would he ever join the KKK to retaliate?

He thinks a minute. He's shaking his head no, but he says: "It's too much sometimes. Sometimes I'd like to be in it. Sometimes I wouldn't. I'm kinda iffy on that. If you know a member, which I don't, you just ask 'em, and they'll give you an application. Just like the Elks club."

* * *

At the graduation ceremony on OP's basketball floor, junior girls in white gloves and lacy dresses usher the graduates to their seats. Tripp Wingard makes it up the aisle in his red socks. As the crowd watches from folding chairs and crammed bleachers, he graduates tenth in his all-white class. He even wins the most prestigious award—the Tommy Wanamaker, given for leadership, character, and school spirit. He holds the three-foot-tall trophy and gives a speech, thanking the faculty and his parents. "God bless you," he concludes.

He's got two parties tonight—a "redneck" one for the public school kids who also graduated tonight, and the OP one where they are roasting a whole pig. But first it's to his mom's, where the cat has eaten part of the decorated cake while everyone else was crammed into the high school auditorium. As aunts, uncles, and family friends watch, he opens a CD player from his mom, a Jimmy Buffett CD from his brother. He fills his wallets with twenties meant for spending on the cruise to the Bahamas he's taking with eight friends starting Sunday. He opens three sets of towels. "I won't be wet at college," he quips. He keeps glancing past his mother, who is quietly overseeing the pouring of Pepsi, the bowls of chips. Tripp keeps beaming at Lindsey, leaning against the counter in a white off-the-shoulder dress and high white pumps.

Lindsey goes with him to the next stop, ten minutes out of town on dark roads to his father's place. The house is full of relatives and computer-generated banners of congratulations; one reads, WATCH OUT CLEMSON, HERE I COME. Tripp's three little half-siblings—all under the age of ten—crawl all over him as he opens a fancy car stereo and huge speakers. He opens a fuzz-buster. Everyone is eating brownies and burrito dip with chips, and his proud dad, who looks just like Tripp, is grousing in jest about how Tripp spends money: $300 on a water ski; $100 on sunglasses. Lindsey stands chatting with cousins, drinking Pepsi from a plastic cup. Tripp is wearing a straw hat that belongs to Lindsey. He comes over for a drink. She rubs his shoulders. He is radiating pride. He grabs a handful of chips.

And then he slips with Lindsey out into the night to do what he has been doing more and more: Partying. Drinking. He feels guilty about it. The teachers don't know. Please don't tell his mom. He's still only been drunk three or four times—the first after the football team won the state championship. He's worried: "Alcohol kills brain cells, which I'm a firm believer of that," he says, "because I've been forgetting things lately." *Buuut* he's a senior this year, and next year he'll be a freshman at Clemson, where there are 15,000 students and keg parties that last from Thursday to Sunday. And besides, he's brought his tent. He can drink and not risk driving till morning.

The moon is full. Sometime later, a lunar eclipse will darken the night. But for now Tripp and Lindsey are cruising fast in the moonlight over the back country roads until he stops where the first party throbs like a monster heart in the night.

Tripp parks behind a long line of cars. He gets out and takes Lindsey by the hand.

"Political Incorrectness"

In the third grade, we got "integration." Twenty years after the ruling in Brown *vs.* Board of Education, *the public schools in Durham, North Carolina, were finally being forced to comply, and so my little brother and I started going by bus across the park and through downtown to East End School, instead of walking five blocks to Club Boulevard. From the first day, it was clear that separate had been very unequal: The jungle gym on the playground was ancient and all rusted, and although we had complained about the grossness of our old cafeteria, this school didn't even have one. So we brought our lunchboxes and ate in the basement. My desk was broken, and the books were worn-out. And, of course, for the first time, I had not only black kids in my classes but a black principal, and a black homeroom teacher, Mrs. Lester.*

There was a lot of tension. I remember rumors that if a black kid and a white kid touched, their skin colors would rub off on each other—making games of tag much more serious. And even the racism that didn't escalate in this new setting just got quieter. Out on the playground, white kids who used to proudly shout out the "nigger jokes" their dads taught them now shut up a lot more. Usually, they waited until we were back on the bus and into our own neighborhoods again to start up with them. Even the white teachers who had been transferred to East End seemed to like these joke sessions. Once when a white girl asked one of the teachers was it true that the black girls put cooking oil in their hair, the teacher laughed and said to crack an egg over her head in the sun and see if it fried. Actually, I'd often heard them commenting about "niggers" back at our old school too. I got the feeling a lot of the teachers, black and white, hoped this whole integration thing would just blow over soon.

But Mrs. Lester was into it. She gave us a long lecture instead of a class one day around a month into the year—all about how we were here together for a reason. She said that most of us were still acting as though we went to separate schools, there was so little interaction between the blacks and the whites. Then she made a big point of exempting from her lecture me and a girl named Lisa, saying, "But there are two girls in this class who are different races, and they're as close as two peas in a pod." It was true. Lisa was my best friend. But it wasn't until I was writing this chapter, remembering all the things we used to do together, that I realized Lisa probably felt like she had to cover up a lot of the differences between us. Neither of our families had a lot of money, but we had our own house while she lived in a duplex with another family. That was just temporary, she said. She also didn't have a father, and the day I first walked home with her to play after school, she made up this elaborate and appealing lie about how her dad was a traveling salesman for a toy company, and was coming back with boxes of those little hairy troll dolls and jacks for both of us. Once Lisa invited me and another girl to sleep over at her house and Valerie's grandmother, whom Valerie lived with, called my mom and asked, "What kind of a girl is Lisa?" "A nice girl," my mom answered, knowing what information the woman actually wanted. "Is she a Negro?" her grandmother finally said. My mom lied and said no. We all three slept over at Lisa's. Lisa and I may have been overlooking our skin colors as much as we could, but other differences that came along with them kept coming up.

Five years later, as a teenager at Carolina Friends School, a Quaker school where my parents transferred us hoping the teachers' philosophies would be more like their own, there was a black student named Ronald Pratt. My paternal grandmother, who belonged to an old North Carolina family, told me that his having the same last name meant Ronald's ancestors had been slaves on our ancestors' plantation, and had taken their masters' family name when they went free. My mom tells me this is the same grandmother who had written a letter to my dad when he was marrying her, saying she knew she should have warned him about immoral races like the Negroes and the Jews. I still don't know if there was any factual basis for what she said about the last names or not, but it totally startled us that our family at some point might have had slaves. Partly because—even though my sister was only joking about telling Ronald, "Hey, slave, get my lunch"—some things hadn't changed all that much since my grandmother grew up. Maybe just the laws.

Many things still haven't changed. I remember a girl at East End that first year confessing to me how she prayed every night to be white. It makes me appreciate even more all the teenagers I know now who, in spite of the racism they experience daily, are proud of the race they are—whether black or white or both.

Rashida is part of an increasing number of kids from mixed-race families, a number that more than tripled between the late sixties and the beginning of the nineties. The population as a whole is just changing, becoming less white as the black population grows and immigration brings in more Asians and Latinos. Schools in most places are more racially mixed, although it is still hard won, not because of legally enforced segregation anymore but because of social and economic segregation in so many areas. In Kansas City, Missouri, a billion-dollar program to entice white kids into inner-city schools is failing. And schools in Oklahoma City have actually reversed integration policies.

It's the same now among teenagers—every good sign countered by a bad one. Here's an example: Forty-two percent of university students surveyed recently thought "helping to promote racial understanding" was an "essential" or "very important" goal. That number was up eight percentage points from a year before, one of the most dramatic increases in the twenty-seven-year run of the

*survey. And racial issues (including "all the racism everywhere,"
interracial dating, and "people telling me I act 'black,' calling me a
'wigger' ") came up more often than anything else when we asked
kids about their biggest issues. But the increasing concern comes
at the same time as—and possibly in reaction to—the fact that
racist attitudes and racially motivated attacks among teenagers
are higher now than ever. As a 1993 study by the Anti-Defamation
League showed, young whites are more biased against blacks than
even older whites.*

*But who needs statistics? You can't escape hearing it every-
where. It comes out in apologetic-sounding whispers. It comes out
in tones and words that are harsh and hard to accept. When Tripp
talks about the KKK it probably sets off alarms for a lot of people
just the way it did when I told my dormmates at Andover about
these guys I knew back home. I'd met them in a Methodist Youth
Fellowship group I had joined for some reason (called boredom)
only to find out they all had business cards in their wallets proving
they were "junior klanners." Of course, some of the kids who were
so shocked at prep school were the same ones who said they were
sorry but they wouldn't want to room with the one African American in our dorm because her hair products smelled. And that's still
true today. People who scoff at extremist groups like the KKK and
think racism is much worse in the South don't realize their brand
of it is just less overt, more insidious. Some teenagers, like
teenagers in the Aryan Nation, say the increase in these more blatant forms of racism and violence among races is proof all this
racial mixing is not working and that we need to segregate "before
we all like kill each other." And then there are teenagers in Afro-
centric groups like Blackwatch, whose leader told a* Sassy *writer,
"If young black people want to do something that motivates themselves, to feel better about themselves, and to unify themselves . . .
once we can get that kind of thing going, then we'll have something
to contribute to the rest of the mess out here. We're going to be
called racists. But we can't afford to be rainbow anymore. It's not
about separatism. We've just got no time."*

You can see how bad it's become. Sure, there are some great grass-roots efforts to promote racial harmony, like Colors, a club in a Massachusetts high school, and like the American Ethnic Coalition, which some Long Island students started. But most kids don't know the history of racial oppression. They don't have personal memories of blacks being hosed down in southern streets, being attacked by police dogs. While I don't either, I did hear a lot of stories from my uncle Joe who was a Freedom Rider and spent a summer in jail in Mississippi (and how grandmother said that meant he owed the state of Mississippi room and board). These kids don't remember Martin Luther King, Jr.'s talk about brotherhood or Bobby Kennedy's. For lots of kids, racial equality is no longer a matter of good versus evil, as it seemed back during the civil rights battle when people like my uncle decided to rebel against his southern heritage and join the "good" side.

Now, it is black versus white versus Native American versus Korean versus Japanese versus Mexican. It's Us versus Them. One of the girls who put racism on her list of concerns, said, "I'm glad we're taught to take pride in our cultural diffs, but sometimes I think we focus so much on that, we don't see what we have in common." Instead of Bobby Kennedy, teenagers are hearing white separatists talk about making the Pacific Northwest into an exclusive enclave. Instead of Martin Luther King, Jr., they're getting Louis Farrakhan and his disciples giving lectures about Jewish "bloodsuckers." Instead of freedom rides, these kids watch CNN report on angry mobs of Jews and blacks facing off in Crown Heights, Brooklyn. These kids remember white policemen brutally stomping on Rodney King, Reginald Denny being pulled from his truck and beaten on the ground, Korean grocers trying to defend their stores against rioting kids from South Central.

And if their view of racism is raw, the way they talk about it is too. Their words can be shocking. They don't speak euphemistically of "the underprivileged" and "the underclass." They say niggers, gangstas, wiggers (for whites who act black), bitches, and hos. They'll tell you that politically correct terms don't say what they mean, don't describe their world. *"I think political correctness is really kind of a bad thing because you can like stifle people, and they can't like express what they mean to without it being misconstrued by someone else,"* one fifteen-year-old told us. *"Plus, you can still be a racist or homophobe and just hide behind political correctness. Instead of nigger lesbo, you can say African American woman of alternative sexual orientation. Sugarcoating it isn't gonna make it better."*

So they strike this uneasy balance. A seventeen-year-old from Great Neck, New York, says that in her liberal high school it's cool to have Asian and African American friends. *"Everyone looks up to minorities."* But, she added, *"there's this tension 'cause of things like applying to college. I mean, African American students are definitely taken over other students. I had two friends—one black, one white—apply to Duke University. Guess which one got in?"*

Racism is just there, whether it's an Athens, Georgia, mother who points to the "porch monkeys" as she drives the kids home from school; whether it's people turning in a Miami pizza parlor to stare at the only two black kids in the whole place; whether it's American Jews snubbing Iranian Jews in a New York high school. It all hurts and destroys. And when kids can't find the words to fight back, they will fight it in other ways. They will try their own solutions.

VALERIE KING'S
NINE REASONS TO FIGHT
IF YOU'RE A
JEWISH SKINHEAD IN L.A.

You see a guy painting swastikas on a grocery store
Valerie King shaved her head when she was fifteen. Two weeks later, she saw a "totally bonehead looking" guy painting swastikas on a grocery store. "HaHa," she taunted him. "You're drawing 'em the wrong way. Backwards." Then, to mock him, she threw up her arm and gave him the Nazi salute: she sieg heiled him.

"Oh, *cool,*" he fired back snidely.

"Down with you, you fucking faggot," she yelled. "You're a faggot. Adolf Hitler was a faggot. Your dad's a faggot." And then she walked away, having upheld what she and her friends believe is the true spirit of being skinheads: fighting racism.

The next day she was walking down the street with two skinhead girlfriends. They met up with six guys riding skateboards and bicycles. One of them was the swastika guy. "Okay, you skinhead," the guy yelled at Valerie. "You're gonna die for your fuckin' beliefs! Are you ready to die for your beliefs?"

Valerie's friend, Sally, who is two years older, stepped in: "She's not a skinhead. I'm a fuckin' skinhead. You go try it with me."

"Shut up," Valerie told her, and she hung back, laughing at the swastika guy, as her friends turned to walk away.

The next thing she knew: "I just hear a POP [from a punch], and I go down on the ground. I was like out for thirty seconds. He knocked me out. But I got right back up. I just went and kicked him in the balls. He punched me, and I reached up and punched him. I kicked him in the balls again. He knocked me down on the ground. The same thing happened about six times," she says.

Then her friends, the guys on skateboards, the guys on bicycles, everybody started looking at Valerie "like really weird." Somebody yelled, "Fuck, you killed her." Valerie was afraid to look down because she thought the swastika guy might hit her again, even though all his friends were starting to walk away. Finally, she looked down anyway and saw blood all over her white T-shirt. He stood over her alone, motionless. He had stabbed her. "I was bleeding and bleeding," she remembers.

At the hospital, they sewed her up with five stitches and told her she was lucky: the knife had just missed her spleen, cutting right above the kidney, right underneath the lung. The cops came to the hospital because the guy who stabbed her had turned himself in. He thought he had killed her. He was part Filipino, part Mexican, neo-Nazi. To prosecute, the cops needed Valerie to cooperate. "I don't want to," Valerie cried. "You'll call my mom."

A fat chick wears the American flag as a skirt

Valerie and a bunch of skins are at a show one night, and they see this 200-pound girl. "This is how she dresses to get into a fight," Valerie says. "She spikes up her hair in her mohawk, puts on like three layers of pancake makeup, eyeliner out to here, heels, and a ripped-up American flag tied around her waist as a shirt. I mean we do not allow the destruction of the American flag. That's one thing we do not allow."

Somebody calls your friend a slut

Last time Valerie had to avenge some rude gossip about one of her friends, she ripped part of a girl's ear off.

Valerie has three friends worth fighting for, and together they hang out in a complicated world ruled by the clashing codes of punk rockers, gangsters, neo-Nazis and SHARPs (Skinheads Against

Racial Prejudice). The four friends don't fit into any of these categories. They don't have an official name, but they model their lifestyle after the culture that grew out of England's Mods in the sixties. They listen to ska music. They have tattoos. They wear Doc Martens. Their favorite mode of transportation is the motorized scooter. They don't use guns and don't like those who do—"You can't do drive-bys with a knife."

"We're just the four skinhead girls," Valerie says. "We would just never back down for one another, never."

Valerie, who has broken six bones as a skinhead, is sitting on the floor in her apartment, where her mom pays part of the $600 rent so Valerie won't have to live at home and fight with her little brother. She's here smoking and drinking Guinness with her friends and a couple of guys. She has a shaved head except for a fringe left long around her face and three tattoos—"skinhead" in Japanese on her back, the Celtic wedding band on her shoulder, and a Fred Perry label just above her left breast. She's also wearing brick-red lipstick, fishnet tights, a micro white skirt, and a tight green sweater. She has braces because she hurt her jaw in a recent fight. Right now, she's an unemployed certified bank teller, so to fill time she just baked two pies from scratch—a chocolate and a peach (Her friends complain that there's too much nutmeg in the peach.) There's homemade lentil soup on the stove and noodles in the oven. "She'll be happy having children and having a home and having her husband support her," one of her friends whispers. Just then, Valerie giggles from the other room. She giggles a lot and speaks in a pink bubblegum voice. Her friends call her Miss Betty Crocker.

Of the four skinhead soulmates, Sally isn't here today. She's the skin who got Valerie into the scene. Sitting on the floor in jeans and a turtleneck is Meg, Valerie's roommate. She has a pixieish red haircut ("a Carol Brady do," Valerie says) she keeps so that she can hang on to her job as an assistant manager at a bookstore. They are waiting for Carmen, the girlfriend they call the "Cindy Crawford of skinheads."

They love to tell Carmen stories. One night the girls were down in San Diego for a show. They ran into this girl who looked at a picture of Carmen and said, "Yeah, I know that girl. She fucks with my friend." It started a feud, because, as Valerie points out: "You talk to Carmen about her feminist views or whatever, how she perceives herself. She's like the least slutty girl I know."

The next week, they were all up in Berkeley for a scooter rally. A good-looking guy kept coming around, looking for Carmen. But Carmen was already passed out in the backseat of a car. Valerie repeatedly told the guy to go away, and later they found out that the San Diego girl had given him a six-pack and said, "Go take advantage of Carmen for me while she's drunk."

As Valerie gets to this point in the story, she's giggling and everyone on the floor starts laughing. They all know Carmen: "I feel sorry for the guy that did that because she'd be wearing his left testicle around her neck now," Valerie screams as her friends howl.

Meg reminds everyone about this porno director who once propositioned Carmen. "I wanna fuck you," he said, pulling out his wallet. "She beat on him so hard," Meg recalls. "He ran so fast, all the way back to his house."

"Grabbing his ass," Valerie says, adding that they were all sorry they hadn't "jacked him for his money" so they could've eaten at Black Angus.

"Speak of the devil," Meg says. Carmen is pounding on the door. They call her in and she flashes a smile. She does look something like Cindy Crawford. Except she has broad shoulders, hair that's buzzcut with bangs, and a pierced belly button.

Valerie tells her: "There's pie in the fridge, soup on the stove, noodles in the oven." Carmen goes in and helps herself as Valerie relates yet another story about how Carmen earned her reputation: Once some guy bumped into Meg's boyfriend at a Chinatown club, and Carmen pounced on him and "kicked the hell out of him." The guy started bleeding out of his shorts, and the bouncer who was trying to swab him up said, "Damn, you got fucked up bad. That guy fucked you up bad."

And the bleeding guy said, "No, man. That was a chick."

Carmen comes out of the kitchen, belches loudly, and grins.

Some male chauvinist pig is slapping a slut around

One night they were all at a party with their boyfriends of the moment (another cool thing about the skinhead scene, according to Valerie, is that there are twenty-five guys for every girl). They saw this guy leaning against a car with his girlfriend. He slapped her, and Meg's boyfriend hurtled after him, sparking a riot that ended when the male chauvinist pig got stabbed.

"His intestines were hanging out," Meg says.

"They had to cut off eight feet of his intestines, and he lost a kidney," Valerie adds.

But to the skinheads the worst thing was that the guy started "pointing fingers" for the cops.

"It's like vigilante law," Valerie explains. "You don't go getting the cops involved in something like that. If you wanna take care of it 'cause that was a friend, whatever."

"But the guy was stabbed," Meg amends Valerie. "He coulda died. So they had to bring someone in."

"They had to bring someone in," Valerie admits. "But they ratted everyone off. They ratted off people that weren't even involved in it. Whatever happens, you don't rat. When I got stabbed, I didn't even call the police. I went, I'm gonna go to the hospital. That guy's gonna get taken care of eventually. If he's on the street, we'll have more of a chance of taking care of him."

The Nazis are recruiting

Top of the list for things to take care of are Nazis. Meg says: "If a Nazi came up to me, no matter if—he could be Mike Tyson size, and if he wanted to fight, I would fight. I would never back down to something like that." If Nazis show up at one of their concerts or scooter shows, they shout insults. If someone says White Power, they kick, throw punches, throw chairs. Whenever they see violent hatred, they retaliate with violence.

The skinhead girls say they are only being loyal to the true skin-heads, the ones that started in England and had nothing to do with hatred. It's about music. And dressing in Crombie coats and Fred Perry shirts and Doc Martens. In their scene, they hang out with black skinheads and Mexican skinheads. Valerie is Jewish.

They say the neo-Nazi skinheads that are "hyped" by the media give the true skinheads a bad reputation. It's easy to do, the skin-head girls say, because fascist leaders go to skinhead rallies and try to recruit "fresh cuts" who are confused about what it means to be a skinhead. "They use what they term as skinheads as their little sol-diers," Valerie says, adding that they end up with the pathetic dregs of the scene. "They're target practice," she proclaims, smirking.

"I've never met a Nazi that was ever going somewhere, that had anything going for them," Meg says.

Valerie adds: "They're always people that have nothing to show for themselves, so they get something to blame it on."

"They're dropouts. They do drugs. They have children very early," Meg says, noting that one eleven-year-old had a baby and claimed it was to "advance the cause."

When Meg still lived in her small hometown, they even tried to recruit her. "It was like, the South will rise again," she says. "I hate using this word, but they said Niggers and Spics don't belong on this earth. It's the exact same stuff you hear on TV. It's a broken record. It's like robots. They've been brainwashed."

"It's just poor white trash basically," Valerie says, then adds, "Excuse the expression, but it's true." She giggles reflexively.

Valerie had as hard a childhood as any. But she came out of it and now, she says, by being a skinhead, she's earned stuff to show for herself—like the T-shirt she was stabbed in. She gets it out of her room so her friends can see the brown blood stain, the gash through it. She holds it up like a trophy.

In junior high, you get ganged up on

After a soccer game against a team of what Valerie describes as "ChaCha chicks," Valerie tried to stick up for a friend who had been robbed in the locker room. The Chicana gang girls chased Valerie outside, where it was raining. They wrestled her umbrella from her as she wallowed in the mud. They beat her until she bled from her ear. She lost 40 percent of her hearing.

Boys beat you up in elementary school

The first fights Valerie fought were self-defense. From the time Valerie was seven, her mother was divorced and working hard to support Valerie and her little brother. She couldn't drive, so every morning she had to get up at four a.m. and take three buses to teach second grade in South Central L.A. Meanwhile, Valerie and her brother were going to their neighborhood school in house slippers. Finally, their mother decided to transfer them to the school where she taught. There, they were the only two white kids at the school.

Not only was Valerie white, she was also the smallest kid in the school and her teeth didn't come in properly until she was nine years old. The boys bullied her. She hid out in her mother's classroom and finally her mother agreed to let her transfer back to her old neighborhood school. But by then, Valerie had lost her place in the magnet program for kids with IQs over 145. So she had to repeat lessons she had already learned.

The Klan burns a cross on your yard

Valerie's mother is Jewish, born and raised on a farm in New Jersey. Her father is Lutheran, born and raised in Iowa. When Valerie was four, her father moved his Jewish wife, daughter, and son back to his hometown. Valerie remembers the rocks through her window, the cross burning on her lawn.

Her mother finally moved out, taking the children to Los Angeles, where Valerie's aunt and uncle lived. Valerie hasn't seen her father since she was seven, hasn't talked to him since she was twelve.

Your grandmother survived a concentration camp

From the time she was four, Valerie heard about the Holocaust. Her maternal grandmother had already died of Hepatitis B, but her mother passed along the stories: how the Nazi's had shaved her grandmother's head; how the Nazis had ordered their German shepherd to maul her for trying to feed another prisoner in the camp; how her grandmother dug her own grave just before the Russians saved her from it.

"If you're in a family that survived the Holocaust, you grow up with the guilt," Valerie says. "You are bombarded with all these stories.

"I've had conversations with Nazis, and they tell you the Holocaust never happened. And I'm like, 'If the Holocaust never happened, why was I bombarded with these stories when I was four years old? It happened. Believe me, it happened.' "

She pauses for a minute. "I don't know what I'm gonna do to my kids. But I hope . . . everyone's forgetting. There's not that many survivors left."

She knows that she wants her kids to be skins. "Hopefully," she says, "my kids will be it, our grandkids will still happen. It moves. It grows. Whatever they are, they are. They better not be Nazis. That's the only thing I will not tolerate is a Nazi."

For now, though, she'll put on a conservative-looking blonde wig to try and nail her interview with Universal Pictures so she can work crowd control for the summer—until she goes off to San Francisco State in the fall. Maybe someday she'll get to transfer to Bennington, where she really wants to go to college. She'll see. She'll keep fighting the fight.

"A lot of people, they go, 'Violence isn't the answer to racism.' But you gotta think, How long did racists keep everyone else down? And what did they use? They used violence. They used intimidation. And I'll use the exact same thing to keep them down.

"Violence isn't the long-term answer," she says, "but it's a quick solution." She giggles again.

WHY RANDY MURRELL
KEEPS COMING HOME

Randy Murrell is coming into the Kentucky county where he was born and where his daddy was born and his daddy before him. Owsley County is in the heel end of the Appalachians, where the land bucks up into high hills and then drops into valleys just big enough for creeks to rattle through. The county seat, Booneville, is dominated by a white church's steeple. There is a grocery store with a plank porch, and there are men whittling away Sunday afternoon talking on some sidewalk benches out front. *"May*berry is bigger than Booneville," says Randy affectionately in the hillcountry drawl that has something of a Scottish lilt leftover from the early settlers.

Here are his grade school, his high school, the little boxy house where he lived until his daddy finally got his dream come true: a fifty-six acre farm up at a scenic point called Travellers Rest. "There's our shop," Randy says, as he goes past a low blue garage that his grandfather Murrell owns and where his father works as a mechanic, where Randy himself has pumped gas on days so hot and steamy the only hope of maybe cooling off was to pull an RC Cola from the corner machine.

Randy motions toward a storefront that serves as the Owsley County Public Library. "I spent a lot of time in there," Randy says. "Boy, I loved that place." It is an unassuming building, its windows decorated like a grade-school classroom. It's where Randy discovered William Tell and Darwin. Randy says his love of reading gave him a way to imagine something beyond hardscrabble life in the poorest county in Appalachia.

"I read a lot of Shakespeare," Randy says. "Hamlet is my Number One A person. That is my top piece of literature. Nothing will ever beat *Hamlet* in my eyes, ever. There's so much more depth to Shakespeare's writing. The tragedies are really tragic and the comedies are really funny, you know. I just think he's an ingenious writer."

From the energy in his voice, you would think he was a baseball fan talking stats: "I could read *Hamlet* seven thousand times and still never lose interest in it. I've read it at least six times, and I've seen the movie. Ophelia is *so tragic.*" He grabs his heart, without sarcasm. "See, Ophelia was the most tragic character of the whole story. I don't care what *any*body says. I mean some people say it was Hamlet, but I don't think so. Ophelia got the worst of everything. Her father died, and I guess her mother had died beforehand because it never really talks much about her mother in the story. But her brother ends up dead. Hamlet ignores her and plays insane . . . *Arrrgghhhh.* Her father's a rotten guy it turns out. Everybody around her dies, you know, and then she goes insane and well they say she falls off a bridge but she probably committed suicide. But she's my favorite character from *Hamlet* 'cause she just had the worst run of luck."

* * *

He passes a small tobacco patch growing near a clapboard house with a La-Z-Boy recliner on its porch. "That's supposedly Owsley County's cash crop right there: Tobacco," he says, pointing at the leafy rows. He's quiet for a minute and then adds: "I say that in kind of a mild tone. 'Cause it isn't." He explains that times are so bad that a lot of "hardworking people have resorted to growing marijuana as a cash crop." There are no factories in the county, no major highways. The coal companies have stopped stripmining because, while the coal is high quality, it doesn't run deep—only about fourteen inches. And tobacco has a shrinking market; Randy says you never could quite make a living off it anyway. But "marijuana can grow just about anywhere," he says. "It's a weed. In all respects, it's a weed. It'll grow just about any way. Grow it in direct sunlight or shade. Just as long as it gets some water."

But what about the law?

"It's hard to get caught," Randy says. "As long as you call in to the National Guard that it's okay if you guys search my place, they can't really press charges on you for any marijuana that's been found on your place—since you've given 'em free permission to search. Almost everybody in the county does that because growers tend to want to grow it on other people's places without the owners knowing. It makes it extra safe for them not to get caught. Unless they get directly caught in the patch.

"I don't believe in it," he says with conviction. "I don't believe in any kind of drug." But in Owsley County, *everybody* knows how the marijuana trade works. They hear the helicopters circling over head. They see the National Guard trucks rumble through town, looking as if they were headed off to war. "They do aerial photography to map out potential areas of growth," he says, "and then they come back in August and they harvest."

He means bust, right?

Randy snickers. "That too," he says, "but you know there's something kind of shady about that deal also. Well, you'll always see these big army trucks goin' through town with marijuana hangin' off of 'em. But you'll never see any buds on it. That's the main part of the plant—as far as the plant goes with makin' the money off of it. [The National Guard guys] are no better than anybody else around here. Most of those people from the National Guard come from around here so . . .

"It's not like everybody in town's a dopehead or anything like that. Most of them are good hard honest working people, it's just they've had to resort to growing the stuff in order to live and that's not good."

* * *

The road to home cuts a steep and rocky ascent over a hillside covered with oak trees and blooming chicory and clover. In spring, the rains wash the road out so much the coal underneath gleams black. When the winter snows come, the family has to walk up the road to their red brick house, which is in a high clearing where even on still nights they can hear the airplanes overhead but not any auto traffic down below.

Randy calls his family part of "the working poor." He is determined to change the "poor" part (not just for his family but for everyone in Kentucky) by making more use of the "working" part. To him, nothing is more noble than work. He calls Karl Marx one of his heroes (along with Bob Dylan and John Kennedy): "Labor is what defines you. Your works are what you are," Randy says. "From what I've read of Marx, that's pretty much what he believes and that's a good way to think. Working together as a single body is a lot better than havin' to compete. Competition has its advantages. I mean, progress is achieved through competition, technological progress anyway. Workin' together you get a lot more achieved, a lot more. You might not get advanced as fast, but I believe you can have a more peaceful work environment that way."

He learned about work from his dad, Roger Murrell. When Randy was eleven, they moved onto fifty-six acres, and Randy helped clear them and fence the place to hold what are now forty-six head of Holstein cattle. Every year, they scrape together the "ridiculous, awful" property taxes. But it's worth it. "My dad, he's kind of a mechanic cowboy," Randy says proudly.

At the top of the hill, his collie, King, runs out to greet him. And almost the minute King has his wet nose in the palm of Randy's hand, his mother is at the back screen door.

"Hi, Mama," Randy calls. "Bet you didn't think you'd see me today."

"No," Wanda Murrell answers. "But then I never do." She looks out to see him walking across the yard in his black Metallica T-shirt, black jeans, and black sneakers. Her only son and oldest child,

Randy has done what few teenagers in his town have ever done and gone away to college.

Berea College, where he goes, is fifty miles away by winding mountain road and has 1,500 students, meaning it's as big as Booneville. There he has learned everything from Hegel to the style of music he calls "head bangin'." ("You just shake your head like you're saying no real fast.") He has had a gay roommate who played too much Madonna. He has chafed over Berea's quota system and stood up for black friends. He has watched the 1992 Presidential debates unfold on CNN and memorized the German version of the Beatles' hit, *I Wanna Hold Your Hand.*

It takes a good hour and a quarter to come home, which is why he says his year-long girlfriend broke up with him just before the senior prom last year. She didn't think a long-distance relationship would work, even though Randy says he felt "perfectly safe with a belief that I could remain faithful and all that."

Anyway, he makes the trip home every two weeks or so in the 1983 forest green Dodge flair-side pickup that he saved up for and bought. His uncle keeps it for Randy near campus, which is "a bit iffy," Randy admits, because students aren't allowed to have vehicles. But Randy says the car's mainly so he can get home and help out his parents if they need it, so he can come eat his Grandma Cooper's chicken and dumplings.

"I don't wanna ever lose touch with my hometown or anything, not this state [of Kentucky] 'cause it needs too much help from its own," he says. "That's kind of why I'm [at Berea] you know. Politics being what it is and all, that's one of the very few ways, my area, this section of this country is gonna get out of the rut it's in now. We're gonna have to get some people from Congress and White House to take notice. I'd like to get into office. I'd like to get into the Senate really bad."

* * *

His mama, Wanda Murrell, is a young-looking slim woman with a blond ponytail. She gives him a Coke to drink and scolds him for not calling her more often. She tried five times on Friday to reach him, starting at seven a.m. His dad, the lanky guy in jeans and a T-shirt in the living room recliner, just shakes his head and grins. Randy tells her he was already at work then, worked from seven to four, renovating one of the dorms—ripping out old tiles, painting, tearing down shelves. At Berea, a college founded to educate former slaves and now dedicated to educating poor Appalachians, students work for their tuition, room, and board instead of having to pay for it.

Randy swigs his Coke and tells his mom and dad about his campaign for the Danforth dorm presidency. "I've done my own advertising, that kind of thing," he says. "I don't get too many people to carry my name around. I like setting down and talking to people on an individual level." Tonight at keycheck is when they're holding the election. "I'm one of three candidates, kinda like last year's national election. It's like I'm Clinton and the other two are Bush and Perot."

"Perot," his mom says. "I like *him*. Clinton? I don't have anything against him, buuuttt. . . ." She grins at her son. "I just kinda like Perot with the big ears."

Randy looks disgusted in a good-natured kind of way.

Roger says: "Perot likes to tell the people the way it's gonna be and if they don't like it . . . he tells them more or less the truth."

As evidence of Perot's truth-telling, Wanda says: "He told them there was gonna be a gasoline tax. And there is. A big one."

Randy whines: "But Clinton said the same thing. He said he told people there'd be a gas tax."

"Not at first," his mom counters.

"Yes, he did."

"He didn't till after little Perot come in there and give him a hard time," she says, grinning.

"Oh, *please*," Randy groans. "Let's not get into this."

"Any man that has made as much money as Perot has can't be all bad," his dad tells him. Then, he explains: "Politics is just something to argue about."

"Good to *talk* about," Wanda echoes, looking pointedly at her son.

"I *like* it," he says.

Roger nods at Randy and tells his wife: "He would make a good lawyer. He would make an excellent lawyer. He will argue to the death if he's wrong."

Randy does a big harumph.

"Well, you do," mama tells him.

"There's no right and wrong though," Randy says. "You learn that in philosophy."

"I don't care," his mother replies, seeming to completely miss the implication that he has studied philosophy and she hasn't. "YOU're wrong if you think Perot wouldn't make a president."

* * *

Randy changes the subject: "I got you a Father's Day present but you won't get it until I come home next week. You have to feed it though."

"You have to feed it?" his mom asks.

"Sounds like you got your mother somethin' then, if we're feedin' it," his dad teases him.

"What is it?" Wanda asks.

"It's only about this big," he says, holding about four inches between his thumb and his index finger.

"What is it?"

"A rat probably," says his younger sister who has been sitting silently on the couch.

"It's not a hamster?" mama probes.

"No it's not a hamster."

"What is it? It's a rat?"

"It's not a rat."

His mother sighs. "Well, what is it?"

"A mouse." Randy says it proudly, like TA DAA.

"Where'd you catch that, in your room?" his mother asks.

"It looks just like one of these cows out here, Mama. It's white with little black splotches all over it."

"A Holstein rat," she says. And the whole family laughs at the idea of a mouse that's the same brand as their cattle.

"Yeah, that's what it is. I'm serious," Randy says, pleased. "It looks just like a little cow. It just caught my eye. I thought, He'll love that. Got it at Animal House, a pet shop in Berea. It didn't cost too much. Only cost about a couple of bucks. A cow mouse is what it is."

"Henry'll take care of him," Wanda teases Randy. Henry is one of the family's rodent-eating cockatiels.

"Oh, mama," Randy tells her, rolling his eyes, smiling, "that's cru-el."

* * *

His mother reminds him always to drive slowly and be wary of other drivers. She can't hardly stand to see him leave, but she knows he has to. Both parents admit that deep-down they know there is no other choice that's any good for Randy. "There aren't a whole lot of jobs out there even if you do go to college. But at least you've got a chance," says Roger.

"That's right," Wanda says, almost as though she's reminding herself. "If they don't leave here and go to college, they're gonna stay around here, and then get married. And they end up on welfare and food stamps. So if you don't push 'em to get out of the county and go to college, you've just . . . that's it."

"A lot of [parents] won't," Roger says.

"Most of 'em won't," Wanda agrees.

"They don't want 'em to . . . they want 'em to be right with 'em," Roger's voice shows he knows that feeling himself. "I mean it would be nice if everybody could stay all together all the time."

"But it don't work like that . . . in this small town," Wanda says.

Roger paints the picture. "Eventually the parents are gonna be gone, and there's gonna set a person that's fifty years old and don't know how to do nothin' . . . "

"Even care for their ownself, you know," Wanda says.

"Was there anybody in your family that went to college?" Roger asks his wife. "There's nobody in my family ever had even the chance to go to college. Anybody in yours? Back when we was growin' up, you didn't even think about it."

"It was just a dream," Wanda says.

"But he really likes it down there," Roger says. "I'd rather for him to like it than to not be satisfied."

"I mean if I thought he was homesick, I would worry to death," Wanda admits.

Randy says: "When we were having orientation in the summer, this guy gave a seminar, and he said eventually you'll kinda get weaned from home a little bit. That's what he said. You won't feel so homesick."

"They weaned you real fast," Wanda teases.

"I like comin' home every now and then, bein' around kinfolk and everything, like over at the garage," Randy says.

"To horse around," she laughs.

"We don't horse around that much. That's part of havin' relatives though, Mama, you gotta goof around a little bit."

His dad winks: "He likes them fried green 'maters."

"Yeah, those are good," Randy says. "Those are real good. Cut 'em up and dip 'em in meal and fry 'em. They're good. They taste kind of sour a little bit, crunchy and sour. Gotta put a little salt on 'em. I put a little salt on everything though. It's probably not good for me, but I do it anyway."

He gets up. "Let's get on back to Berea town."

* * *

On the ride back, Randy describes this "hillbilly science fiction" he writes just for fun. But never horror, he says: "The thing that America doesn't need is a reason to get depressed or scared." He also listens to heavy metal (through headphones so he won't disturb the rest of the dorm). He got into it 'cause of an Iron Maiden song that set the Coleridge poem, "Rime of the Ancient Mariner," to clashing music. He started researching the band. Now, whenever he can, he goes to the library and pores over old *Rolling Stone* magazines on computer microfiche looking for stories on his eclectic list of favorites—Metallica, Guns N' Roses, Aerosmith, Jimi Hendrix, Bob Dylan, Janis Joplin, and the Grateful Dead (although he doesn't approve of the Dead's association with the drug culture).

For him, reading has been a rescue. He was always sort of outside the cliques in high school, and when he quit smoking, he gained weight and became real self-conscious. So he started sitting in the back of the classroom and reading the business sections of the Lexington *Herald*—"to look cool," he says. *"Well, what's the stocks doing today?* But I got to really reading it, and it caught my eye. And that's what kind of tipped me off, you know, watching the dollar and how much it's worth internationally and then here, what interest rates were. It's some fascinating stuff. I was reading statistical information when I was twelve or thirteen about what the unemployment rate was, and frankly, I just knew it wasn't gonna get much better. So I've just gotta get ahead. You've gotta have the sheepskin before you can get a job anywhere."

Then during his junior year, he met this local civil engineer named Danny Barrett, who got the idea to bring together top students from Kentucky schools to study their state. Danny got local banks to support him, took nominations from teachers around the state, and called the group the Youth Environmental Leadership Program. Randy says YELP changed the course of his life.

"Danny brought a lot of realism to where I was and where I was gonna be in the future," Randy says. "How to perceive things nowadays: look for the details. Always dig under a little deeper, just dig up the facts, never take anything at face value, he taught me that." YELP studied the pollution in the Kentucky River. The kids hiked the Appalachian Trail. "It's helping us to help ourselves," Randy says. "It's just so hard to find anybody my age or younger that just gives a damn about anything anymore. Nothin' bothers them anymore. It's our country. We've gotta like preserve some of this stuff. Help it, nurture it, let it grow."

He grins at his own passion. "I love leadership," he says. "Leadership is a really big characteristic. Everybody should have some of it. Leadership's easy. It's just *so easy.*" Then he amends himself: "It's easy in one respect and it's a little nervating in another— because you've gotta be, you've gotta have some real faith in what you believe in before you can spread it across anyone else's mind and have them follow you in that idea. And you've gotta have the right tools and the motivations. You gotta know how to say something that's gonna provoke somebody to perform an action that will go along with your thought process. It's like, I hate to bring it up as an example but, Adolf Hitler. He knew how to motivate peole. He used economics to stimulate people to turn against a whole race.

"But you gotta know the problem before you can ever start to lead anybody, and you've gotta know your problem well. You've gotta let them know. And information is the greatest source of power in the world. If you withhold it from somebody, that causes problems. Curiosity killed the cat."

So how does he plan to lead, assuming he wins the dorm election and becomes president? "Gettin' the job done is basically my policy," he begins. "I'm big on priorities. Number one, keep the thing clean and keep it in reasonable shape. Number two is unity in the dorm. 'Cause ever now and then you'll have an incident of discrimination or racial tension or some guys pickin on the gay people and stuff like that."

He gives an example. "Last summer, there was a guy from Florida, southern Florida, really the heart of Florida, and this other dude from Alabama and he's a black guy. He's one of my friends. They got into a little argument one day over suite duties and one thing led to another and the white guy from Florida says, 'Why don't you just pull a gun? That's what your kind does anyway.' *That's* the kind of incident I'm talkin' about. It doesn't happen often, but when it does, it really bothers a lot of people. And that's one of the things I'm trying to work against, tryin' to get rid of that kind of tension, that kind of thinking. It's just horrible.

"I talked to both of them about it. The guy from Alabama, he was just being pushed around. Now I talked to [the guy from Florida] and . . . It's the way he was raised for one thing. He's from one of those families that's prejudice kind of . . . that way. And I tried to bring it to mind, 'This guy probably grew up the same way you did, wantin' a car all of his life, doin' the same kind of labor and tasks you had to do. You just gotta look at that and take it for what it's worth and look beyond the skin, man. Because that's not what's there. That's not the real thing about a person. It's inside that matters.' "

But Randy is frustrated because all he could do was talk. "If I'd had real control of the situation," he says. "I woulda had 'em *work* together. That would've been a fairly good solution in my opinion. Because then you could see what each is made of. Then they could find their own similarities and appreciate that for what it's worth."

Randy also points out that the racial tension runs both ways at Berea, although he thinks most of the students—largely from poor families—have come to the conclusion that he has come to: "Your story is your brother's story, it's just painted a different color." It pains him to explain this, but he tries: "Well black students tend to use racism—some of them do, I'm not saying all of them do—some of them use racism as kind of a defense. It's like if a person does a poor job at work. This is a black person doin' a poor job at work, and he gets fired from that department. He'll use the excuse, Well, I'm just gonna take you to [student justice council] and accuse you of racism. That's kind of what I mean," he says.

"And another thing they control—when I say *they* I don't mean the whole group, I just mean the ones who are doing it—whenever we have a dance over here that happens to be anything but rap, certain individuals that walk in, they say, *Well you're racist man, you're not playing any black music.* And they'll give you that kind of argument. They did that to a country dance one time. I don't like country music that well, that Heehaw kind of stuff, I bite my nails whenever I get close to it. I love Latin opera more than I do country music. But we had a pretty good dance and then we had a guy come in and start mouthin' off and we had to call Safety and Security. Callin' us racist and all that kind of thing. It's stressful, man. Pardon my French, but it's kind of damned if you do, damned if you don't."

He knows these are the same issues that are plaguing the whole country. Since there is only one extended black family in Owsley County, prejudice wasn't something that Randy dealt with much before he came to college. Now, he says he's studying it. "There's no use as to be so extreme as to go completely the other way on an issue," he says of those students who are "all the time yelling racism. That's never a good idea. I mean I've read Malcolm X, his books, his writings. And I know he was kind of extreme, but he didn't go so far as to say, Let's commit genocide on the white race. Later on in his other writings, he began to believe in brotherhood too. Martin Luther King, Jr., that was a great man. You know, it's just like the old song says. You've just gotta come together. We're stuck on this little mudball planet, and there's no gettin' away from one another.

"I was watching something on MTV last night about hate rock, neonazis and that kind of thing. I just can't believe this thing is flaring up again. I just can't believe these kind of people are walkin' around with the attitude they have about blacks and homosexuals and they've got computer nets up right now, that you get mail and stuff off them for Nazi organizations. Hitler," he screeches in disbelief. "Hitler. They proved the man was insane."

He says he feels sorta hopeful, though. "There's a lot of people out there like me who want to see it change, who want to see us move toward a common ground rather than struggle off onto separate islands. It's awful when you just want to get away from one another. That's horrible. I feel a responsibility just . . . we should all find some brotherhood.

"The KKK, they go down to some small towns here in eastern Kentucky, and they don't get any response at all. Oh it's beautiful. I went down to Laurel County, Kentucky, and they had a KKK march and nobody showed up. *Nobody.* Nobody showed up. They were marching down the street, little sheets on, little signs and no one was there. Nobody showed up. I was just passin' through the town. It was horrible. I felt so much like gettin' out and tossin' some rocks. But I'd be no better than they were. That'd be violence. You can't achieve anything through sheer and blatant violence."

*   *   *

Randy is hoping to get back to campus before the cafeteria stops serving dinner. "We oughta get back by dark." As the cattle-strewn fields fall past, as the car passes a nuclear missile site, Randy turns his head to look at everything.

"I'm learning more about the lay of the land, what the real problems are, getting the issues together," he volunteers. "I'm studying the political process just on the state level, how things happen here, how money's appropriated, where it goes, who gets it, who spends it, and basically I'm tryin' to study the connection between the state and the national, federal government.

"And you've gotta climb that ladder you know. I'll be kinda old I guess before I ever make it to the Senate." Then hearing how he sounds, "Or even *if* I ever make it to the Senate. I've got wishful thinking," he demurs.

And if he did get there, what would he want to accomplish? "Business," he answers like a shot. "Bringing businesses here. I know that Kentucky is synonymous with tourism and country scenes and green grass and all that. I don't wanna cut out every tree or anything like that but there's still gotta be progress. I feel that you could bring the computer industry here, I really do. Just technology in general. It's just hard to get the land to do it with 'cause it's tied up, and people don't want to let loose of their property."

He says he's already kind of started his campaign, down at his family's garage when all the guys are loafing. "I can always help to promote some of the ideals and things. The only thing I can really do is put the idea there and let people know this is the way this has gotta be done, in order to get out of this mess. We've gotta try hard, work hard.

"Whether they do listen or they don't, I make a conscious effort. I talk to a lot of my friends and a lot of the older citizens of Owsley and Booneville, people who own the businesses and own the property. They usually know my grandpa pretty well and I hang out with my grandpa. So I talk to them through him kind of. And he's got a little more credibility with them than I do. So they'll listen to him more than me. Youth is kind of overlooked amongst the old, the elderly. Ideas are just that, for them. You're being an idealist and all. I'm just tryin to put something that could be real there. As soon as possible. They're pretty open to ideas. They 'bout have to be. It can only get so bad. They've got their traditions and all but they're ready to improvise a little and bring in some fresh ideas."

* * *

Randy is home in time for supper. He still has a few hours to talk to some of the guys who will be voting in the election tonight. They're already filing into the dining hall. But even in his anxiousness to go eat with them, he pauses to answer one last question for this book.

Has there every been a Senator from Owsley County?

"No," Randy says. "I'll be the first." No if.

November 10, 1982

Well, I am about to not be a teenager anymore. Sounds more significant than it feels, but I thought I should write it down. Maybe it'll mean something to me later. My friend M. says that the four college-age years are your last formative years. I don't know where that theory comes from, but I feel

*pretty formed. Actually, when I read back over stuff I wrote
even when I was 13, 14, 15, I see I was exactly exactly the
same then. I've changed in some ways, know more what I
want.*

God, so many things: to run the marathon
                      to dance with Twyla Tharp
                      to counsel battered women, rape
                            victims, other women, young
                            women
                      to make documentaries that are art
                            too
                      to cure progeria, anorexia, bulimia,
                            Tourrette's, narcolepsy
                      to live on Dolores St. in San Francisco
                      to co-anchor 60 Minutes
                      to act
                      to have beautiful babies
                      to document abuses in prisons, other
                            countries, our country
                      to have my own magazine, or with a
                            friend
                      to have a family, all living together
                      to write a novel
                      to be continued

*But that's all superficial in a way, outward manifestations
of much other deeper wants.*
Yeah, at 13, I knew it all.

A Nonsuperfluous Conclusion

Teenagers like Randy make me cry. And I can't help it, they make me recall the quote from that most famous inspirational teenager, Anne Frank, 'cause in spite of everything they've seen and dealt with—AIDS, drive-bys, bleak job futures—they still believe in people, still believe in themselves, still believe that the world is a hopeful place. When, like Jon, they take the adversity they face and rather than feeling defeated or bitter, they feel like working to make things more tolerant, healthier, more secure—then they make me that hopeful, too. Especially when I see them pouring their often novel ideas and their usually boundless energy into it.

It's Valerie planning to go to Bennington and raise a family someday. Gabriel still trying to get a job. Kyle's aspiration to be a social worker and help someone else down the line. Their potential may not be the obvious thing about them. It's certainly not the thing that makes them part of all those statistics that often become the only way teenagers are seen. So it's up to the rest of us to look past those numbers and the "15-Year-Old Kills Brother" headlines. It's up to us to look at any kid anywhere and see an individual and not a stereotype.

What I've shown you of American teenagers may not have been the picture you wanted to look at. It's probably not the way a lot of ex-teenagers choose to remember that time in their own lives. And it's probably really not the way some kids and parents and grandparents and teachers would like to think that kids' lives are today.

Because I fear that a lot of people sort of hold a snapshot of a teenager they care about in their minds, a picture of getting the kid dressed for the prom or some simple time like that. That's easiest. But it's not real.

Kids know so much. They're leaps and bounds ahead of where I was when I was a teenager. Even feeling eternally fifteen in many ways, and I know I'm not the only one, still I compare myself, and there's no way at that age I was half as aware, or had any understanding of the complicated issues that they grapple with now and often overcome. I'm amazed at teenagers like Erin who gets so upset about drunk driving that she sends letters to the editor of her town's paper and others who care so much about Russia or welfare reform that they write to President Clinton about it, when I reserved such upset for myself, my friends, my school. I feel more confident leaving this world in their hands than with any previous generation of teenagers I can think of.

They already know what's missing—job security and AIDS research and gun control—because they're out front with most issues and trends. Plus so many of them, like Amber, have that great trait of just blurting out what they feel at the moment (even if it may change the next) without worrying about how to say it correctly. So we need to hear their ideas for how to do things differently. Especially because they're not tainted by having tried old methods. They're fluent in all these new technologies and we're not. They're often not bridled by practicality or mainly motivated by their own financial or political gain. They more than anyone are who we need to look to, learn from. To support and to give them the autonomy they need to make the changes that will affect their lives. If we can't always find a way to make things better for them, I believe they'll find a way for themselves. For all of us. For real.

Where They Are Now (Or At Least Where They Were Last Time We Checked)

Nick Plummer has just *one* girlfriend, and they've been together "just me and her" for a year. He also has a new stepmom, a new house (where "I basically hide out in my room"), and a new $1,700 Leading Edge computer. And since he "blew his knee out" playing hockey early in the season, he spends a lot of time hitting the computer games and posting stuff on computer network bulletin boards. He's even thinking of starting his own humor-oriented computer service.

Amber has a girlfriend. They met at an AIDS dance-a-thon when everybody was so hot they stripped and danced in their bras. "She was undecided about her sexuality too," Amber says. "We'd both been burned by guys and wanted to know how a relationship with a girl would differ. I thought it wouldn't be as harsh. Nothing sexual has happened at all. All we really do is talk on the phone and meet in public. I never really appreciated how hard a time people who are not heterosexual have. When I had to go home on the train, I gave her a big hug, and I wanted to kiss her so badly. It's an incredible level of intimacy, emotionally."

Amber is also doing the "college search thing," and she just completed 140 hours of volunteer work. Last month, she pierced her nose, which fascinates the little kids she babysits. "It hurt," she says. "It hurt a lot."

She's seeing four guys. "Yeah, four. Nothing really serious," she says.

Nicole Woolf is a sophomore in college, where she's not sure yet what to major in. She's still saving money to study in Jerusalem, through Brigham Young University. Until then, her major passion is participating in triathlons. Jake is still away on his mission, and he sends her letters. She had a steady boyfriend last year, but that's all over. Her mom did get married, though. "Now we have 16 kids in our family," she says, and then she laughs.

Kyle TwoHorses is still in school, on his way to becoming the first TwoHorses to graduate.

James Colzie is headed into his junior year at Florida State University, where he has played in both the Orange Bowl and the Sugar Bowl. His first year he played more than any freshman ever, and as a sophomore he became a starting corner back. He was named one of the top eight defensive backs in the country by *Sports Illustrated.* But he still goes home to watch his sisters when they play basketball in the Districts. He's majoring in business and minoring in drama, which he hopes will pay off when he goes to Chicago to audition for an upcoming movie. James says that he still hasn't had a taste of beer: "I still can't do it."

Gabi Phillips is playing her violin in quartets and a symphony orchestra at the Cleveland Institute of Music. She has her own apartment and a boyfriend, who happens to play the cello, just like her dad. "My dad loves him," she says, laughing. "We're always looking for our dads, aren't we?"

Erin Conrad just finished her freshman year at Macalester College in St. Paul, Minnesota, where every day she got three e-mail letters from her dad. "We've worked everything out. I love him *so much.*

And I love that invention," she says of the computer network that links her IBM with modem to her dad's back home in Madison. "My mom writes once a week to tell me to take my vitamins. My grandparents write every day. It's great." Right now, she has a double major in political science and anthropology. Eventually, she wants to go to law school (at Harvard, she hopes) and practice international law. Partly in preparation for that, she and a friend are going backpacking this summer in Equador, where they plan to live with an indigenous tribe and visit with members of the Peace Corps.

Cassidy Hill is still hanging out in Santa Fe. His friend Max moved away, but they write letters.

Chicken Hawk is on hiatus. **Andy Lewis** studies "cool political science stuff" at Shoreline Community College. **Dane Brandon** is working six days a week, getting ready to travel around Europe. **Alex Newman** is finishing up high school. They've gone their separate ways, musically speaking. "But we're gonna play this summer and do more recording," Andy says. "We're just takin' a break, givin' each other space." No word on Mack.

Gabriel is still in the neighborhood.

Jessica Miller started high school in Anchorage at an alternative school she loves. But she does miss being at home in the bush. An apartment just isn't the same. It helps having her cat, Garf, with her and knowing her dog Willow is staying with a friend nearby. Recently, one of her assignments was to do an art project representing herself. Jessica was thinking of doing a poster with pictures on each side—one about "home," one about living in Anchorage. "To show both sides of me," she says.

John Robert Hunt is out of high school and "punchin' cows" on the ORO Ranch. He went out on the fall wagon last year, and "the wagon boss should be holdin' my horses for this spring wagon," John Robert says adding, "I'm on horseback constantly."

His other form of transportation has changed: "The Very Special truck is dead," he says. "I survived, but the truck was totaled after the sixth wreck." Its replacement is a tan 1989 Ford two-wheel drive pickup. "I even put a little bit of a stereo system in it. The only thing it's missing is chrome rims. I'm goin' a lot slower now. I haven't even come close to my record time."

As far as a new girlfriend goes, he's still looking. "I went out with a zero last week," he says. "I haven't had a worse time in my whole life. If I wasn't talkin' there was nothing to listen to but the stereo."

Kathleen Doxey broke up with Mark. After she graduates, she's going "straight to Ole Miss," where she plans to study law. "Just like my daddy," she says. Is she going to take up practicing on that same corner of the square in Holly Springs where her family has been for three generations? "Depends on if my daddy'll have me."

Lynn Thomas had another baby, a boy named Dominick. She and Kenny now live together, which is great with Cameron, now three. Lynn is closing in on a degree in accounting from Parkland College.

Jon moved to another part of the country to study acting.

Chana Abehsera and her family moved to Israel. She just got married to a guy who studies with her father. "He's just like me," she says, "So *open*."

Cindy Parrish is seventeen now and got married in January. She's expecting a baby this August. She says her parents were shocked at first, and it was sad when her daddy stood up at the wedding and said, "Now I don't have anything else to give away." But her mama's excited about buying new things for the baby, and her husband gets along well with both her parents, which is great because the newlyweds are living in Cindy's old room. "He's like the good Samaritan around here," Cindy says. "He takes out the garbage. He'll do the laundry if it needs doing."

Right now, Cindy is finishing high school through a "home school" program, which she likes because she doesn't have to get up early. Even though she doesn't go to the private church school anymore, she still belongs to the Pentecostal Church.

Ashlee Levitch is eighteen, still in Hollywood, and still living with her mom, dad, and sister. Her sitcom, *Family Album,* got cancelled, but since then she's done a movie-of-the-week called *Kids Killing Kids* and an HBO movie called *Tyson.* George C. Scott was also in that, and they had a scene together. "It was very cool to work with George C. Scott," she says. "He's really, really serious." Right now, she's hoping her new drama series, *McKenna,* will get picked up on ABC. It shoots in Bend, Oregon, and she got to go away and be on the set by herself for the first time. "My phone bill was enormous," she said. "I'm such good friends with my parents, and I missed everybody back here."

Rashida Jones is a sophomore at Harvard, where she's studied quantitative reasoning and Descartes meditations. She's also been in several plays. People teased her when LLCoolJ and Quincy Jones helped her move into the dorm. But now she's settled in and loves it. "When I go back to LA, I feel like this rugged East Coast kid," she says.

Tripp Wingard is vice president of the Pep Club at Clemson University. He's also president of the Accounting Club. He has a new girlfriend back home in Orangeburg, but he says he still wants to stay away from that part of the state after he gets his accounting degree. "Too much tension between whites and blacks," he says. "I wanna stay up here. It's a liberal college, and it's all whites in this part of the state."

Valerie King went two years to San Francisco State University. And then she joined the Air Force. She was in boot camp, so we couldn't speak to her, but one of her old friends told us that Valerie wants to be a nurse someday. Her old roommate, Meg, just had a baby. And Carmen is in college.

Randy Murrell got married to a "nice Kentucky girl" and is still pursuing his degree at Berea.

Who to Call

If you need confidential help or just have a question, here's where you can go:

National Youth Crisis Hotline
800-448-4663
Open 24 hours, seven days, with counseling and referrals to more specific help numbers.

Boys Town National Crisis Line
800-448-3000
800-448-1833 (for the hearing impaired)
Open 24 hours, seven days, for help with any kind of personal crisis.

Florida Tech Hotline
800-544-1177
For help with food or drug addiction or depression.
Open 8 a.m. to 9 p.m. (Eastern Standard Time), Monday through Friday; 9 a.m. to 6 p.m., weekends.

The American Anorexia/Bulimia Association
212-891-8686
Open working hours, Monday through Friday.

Planned Parenthood Locator
800-230-7526
This number automatically connects you to your local branch of
Planned Parenthood, where you can get information and referrals
on reproductive health and birth control. Clinics keep regular working hours.

The Hetrick-Martin Institute
212-674-2400
For information on lesbian, gay, and bisexual youth.

The Children's Aid Society
National Adolescent Sexuality Training Center
212-876-9716

Centers for Disease Control and Prevention National HIV/AIDS Hotline
800-342-AIDS
Open 24 hours, 7 days, with information and referrals to local hot-
lines, testing centers, and counseling.
800-344-SIDA (in Spanish)
Open 8 a.m. to 2 a.m., 7 days

Centers for Disease Control and Prevention National Sexually
Transmitted Disease Hotline
800-227-8922
Information and referrals to public clinics.
Open 8 a.m. to 11 p.m. (Eastern Standard Time), Monday through
Friday.

National Drug Information Treatment and Referral Hotline
800-662-HELP
800-66-AYUDA (in Spanish)
800-228-0427 (for the hearing impaired)
Information, support, and referrals to local rehab centers.

Open 9 a.m. to 3 a.m. (Eastern Standard Time), Monday through Friday; noon to 3 a.m., weekends.

National Cocaine Hotline
800-COCAINE
Open 24 hours, 7 days, for help with all kinds of drug dependency, including information and referrals to local rehab center.

Local branches of Alcoholics Anonymous or Narcotics Anonymous can be found in the phone book.

Suicide Prevention numbers can be found in the Yellow Pages under "suicide." Or you can find someone to help at these two services 24 hours a day, seven days a week:

Suicide Prevention and Crisis Hotline (Los Angeles)
213-381-5111

Suicide Prevention and Crisis Hotline (New York)
212-673-3000

Children of the Night
800-551-1300
For teenage runaways and their parents.

Research Notes

We didn't want to bog you down with research notes in the text, but in case you want more information, here are some of the places we found our facts and figures.

Step–Grand–Surrogate–Adoptive–Dysfunctional–Test-Tube–Parents
"Mental Health," by Marjorie Ingall, *Rock the System: A Guide to Health Care Reform for Young Americans,* 1994.
Vital Statistics of the United States.

"Abs of Steel"
The American Anorexia/Bulimia Association, Inc.
    c/o Regent Hospital
    425 East 61st Street
    Sixth Floor
    New York, NY 10021
U.S. News & World Report, June 1, 1992
The Harvard Center for Eating Disorders
The Medical University of South Carolina
    Studies on eating disorders among preteens
Vogue, May 1994.

"Superbud"
"Notes from a Psychedelic Revival Meeting," by Richard Gehr, writing in the *Village Voice,* July 5, 1994.

"The Young and the Reckless," by Peter Wilkinson, writing in *Rolling Stone,* May 5, 1994.

"Heroin Finds a New Market Along Cutting Edge of Style," by Trip Gabriel, writing in the *New York Times,* May 8, 1994.

"The Year of the Cat," by Seth Hettera, writing in *Spin* Magazine, February, 1995.

Centers for Disease Control, *JAMA,* December 18, 1991, Vol. 266, No. 23.

"Wasted Youth: More Students Are Starting to Use Drugs and Sniff Glue at an Early Age," *Time,* April 26, 1993.

The University of Michigan's Institute for Social Research Study on drug use among teenagers.

"Condoms"
Planned Parenthood, New York

"Pregnancy," by Lisa Ruppel Benenson, writing in *Rock the System,* 1994.

"Absolut Queer"
The Hetrick-Martin Institute
2 Astor Place
New York, NY 10003
For information on lesbian, gay, and bisexual youth.

The Children's Aid Society
National Adolescent Sexuality Training Center
350 East 88th Street
New York, NY 10128

"At the Prom," by Adam Mastoon, writing in *The Village Voice,* June 28, 1994.

"Bid to Include Gay Students in Anti-Bias Policy Stirs Little Protest," the *New York Times,* June 20, 1994.

"Out and Organized: As the National Gay Movement Shies Away from the Subject of Homosexuality Among the Young, Some Gay Teenagers Are Determined to Open the Subject Up," by Jesse Green, writing in the *New York Times,* June 13, 1993.

"Tune In, Come Out," by David Gelman, writing in *Newsweek,* November 8, 1993.